CAPITALISM'S LAST STAND?

About the Author

WALDEN BELLO is a member of the House of Representatives of the Republic of the Philippines. He is currently also an adjunct professor at the State University of New York at Binghamton and at St Mary's University in Halifax, Canada; he has also been professor of sociology at the University of the Philippines. He was founding director of the Bangkok-based Focus on the Global South and the Institute for Food and Development Policy (Food First) in Oakland, California. He is the author or co-author of seventeen books, including *Dilemmas of Domination: the Unraveling of the American Empire* (London: Zed Books, 2006) and *Deglobalization: Ideas for a New World Economy* (London: Zed Books, 2004). He obtained his Ph.D. in sociology from Princeton University.

CAPITALISM'S LAST STAND?

Deglobalization in the Age of Austerity

———————————

WALDEN BELLO

Zed Books

LONDON & NEW YORK

*For my colleagues and dear friends in Akbayan
and Focus on the Global South*

Capitalism's Last Stand? Deglobalization in the Age of Austerity
was first published in 2013
by Zed Books Ltd, 7 Cynthia Street, London N1 9JF, UK
and Room 400, 175 Fifth Avenue, New York, NY 10010, USA

www.zedbooks.co.uk

© Walden Bello 2013

The right of Walden Bello to be identified as the author
of this work has been asserted by him in accordance with
the Copyright, Designs and Patents Act, 1988

FSC
www.fsc.org
MIX
Paper from
responsible sources
FSC® C013056

Designed and typeset in ITC Bodoni Twelve
by illuminati, Grosmont
Index by John Barker
Cover design: www.roguefour.co.uk
Printed and bound by TJ International Ltd,
Padstow, Cornwall

Distributed in the USA exclusively by Palgrave Macmillan, a division of
St Martin's Press, LLC, 175 Fifth Avenue, New York, NY 10010, USA

A catalogue record for this book is available from the British Library
Library of Congress Cataloging in Publication Data available

ISBN 978 1 78032 046 5 hb
ISBN 978 1 78032 045 8 pb

CONTENTS

INTRODUCTION

GLOBALIZATION'S DEBACLE: CRISIS AND OPPORTUNITY

The economic freefall of the last few years has brought tremendous economic misery to millions. It has also exposed the failure of traditional economic approaches to come up with a solution. Both neoliberalism, which brought on the crisis, and Keynesianism, which was the initial response to it, failed to bring Europe and the United States out of the doldrums. Thus the hunger for innovative solutions, along with a demand for alternative explanations for the emergence of the worst economic crisis since the Great Depression.

People's concerns were not limited to growth and jobs, but to more fundamental questions like what brought about the crisis and how could the economy be better organized to meet the needs of people and the environment. It is in this context that the mainstream began to show interest in what it once regarded as a fringe idea when we first explored it in the book *Deglobalization: Ideas for a New World Economy*, published by Zed a decade ago. Attributing the term 'deglobalization' to the author, *The Economist* noted that, contrary to the accepted dictum that globalization was irreversible, 'the integration of the world economy is in retreat on almost every front.'[1]

---

1. 'Turning Their Backs on the World,' *The Economist*, February 19, 2009, www.economist. com/node/13145370.

Even more interesting, deglobalization became a central part of the presidential debate in France in 2011-12. It became the platform of Arnaud Montebourg of the Socialist Party, who said he got the idea from me. Various political parties, including those from the right, then tried to claim it as their own approach.[2] Deglobalization's entering the mainstream of economic and political debate has compelled me to clarify what it means, how I have employed the paradigm in my efforts to understand various aspects of the contemporary economic crisis, and what it may offer in the way of bringing about a transformation of social and economic relations towards more equality, justice, and sustainability. Deglobalization, in my view, offers a way out of the crisis, though perhaps not the only way.

This volume brings together essays written over the last six years, a period that saw the unraveling of globalization, the financial implosion, and a plunge into deep recession in the United States and Europe. Written in response to fast-moving developments, the articles appear here largely as they were originally published, with a few explanatory comments to place them in context. While some figures may need some adjustment, the analysis in these pieces retain, in the author's view, their validity and urgency.

The purpose of this introductory essay is to guide the reader in navigating this volume. It discusses, sums up, and attempts to further clarify the ideas presented in the three parts into which this book is divided. In Part I, the writings focus on the origins and dynamics of the financial and economic crisis that broke out with Wall Street's collapse in 2008. Part II looks at other key dimensions of global capitalism apart from the financial meltdown: the continuing export of industrial facilities and jobs from the North to the South; labor trafficking from the South to the North, which some have called 'the new slave trade'; and the dynamics of the global food

2. Pierre Haski, 'Is France on Course to Bid Adieu to Globalization?', YaleGlobal Online, July 21, 2011, http://yaleglobal.yale.edu/content/france-bid-adieu-globalization.

price crisis of 2006-08. In Part III, the essays discuss the different perspectives which analysts have used in their effort to understand the crisis of globalization and the alternatives to current social and economic arrangements proposed by these paradigms.

The destructive dynamics of finance capital

For those from Southeast Asia, like me, the financial collapse in New York and Europe in 2008 probably came as less of a surprise than to people in these places. I still remember the swift unraveling of economic life in Bangkok, the 'ground zero' of the crisis, when, taking advantage of the collapse of the real-estate sector owing to overinvestment, speculators hit the baht and forced its value to spiral from 25 to 55 baht to the dollar. In the brief span of a few weeks in the summer of 1997, over $100 billion left the East Asian economies in probably the biggest financial panic until then, bringing Thailand, Indonesia, the Philippines, and South Korea to an economic standstill and dragging 22 million Indonesians and 1 million Thais under the poverty line.[3]

Just as Asians should have worried that the financial crises that had hit global markets since the liberalization of capital markets in the early 1980s might one day engulf them, the Asian financial crisis should have been seen, as in the rest of the world, as a portent of things to come, but apparently the only ones to learn from it were Asian governments, which began to stockpile their dollar reserves, largely earned from their exports, to ward off future attacks on their currencies by speculators. In contrast, in the world's leading economy, by the middle of the first decade of the twenty-first century the key reforms to ensure financial stability that had been put in place during the Great Depression, including the landmark Glass–Steagall Act, which built a Chinese wall between investment

---

3. Walden Bello, *Dilemmas of Domination* (New York: Henry Holt, 2005), p. 121.

banking and retail banking, had been dismantled, and a new, hyperactive unregulated financial sector dealing with new financial instruments called derivatives had sprung to life. Surprisingly, among the bearers of warnings that went unheeded was former treasury secretary Robert Rubin, one of the architects of financial deregulation in the administration of President Bill Clinton. 'Future financial crises,' he warned cynically, 'are almost surely inevitable and could be even more severe.'[4]

Why had finance become so central in the global economy? Why did credit, in the form of subprime bank loans and credit cards, become so prominent a feature of global capitalism's leading economy in the last two decades? Why did speculative activity that saw staid investment vehicles like stocks and bonds mutate into all sorts of esoteric financial instruments, like derivatives and 'collateralized debt obligations,' become the driving force of the capitalist economy? One financial corporation chief writing in the *Financial Times* claimed that 'there has been an increasing disconnection between the real and financial economies in the past few years. The real economy has grown ... but nothing like that of the financial economy, which grew even more rapidly – until it imploded.'[5]

The rise of the finance-driven economy

But was there really a 'disconnect' between the real economy and the financial economy? Or did the financial economy explode to make up for the stagnation of the real economy?

One cannot understand the emergence of the finance-driven economy without going back to the state of the US economy in the 1970s, when the so-called 'golden age of capitalism,' driven by post-

---

4. Robert Rubin and Jacob Weisberg, *In an Uncertain World* (New York: Random House, 2003), p. 296.

5. Francisco Gonzalez, 'What Banks Can Learn from the Credit Crisis,' *Financial Times*, February 4, 2008, www.ft.com/intl/cms/s/93b9ccoc-d346-11dc-b861-0000779fd2ac,Authorised=false.html.

war consumer demand, the reconstruction of Europe, US military spending, and rapid economic development in the decolonized world, came to an end in the twin crises of stagnation and inflation, which according to orthodox economic theory were not supposed to occur simultaneously. 'Stagflation,' however, was but a symptom of a deeper problem: the reconstruction of Germany and Japan and the rapid growth of industrializing economies like Brazil, Taiwan, and South Korea had added tremendous new productive capacity and increased global competition, but continuing social inequalities within countries and between countries worldwide limited the growth of purchasing power and demand. This contradiction eroded profitability.

But while economists of the reigning Keynesian school were puzzled by stagflation, to progressive analysts this phenomenon was a symptom of the classic capitalist crisis of overproduction or over-accumulation, which Marx had described thus: 'The real barrier of capitalist production is capital itself. ... The means – unconditional development of the productive forces – comes continually into conflict with the limited purpose, the self-expansion of existing capital.'[6]

The limits of neoliberal restructuring

Capital tried three escape routes from the conundrum of overproduction: neoliberal restructuring, globalization, and financialization. Neoliberal restructuring was also known as Reaganism and Thatcherism in the North and structural adjustment in the South. Its aim was essentially to invigorate capital accumulation, and this was to be done by (1) removing state constraints on the growth, use, and flow of capital and wealth, including geographic barriers; (2) tearing up the 'class compromise' between Big Capital and Big Labor that was the central social feature of the Keynesian state; and

---

6. John Elster, ed., *Karl Marx: A Reader* (Cambridge: Cambridge University Press, 1986), p. 120.

(3) revising the tax laws to favor the rich on the theory that the rich would then be motivated to invest and reignite economic growth.

What this amounted to was a redistribution of income from the poor and the middle classes to the rich. The figures are eloquent: the top 1 percent of the population cornered nearly 30 percent of the national income in 2007, up from 10 percent in 1957.[7] The problem with this solution to overproduction was that it gutted the incomes of the poor and middle classes, thus restricting demand, while not necessarily inducing the rich to invest more in production. In fact, what the rich did was to channel a large part of their redistributed wealth into speculation.

The truth is that neoliberal restructuring, which was generalized in the North and South during the 1980s and 1990s, had a poor record in terms of growth. Angus Maddison's statistical work – regarded as the most reliable – showed that the annual rate of growth of global GDP fell from 4.9 percent in 1950-73 to 3 percent in 1973-99, a drop of 39 percent.[8] The United Nations confirmed this trend, estimating that world GDP grew at an annual rate of 5.4 percent in the 1960s, 4.1 percent in the 1970s, 3 percent in the 1980s, and 2.3 percent in the 1990s.[9] Neoliberal restructuring could not shake off stagnation.

Globalization: exacerbating overproduction

The second escape route global capital took to counter stagnation was 'extensive accumulation' or globalization, or the rapid

---

7. Robert Reich, 'Why the Economy Can't Get Out of First Gear,' June 13, 2012, http://reader-supportednews.org/opinion2/279-82/11902-why-the-economy-cant-get-out-of-first-gear.

8. Angus Maddison, cited in James Crotty, 'Why There is Chronic Excess Capacity,' *Challenge*, November-December 2002, p. 25.

9. Ibid. Also, according to the Center for Economic Policy Research, globally per capita GDP growth was slower in the period 1980-2000 than in the period 1960-80, with the poorest group going from a per capita GDP growth rate of 1.9 percent annually in 1960-80, to a decline of 0.5 percent per year in 1980-2000. 'For the middle group (which includes mostly poor countries), there was a sharp decline from an annual per capita growth rate of 3.6 percent to just less than 1 percent.' CEPR, *The Scorecard on Globalization, 1980-2000* (Washington DC: CEPR, July 11, 2001), p. 1.

integration of semi-capitalist, non-capitalist, or pre-capitalist areas into the global market economy. Rosa Luxemburg, the famous German Marxist economist, saw this long ago as necessary to shore up the rate of profit in the metropolitan economies. How? By providing capital access to cheap labor; by gaining new, albeit limited, markets; by gaining new sources of cheap agricultural and raw material products; and by bringing into being new areas for investment in infrastructure. Integration is accomplished via trade liberalization, removing barriers to the mobility of global capital, and abolishing barriers to foreign investment.

China is, of course, the most prominent case of a non-capitalist area to be integrated into the global capitalist economy over the past twenty-five years.

To counter their declining profits, a sizable number of the Fortune 500 corporations moved a significant part of their operations to China to take advantage of the so-called 'China price' – the cost advantage deriving from China's seemingly inexhaustible cheap labor. By the middle of the first decade of the twenty-first century, roughly 40-50 percent of the profits of US corporations were derived from their operations and sales abroad, especially in China.[10]

The problem with this escape route from stagnation is that it exacerbated the problem of overproduction because it added to productive capacity. A tremendous amount of manufacturing capacity has been added in China over the past twenty-five years, and this has had a depressing effect on prices and profits. Not surprisingly, by around 1997 the profits of US corporations had stopped growing. According to another index, presented by economist Philip O'Hara, the profit rate of the Fortune 500 went from 7.15 in 1960-69 to 5.30 in 1980-90 to 2.29 in 1990-99 to 1.32 in 2000-02.[11]

10. 'Wall Street Meltdown Primer,' *Common Dreams,* September 26, 2008, www.commondreams.org/view/2008/09/26-5.

11. Philip Anthony O'Hara, 'The Contradictory Dynamics of Globalization,' in B.N. Ghosh

Financialization: credit creation and speculation

Given the limited gains in countering the depressive impact of overproduction via neoliberal restructuring and globalization, the third escape route became critical for maintaining and raising profitability: 'financialization' or the increasing reliance of capital on lending and investment in the financial sector to maintain profitability. As Marx put it in one of his more insightful observations:

> To the possessor of money capital, the process of production appears merely as an unavoidable intermediate link, as a necessary evil for the sake of money-making. All nations with a capitalist mode of production are therefore seized periodically by a feverish attempt to make money without the intervention of the process of production.[12]

Financialization had two key activities in the period leading up to the collapse of 2008: credit creation and speculation. Both were responses to the stagnation of the real economy.

Driven by the banks and government policies, the thrust of credit creation was to sustain demand in the face of the stagnation in the growth of real income owing to neoliberal policies that had promoted a reconcentration of wealth.

In the three decades prior to the crash of 2008, the wages of the typical American hardly increased, and actually dropped in the 2000s, as a result of neoliberal policies.[13] A big part of the problem was the elimination of high-paying manufacturing jobs through the export of jobs to cut down on labor costs. It is estimated that 8 million US manufacturing jobs were eliminated between June 1979 and December 2009. One report describes the grim process of deindustrialization:

and Halil Given, eds, *Globalization and the Third World* (Basingstoke: Palgrave Macmillan, 2006), p. 120.

12. Karl Marx, quoted by John Plender, 'Shut Out,' *Financial Times*, October 18, 2008.

13. Robert Reich, *Aftershock* (New York: Alfred Knopf, 2010), p. 19.

Long before the banking collapse of 2008, such important U.S. industries as machine tools, consumer electronics, auto parts, appliances, furniture, telecommunications equipment, and many others that had once dominated the global marketplace suffered their own economic collapse. Manufacturing employment dropped to 11.7 million in October 2009, a loss of 5.5 million or 32 percent of all manufacturing jobs since October 2000. The last time fewer than 12 million people worked in the manufacturing sector was in 1941. In October 2009, more people were officially unemployed (15.7 million) than were working in manufacturing.[14]

Elimination of high-paying manufacturing jobs eroded a pillar of the mid-century Keynesian economy: the maintenance of effective demand.

This stagnation of income posed a threat to both business and the state. To the first, the slow growth of demand would translate into overproduction and, thus, diminished profits in the corporations' key market. To the state, it posed the specter of rising social conflict and instability.

The threat of a stagnant market was thwarted – temporarily – by the private sector via a massive increase in credit creation by banks, which lowered lending standards and hooked millions of consumers into cheap housing loans, student loans, auto loans, and multiple credit cards. Credit kept consumption up and fueled the boom in the 1990s and the middle of the first decade of the twenty-first century. And where did the American financial institutions derive the wherewithal to create a seemingly inexhaustible stream of credit in the go-go years of the 1990s and the last decade? From foreign loans and the purchases of securitized products by foreign creditors and investors. Between 40 and 50 percent of the securities packaged from credit-card debt, home equity loans, auto loans, student loans, and mortgages by American financial institutions ended up in the investment portfolios of American financial

14. Richard McCormack, 'The Plight of American Manufacturing,' The American Prospect, December 21, 2009, http://prospect.org/article/plight-american-manufacturing.

institutions, prompting Nouriel Roubini and Stephen Mihm to remark that by 'making those purchases, foreign creditors helped finance the borrowing binge that drove the bubble.'[15]

Washington tried to ward off political resentment by adopting a strategy of 'populist credit expansion'; that is, making easy credit for housing available for low-income groups via Freddie Mac and Fannie Mae, the two quasi-government agencies that made housing loans. Political stability was not the only outcome of this approach; it was accompanied by greater profitability for speculative capital. As Raghuram Rajan noted,

> As more money from the government flooded into financing or supporting low income housing, the private sector joined the party. After all, they could do the math, and they understood that the political compulsions behind government actions would not disappear quickly. With agency support, subprime mortgages would be liquid, and low-cost housing would increase in price. Low risk and high return – what more could the private sector desire?[16]

One of the consequences of using credit as a substitute for rising wages in order to shore up living standards and thus defuse political resentment was to make the citizenry participants in financialization and thus legitimize the hegemony of finance capital. As Colin Crouch pointed out,

> [T]he bases of prosperity shifted from the social democratic formula of working classes supported by government intervention to the neoliberal conservative one of banks, stock exchanges, and financial markets. Ordinary people played their part, not as workers seeking to improve their situation through trade unions, legislation protecting employment rights and publicly funded social insurance schemes but as debt holders, participants

---

15. Nouriel Roubini and Stephen Mihm, *Crisis Economics: Crash Course in the Future of Finance* (New York: Penguin, 2010), p. 81.
16. Raghuram Rajan, *Fault Lines* (Princeton NJ: Princeton University Press, 2010), pp. 38-9.

in credit markets. This fundamental political shift was more profound than anything that could be produced by alternations between nominally social democratic and neoliberal conservative parties in governments as a result of elections. It has imparted a fundamental rightward shift to the whole political spectrum, as the collective and individual interests of everyone are tied to financial markets, which in their own operations act highly unequally, producing extreme concentrations of wealth.[17]

Hand in hand with credit creation to keep up demand that could no longer be sustained by rises in real income and real wages was speculative activity to achieve profitability that could no longer be sustained via investment in the real economy. In the ideal world of neoclassical economics, the financial system is the mechanism by which the savers or those with surplus funds are joined with the entrepreneurs who have need of their funds to invest in production. In the real world of late capitalism *circa* 2000, with investment in industry and agriculture yielding low profits owing to overcapacity, large amounts of surplus funds were circulating and being invested and reinvested in the financial sector – that is, the financial sector was turning in on itself.

The problem with investing in financial sector operations was that it was tantamount to squeezing value out of already created value. It could create profit, yes, but it did not create new value – only industry, agriculture, trade, and services create new value.

Because profit is not based on value that is created, investment operations become very volatile and prices of stocks, bonds, and other forms of investment can depart very radically from their real value – for instance, the stock of Internet start-ups that keep on rising, driven mainly by upwardly spiraling financial valuations, and that then crash.

---

17. Colin Crouch, *The Strange Non-Death of Neoliberalism* (Cambridge: Polity Press, 2011), p. 116.

Profits then depend on taking advantage of upward price departures from the value of commodities, and selling before reality enforces a 'correction' – that is, a crash back to real values. The radical rise of prices of an asset far beyond real values is what is called the formation of a bubble.

Profitability being dependent on speculative coups, it is not surprising that the finance sector lurches from one bubble to another, or from one speculative mania to another.

Because it is driven by speculative mania, finance-driven capitalism has experienced some fourteen major financial crises since capital markets were deregulated and liberalized in the 1980s. We have already mentioned the Asian financial crisis. But there were other outbursts that showed the volatility that had been injected into the global economy by unregulated finance capital. Prior to the current Wall Street meltdown, among the most explosive of these were the Third World debt crisis in the early 1980s, the Japanese asset/price bubble collapse in the early 1990s, the Mexican financial crisis of 1994-95, the Russian financial crisis of 1996, the Wall Street stock market collapse of 2001, and the Argentine financial crisis of 2002.

The two dimensions – credit creation to sustain demand and dampen political dissent, and speculation to achieve super-profits that were not available in the real economy – came together in the so-called securitization of subprime and other real-estate loans. Looking at the process more closely, the subprime mortgage crisis was not a case of supply outrunning real demand. The 'demand' was largely fabricated by speculative mania among developers and financiers who wanted to make great profits from their access to foreign money – lots of it from Asia – that flooded the US in the last decade. Big-ticket mortgages or loans were aggressively made to millions of people who could not normally afford them by offering low 'teaser' interest rates that would later be readjusted to jack up payments from the new homeowners.

These assets were then 'securitized' with other assets into complex derivative products called 'collateralized debt obligations' (CDOs), by the mortgage originators working with different layers of middlemen who understated risk so as to offload them as quickly as possible to other banks and institutional investors. These institutions in turn offloaded these securities onto other banks and foreign financial institutions. The idea was to make a sale quickly, make a tidy profit, while foisting the risk on the suckers down the line.

When the low teaser rates came to an end and interest rates were raised on the subprime loans, adjustable mortgages, and other housing loans, the game was up. When the crisis broke in 2007-08, there were about 6 million subprime mortgages outstanding, 40 percent of which were likely to go into default in the next two years.[18]

And 5 million more defaults from adjustable-rate mortgages and other 'flexible loans' were expected to occur in the next several years. But securities whose values run in the trillions of dollars had already been injected, like a virus, into the global financial system. Global capitalism's gigantic circulatory system was fatally infected.

For investment banks Lehman Brothers, Merrill Lynch, and Bear Stearns, and the quasi-governmental housing credit agencies Fannie Mae and Freddie Mac, the losses represented by these toxic securities simply overwhelmed their reserves and brought them down.

And many others joined them as other speculative operations, such as credit cards and different varieties of risk insurance, seized up. American International Group (AIG) was felled by its massive exposure in the unregulated area of credit default swaps, derivatives that make it possible for investors to bet on the possibility that

---

18. 'The Financial Crisis: An Interview with George Soros, *New York Review of Books*, May 15, 2008, www.nybooks.com/articles/archives/2008/may/15/the-financial-crisis-an-interview-with-george-soro/?pagination=false.

companies would default on repaying loans. Such bets on credit defaults made up a $45 trillion market that was entirely unregulated. It amounted to more than five times the total of the US government bond market. The mega-size of the assets that could have gone bad had AIG gone bankrupt was what made Washington change its mind and salvage it after it let Lehman Brothers collapse.

Lehman's collapse in September 2008 triggered panic on Wall Street and abroad that a whole host of commercial and investment banks that had trillions of dollars' worth of toxic subprime assets on their books would follow suit. Washington, however, stepped in, and Congress passed the Troubled Asset Relief Program, which injected massive infusions of capital into US private financial institutions, in effect saving many of them from colossal mismanagement with US taxpayers' money that in the end cost some $1.1 trillion.[19]

As the financial crisis spread, consumer lending spiraled down and bank lending to enterprises nearly ground to a halt. Consumers themselves refrained from more borrowing as they tried to dig themselves out of debt. The outcome was a crash in demand that led to a crunch in the real economy. The coming years were of recession, then very weak recovery that elicited from financier Warren Buffett the comment 'This is not a recovery.' Indeed, with unemployment failing to go below 8 percent – a figure that would have been higher had many not been discouraged and stopped looking for work – the unemployment rate would have been much higher.

Banks and the European crisis

In Europe, though there were important differences in the conditions of the different countries relative to the United States, the similarities were more prominent: property bubbles in Spain, Britain, and Ireland; distressed industries in most European Union countries owing partly to the export of jobs to China and other developing

---

19. Andrew Ross Sorkin, *Too Big to Fail* (New York: Penguin Books, 2010), p. 538.

countries; stagnation in real wages, which was counteracted by rising levels of consumer indebtedness. Essentially, it was the same crisis of overaccumulation, overproduction, and profitability. And, crucially, the financial crisis was a supply-driven crisis, as the big European banks sought high-profit, quick-return substitutes like real estate for industrial and agricultural investment.

In Ireland – once the darling of global capital as the so-called 'Celtic Tiger' – entry into the eurozone gave access to 'huge sums of money inexpensively on international markets with nearly no exchange rate risk, an activity that was barely regulated by policymakers. With easy access to these funds, banks ... lent huge amounts to prominent Irish developers, leading to a frenzy of overdevelopment.'[20]

German and French banks held some 70 percent of Greece's $400 billion debt. German banks were great buyers of the toxic subprime assets from US financial institutions, and they applied the same lack of discrimination to buying Greek government bonds. For their part, even as the financial crisis unfolded, French banks, according to the Bank of International Settlements, increased their lending to Greece by 23 percent, to Spain by 11 percent, and to Portugal by 26 percent.[21] Indeed, in their drive to raise more and more profits from lending to governments, Europe's banks poured $2.5 trillion into Ireland, Greece, Portugal, and Spain.

Prior to the Third World debt crisis of the early 1980s, bankers used to compete savagely in lending the money recycled to their coffers by the OPEC countries, motivated by the so-called 'Wriston doctrine' – named after the man who formulated it, former Citibank chairman Walter Wriston – that asserted that 'countries don't go bankrupt.' The equivalent of this in the case of Europe in the first decade of the twentieth century was that membership of the

---

20. 'Europe Approves Irish Rescue and New Rules on Bailouts,' *New York Times*, November 28, 2010, www.nytimes.com/2010/11/29/business/global/29euro.html?pagewanted=all.
21. 'Worse than Wall Street,' *Newsweek*, July 12, 2010.

eurozone was a guarantee against bankruptcy of any one country since all the other governments would have a strong interest in maintaining the viability of the common currency. That is, the doctrine provided the much-needed justification for unleashing surplus funds that would create no profits by simply lying in bank vaults.

Invulnerable Asia?

As the fallout from the financial crisis spread over the real economy of Europe and the United States in 2008 and 2009, the development threatened the East Asian countries that had avoided entanglement in the speculative frenzy in the North owing to the hard lessons they had learned during the Asian financial crisis of 1997. But their financial caution was undercut by their great dependence on exports to Europe and the United States. Late 2008 saw the beginning of downturn in the Asian economies, with recession spreading throughout the region as exports collapsed. In China, for instance, some 20 million of 130 million migrants workers were said to have been laid off, a great many in South China's export processing zones.[22]

The response to this throughout the region was deficit spending by governments to stimulate their domestic economies to make up for the shortfall in the export sector. China launched the biggest stimulus, which at $585 billion was the largest ever relative to the size of the economy. With their economies in varying degrees of integration into China's economy, many of the region's countries bounced back by late 2009.

Keynesianism's brief moment

Stimulus spending was also the watchword in the United States and Europe in 2009. At the G20 meeting in Pittsburgh in September

---

22. 'China Puts Joblessness for Migrants at 20 Million,' *New York Times*, February 2, 2009, www.nytimes.com/2009/02/03/world/asia/03china.htm.

2009, the advanced capitalist countries and the so-called new emerging economies endorsed stimulus spending to make up for the shortfall in demand in the private sector. The newly elected Obama administration embraced stimulus spending and was able to push through a $787 billion package in the US Congress, while French president Nicolas Sarkozy declared that 'laissez-faire capitalism is dead' and created a strategic investment fund of €20 billion to promote technological innovation, keep advanced industries in French hands, and save jobs. Keynesianism appeared to have made a stunning comeback, an impression that was conveyed by the neoliberal University of Chicago Nobel laureate Robert Lucas, who famously observed that every economist was 'a Keynesian in the foxhole.'

Obama got Congress to approve his stimulus in his first year in office in 2009. A few months later, however, his cautious Keynesianism was embattled. On the left, liberal economists like Paul Krugman, who had demanded a bigger package, asserted that the stimulus, 'clocking in at $787 billion, was far too small for the job. It surely mitigated the recession, but it fell far short of what would have been needed to restore full employment, or even to create a sense of progress.'[23] While the stimulus plan was being drafted early in 2009, Krugman had presciently warned:

> I see the following scenario: a weak stimulus plan, perhaps even weaker than what we're talking about now, is crafted to win those extra GOP votes. The plan limits the rise in unemployment, but things are still pretty bad, with the rate peaking at something like 9 percent and coming down only slowly. And then Mitch McConnell [the Republican Senate leader] says 'See, government spending doesn't work.'[24]

23. Paul Krugman, *End this Depression Now* (New York: W.W. Norton, 2012), p. 117.
24. 'Stimulus Arithmetic (Wonkish but Important),' January 6, 2009, *New York Times*, http://krugman.blogs.nytimes.com/2009/01/06/stimulus-arithmetic-wonkish-but-important.

But how big a stimulus was needed? Christina Romer, the incoming head of the Council of Economic Advisers, had recommended $1.8 trillion – more than twice what the president eventually proposed to Congress.[25] Krugman did not give a specific figure, but said that it had to be big enough to counter the natural dynamics of an economy that gets into trouble owing to too much debt, like the US economy: if too many people and institutions find themselves in debt, their aggregate efforts to get themselves out of debt would create a worse situation for themselves collectively. As he explained it,

> If millions of troubled homeowners try to sell their houses to pay off their mortgages – or, for that matter, if their homes are seized by creditors, who then try to sell the foreclosed properties – the result is plunging home prices. If banks worry about the amount of Spanish and Italian debt on their books, and decide to reduce their exposure by selling off some of that debt, the prices of Spanish and Italian bonds plunge – and that endangers the stability of the banks, forcing them to sell even more assets. If the consumers slash spending in an effort to pay off their credit card debt, the economy slumps, jobs disappear, and the burden of consumer debt gets even worse.[26]

Government therefore had to spend massively to make up for the shortfall in demand owing to consumers' and businesses' natural tendency to save and to allow the economy to grow again, spreading confidence and encouraging consumers and businesses to spend again.

Disaffection on the left was further stoked by the failure of serious financial reform, which had been promised after the huge bank bailout 'to save the economy,' as its promoters had put it. The Dodd–Frank reform did not have the minimum conditions for a

25. Sam Stein, 'The Escape Artist': Christina Romer Advised Obama to Push $1.8 Trillion Stimulus,' *Huffington Post,* February 14, 2012, www.huffingtonpost.com/2012/02/14/escape-artist-noam-scheiber_n_1276998.html.
26. Ibid., p. 45.

reform with real teeth: the banning of derivatives; a Glass–Steagall provision preventing commercial banks from doubling as investment banks; the imposition of a financial transactions tax or Tobin tax; and a strong lid on executive pay, bonuses, and stock options. As the *New York Times* saw it, '[N]early four years after the crash, and nearly two years since the passage of the Dodd–Frank law, the multi-trillion-dollar derivatives market is still dominated by a handful of big banks, and regulation is a slow work in progress.'[27]

The Republican recovery

The larger challenge, however, came from the right. Put on the defensive by the swift unraveling of economies brought about by the unregulated financial sector in 2008 and 2009, conservative political forces had recovered by 2010. The rising debt levels and budget deficits brought about by the stimulus programs in Europe and the US, coupled with the failure of these limited programs to bring about significant reductions in the unemployment rate, became the springboard for the conservative counteroffensive.

The deficit came to 9 percent of gross domestic product - large but hardly a runaway deficit. Moreover, as Keynesians like Paul Krugman argued, when depression was the big threat, fear of government spending was misplaced. The idea of burdening future generations with debt was odd since the best way to benefit tomorrow's citizens was to ensure that they inherited healthy growing economies, and growth depended in the short term on vigorous stimulus spending. Moreover, government default was not a real threat for countries that borrowed in currencies they themselves issued, like the United States, since, as a last option, they could simply repay their debts by having their central banks print more money.

---

27. 'A Long Road to Regulating Derivatives,' *New York Times*, March 24, 2012, www.nytimes.com/2012/03/25/opinion/sunday/a-long-road-to-regulating-derivatives.html?_r=1.

Keynesians might have had the intellectual edge, but the political momentum belonged to the right. The anti-deficit perspective gained ascendancy in the United States despite high unemployment for a number of reasons.

First, as many had expected, the limited results of the stimulus provided ammunition for the opponents of fiscal activism. Second, the anti-deficit stand appealed to the anti-Big Government sentiments of the American middle class. Third, Wall Street opportunistically embraced anti-deficit policies to derail Washington's efforts to regulate it. Big Government is the problem, it screamed, not the Big Banks. Fourth – and not to be underestimated – was the re-emergence of the ideological influence of doctrinaire neoliberals, including those who, as Martin Wolf put it, 'believe a deep slump would purge past excesses, and so lead to healthier economies and societies.'[28] In other words, the neoliberals had left the foxhole, unrepentant as ever. Finally, anti-spending economics had a mass base, the Tea Party movement. In contrast, the pro-stimulus position was advocated by progressive intellectuals without a base or whose potential base has become disillusioned with Obama's weak stimulus and soft approach to Wall Street.

Towards austerity in Europe

In Europe, the narrative changed even more radically. In the case of Greece, the new narrative went this way: this country piled up an unsustainable debt load to build a welfare state that it could not afford. This was a case of a spendthrift that had now to be forced to tighten its belt. Germans were presented as the dour Puritans who were well within their rights to exact penance from the Mediterranean hedonists for living beyond their means and committing the sin of pride by hosting the costly 2004 Olympics.

---

28. Martin Wolf, 'Why the Battle Is Joined over Tightening,' *Financial Times,* July 18, 2010, www.ft.com/intl/cms/s/0/f3eb2596-9296-11df-9142-00144feab49a.html#axzz1y71pz RO3.

That foreign money had flocked to Greece owing to the illusion that the membership of the eurozone guaranteed repayment, that much of the money that came in did not finance government deficits, that Greece did not have a runaway welfare state, and that Greeks worked longer hours than 'almost anyone else in Europe, and much longer hours than the Germans in particular'[29] – all this was missing in the new narrative.

Penance came in the form of a European Union–International Monetary Fund program that increased value-added tax to 23 percent, raised the retirement age to 65 for both men and women, made deep cuts in pensions and public-sector wages, and eliminated practices promoting job security. The ostensible aim of the exercise was to slim down radically the welfare state and get the spoiled Greeks to live within their means.

The main beneficiaries of the change in narrative were the big banks, especially the German ones. They were now truly worried about the awful state of their balance sheets, impaired as they were by the toxic subprime assets they had taken on and realizing that they had severely overextended their lending operations. The principal way they sought to rebuild their balance sheets was to generate fresh capital by using their debtors as pawns. The centerpiece of this strategy was getting the public authorities to bail them.

How would they do this? The threat that Greece and the other highly indebted European countries would default was never taken seriously by the banks since they assumed that the dominant eurozone governments would never allow the collapse of the euro that this would bring about. But by having the markets bet against Greece and raising its cost of borrowing, the banks gambled that the eurozone governments would come out with a bailout package, most of which would go towards servicing the Greek debt to them. Promoted as rescuing Greece, the massive €110 billion package

29. Paul Krugman, 'Greece as Victim,' *New York Times*, June 17, 2012, www.nytimes.com/2012/06/18/opinion/krugman-greece-as-victim.html?_r=1.

that was put together by the dominant eurozone governments and the IMF was expected actually to go largely towards rescuing the banks from their irresponsible unregulated lending frenzy.

As for Ireland, in return for an €85 million loan to repay European banks, it accepted what the *New York Times* characterized as the 'toughest austerity program in Europe,' involving 'the loss of about 25,000 public-sector jobs, equivalent to 10 percent of the government work force, as well as a four-year, $20 billion program of tax increases and spending cuts like sharp reductions in state pensions and minimum wage.'[30] The adjustment was, in many ways, more savage than that imposed on Greece. The program, being essentially, as in Greece, a draconian effort to rip off resources to pay off the banks, ended up choking off growth. And, not surprisingly, after two years, in 2012, the IMF was warning that significant additional fiscal adjustment in a low-growth environment would risk a 'pernicious cycle of rising unemployment, higher arrears and loan losses.'[31]

By the middle of 2012, in fact, two years of austerity programs had merely reinforced a downward spiral not only in Greece and Ireland but in Britain, Spain, Italy, and the Netherlands. Only Germany seemed invulnerable, but German leader Angela Merkel could not seem to bring herself to tell her compatriots, who continued to see the bailout in Greece as a waste of hard-earned German taxpayers' money, that Germany's prosperity was dependent on the rest of Europe consuming its exports, and that austerity programs would inevitably destroy its neighbors' capacity to consume its exports. Greece was simply the cutting edge of a continent-wide drive toward the abyss, followed closely by Spain, Portugal, and Italy.

---

30. 'Demonstrators in Ireland Protest Austerity Plan,' *New York Times*, November 27, 2010, www.nytimes.com/2010/11/28/world/europe/28dublin.html?_r=2.
31. Conor Humphries, 'IMF Urges Europe to Help Ireland Refinance Crippling Bank Bailout,' *Irish Examiner,* June 16, 2012.

Crumbling BRICS?

By the middle of 2012, in fact, not only Europe and the United
States were mired in crisis. In 2010 and early 2011, East Asia and
the big 'newly emerging economies' known as the BRICS (Brazil,
Russia, India, China, South Africa) were regarded as bright spots
in the global economy, exhibiting resilience and growth even as the
North stagnated. Indeed, to economists like Nobel laureate Michael
Spence, 'With growth returning to pre-2008 levels, the breakout
performance of China, India, and Brazil are important engines of
expansion for today's global economy.'[32] In a decade, the emerging
economies' share of global GDP would pass the 50 percent mark,
he predicted. Much of this growth would stem from 'endogenous
domestic-growth drivers in emerging economies, anchored by an
expanding middle class.'[33] Moreover, as trade among the BRICS
increased, the future of emerging economies is one of reduced dependence on industrial-country demand.'[34] 2012, however, seemed
to be the year the emerging economies would yield to the turbulent waves emanating from the sinking economies of the North.
Economies were slowing down, with India's growth in 2011 falling
5 percent relative to 2010. Brazil's growth was under 3 percent
lower, as *The Economist* noted, than sickly Japan's.[35] China's first
quarter growth in 2012 plunged to 8.1 percent, its slowest pace in
three years. The main reason appeared to be the continued great
dependence of these economies on Northern markets and their
inability to institutionalize domestic demand as the key engine of
the economy.

Being the world's second largest economy, China's downshifting
was particularly alarming. In 2008, in response to the crisis, China

32. Michael Spence, *The Next Convergence: The Future of Economic Growth in a Multispeed World* (Crawley, Western Australia: University of Western Australia, 2011), p. 187.

33. Ibid., p. 188.

34. Ibid.

35. 'Start the Engines, Angela,' *The Economist*, June 9, 2012, www.economist.
com/node/21556577?scode=3d26b0b17065c2cf29c06c0101840684.

launched a $585 billion stimulus program to enable the domestic market to make up for the loss of export demand. Achieving some success at first, China, however, reverted back to export-led growth oriented towards the US and European markets. The reason for the retreat was explained by the respected Chinese technocrat Yu Yongding:

> With China's trade-to-GDP ratio and exports-to-GDP ratio already respectively exceeding 60 percent and 30 percent, the economy cannot continue to depend on external demand to sustain growth. Unfortunately, with a large export sector that employs scores of millions of workers, this dependence has become structural. That means reducing China's trade dependency and trade surplus is much more than a matter of adjusting macroeconomic policy.[36]

The retreat back to export-led growth, rather than merely a case of structural dependency, reflected a set of interests from the reform period that, as Yu put it, 'have morphed into vested interests, which are fighting hard to protect what they have.'[37] The export lobby, which brings together private entrepreneurs, state enterprise managers, foreign investors, and government technocrats, remains the strongest lobby in Beijing.

Indeed, according to Yu, only crisis beckoned in the future since China's 'growth pattern has now almost exhausted its potential.'[38] The economy that most successfully rode the globalization wave, China 'has reached a crucial juncture: without painful structural adjustments, the momentum of its economic growth could suddenly be lost. China's rapid growth has been achieved at an extremely high cost. Only future generations will know the true price.'[39]

---

36. Yu Yongding, 'A Different Road Forward,' *China Daily*, December 23, 2010, www.chinadaily.com.cn/opinion/2010-12/23/content_11742757.htm.
37. Ibid.
38. Ibid.
39. Ibid.

Globalization in crisis

The financial collapse and the ensuing deep recession have been the most salient dimensions of the global economy. But there were other dynamics of globalization that were already spawning widespread distress even before the current finance-triggered crisis broke out in 2007. As Susan George has written,

> Although the financial part of the crisis has received the most attention and largely pushed the others off the front pages and the mental landscape, in reality we are in the midst not of a single crisis but of a multifaceted one, which already touches, or will soon touch, nearly every aspect of nearly everyone's life and the destiny of our earthly habitat.[40]

TNCs and the export of jobs

Globalization, while in crisis, was not yet reversed, and a number of the processes that had been set in motion continued on their destructive course, like the proverbial hand of a dead engineer on the throttle of a speeding train. One of these was the continuing transfer of jobs to cheap labor areas by transnational corporations (TNCs), which had been the spearhead of a process of global integration of production and markets. The financial implosion led to the widespread portrayal of investment banks as the villains of the piece, with iconic status accorded to Matt Taibbi of *Rolling Stone* magazine for his description of Goldman Sachs as 'a great vampire squid wrapped around the face of humanity, relentlessly jamming its blood funnel into anything that smells like money.'[41]

TNCs specializing in production, on the other hand, by and large escaped the early negative fallout, despite the fact that the export of jobs had been one of the key reasons for the stagnation of real wages in the US that had to be counteracted through debt creation.

---

40. Susan George, *Whose Crisis, Whose Future?* (Cambridge: Polity Press, 2011), p. 2.
41. Matt Taibbi, 'The Great American Bubble Machine,' *Rolling Stone*, April 5, 2010, www.rollingstone.com/politics/news/the-great-american-bubble-machine-20100405.

Indeed, information industry leaders like Apple were endowed with the reputation of being unrivaled innovators that created prosperity and jobs for Americans. The reality was, however, different.

Apple employed relatively few workers in the US, with the bulk of the workforce that assembled iPhones and iPads located overseas, most of them in South China, where they worked for a pittance for notorious labor-rights violators like the gigantic contractor Foxconn. In terms of profit per employee, Apple is more profitable than Goldman Sachs or GM, but the source of that profit is the low wages of Chinese contract workers who labor in facilities with high accident rates and where miserable conditions have driven some of them to suicide.

The Slovenian philosopher Slavoj Žižek has described China, with its tight control of labor and privileges for transnational capital, as the 'ideal capitalist state.'[42] But at the end of the first decade of the twenty-first century, spontaneous strikes in South China and rising wages as the rural migrants that replenished the urban workforce in the coastal areas began to dry up, made China less attractive as an investment site. Indeed, investors began to locate their operations to other sites such as Indonesia and Brazil. On Brazil, *The Economist* noted, 'Foreign investment is pouring in, attracted by a market boosted by falling poverty and a swelling lower middle class. The country has established some strong political institutions. A free and vigorous press uncovers corruption – though there is plenty of it, and it mostly goes unpunished.' It concluded: 'Its take-off is all the more admirable because it has been achieved through reform and democratic consensus-building. If only China could say the same.'[43]

A major attraction of these areas in the eyes of corporations was apparently not just cheap wages but also more open political

42. Slavoj Žižek, *In Defense of Lost Causes* (London: Verso, 2008), pp. 190–91.
43. Brazil takes off, *The Economist*, November 12, 2009, www.economist.com/node/14845197.

systems that could act as a safety valve for destabilizing labor dissent. This raised several interesting questions about the relationship of capital and formal democracy in creating conditions for the stable reproduction of the capitalist mode of production. Cheap labor is not enough, increasing numbers of investors seemed to be saying. Freer political processes and even limited labor rights provided, in their view, some measure of political legitimacy to governing institutions that was a *conditio sine qua non* for economic stability.

The new slave trade

The freer flow of commodities and capital has been one of the features of the contemporary process of globalization. Unlike in the earlier phase of globalization in the nineteenth century, however, the freer flow of commodities and capital has not been accompanied by a freer movement of labor globally. The dynamic centers of the global economy, after all, have imposed ever tighter restrictions on migration from the poorer countries. Yet the demand for cheap labor in the richer parts of the world continues to grow, even as more and more people in developing countries seek to escape conditions of economic stagnation and poverty that are often the result of the same dynamics of a system of global capitalism that have created prosperity in the developed world.

The number of migrants worldwide grew from 36 million in 1991 to 191 million in 2005. Labor export is big business, having spawned a host of parasitic institutions that now have a vested interest in maintaining and expanding it. The transnational labor export network includes labor recruiters, government agencies and officials, labor smugglers, and big corporate service providers like the US multinational service provider Aramark. Labor trafficking is expanding to become just as big and profitable as sex trafficking and the drug trade. Indeed, since large numbers of women are among those trafficked, rape and sexual abuse have become part and parcel of all phases of the business, from the moment the women are in the hands of the smugglers.

The spread of free wage labor has often been associated with the expansion of capitalism. But what is currently occurring is the expansion and institutionalization of a system of unfree labor under contemporary neoliberal capitalism, a process not unlike the expansion of slave labor and repressed labor in the early phase of global capitalist expansion in the sixteenth century, as elaborated in the work of sociologists like Immanuel Wallerstein.[44]

A major destination of labor export, especially from Southeast and South Asia, has been the new centers of global capital accumulation like the Gulf States in the Middle East. The combination of a lightly populated indigenous Arab population, a foreign workforce that in many instances constitutes the majority of the population, and a culture still infused with many of the attitudes of a slave-owning society has created an extremely repressive labor system, particularly for female domestic workers practically bereft of all rights, including freedom of movement, and exposed to both labor and sexual exploitation.

The food price crisis and the peasantry

A major source of labor migration, be this within or across national borders, has been peasants or agricultural workers. The reason has been the restructuring of global food production. Neoliberal reforms have subverted small-scale peasant farming in favor of capitalist agriculture, making much peasant labor superfluous. But the erosion of peasant agriculture via structural adjustment and trade liberalization had wider implications. It was a central cause of the food price crisis of 2006–08, which saw the price of basic food commodities skyrocket beyond the reach of ordinary

---

44. See Immanuel Wallerstein, *The Modern World System* (New York: Academic Press, 1974), pp. 66–131.

people, in the case of rice by 300 percent in just three months at the beginning of 2008.

More profoundly, the uprooting of the peasantry was part of a broader process whereby food production came to be increasingly concentrated in the hands of transnational agribusiness corporations that controlled seed, land, production, and marketing. The focus of production became global markets catering mainly to the elites and middle classes, whose needs could be serviced from distant production sites. This globally integrated system of food production disenfranchised not only farmers but the urban poor as well, and imposed severe ecological and health costs owing to its dependence on fossil fuels and genetic engineering.

The ecological limits of capitalism

The ecological crisis has worsened over the last decade, especially in the form of climate change. An increasing awareness has grown of the relationship between capitalism and environmental degradation, rooted in capitalism's inherent drive to turn living nature into dead commodities in order to gain profit. There are, it is now clear, limits to the shrinking of ecological space to accommodate the geometric expansion of the economy. That tipping point is now with us in the form of climate change.

The North–South dimension has added a deadly dynamic to this process, as the so-called emerging capitalist economies of the South make their claims to their share of ecological space to grow while the capitalist economies of the North continue to refuse to give up any of the vast ecological space they now occupy and exploit. Overconsumption, which keeps the advanced capitalist economies afloat, is a central part of the problem, but neither the European Union nor the US see consumption as an issue to be negotiated. The EU governments may entertain limits to greenhouse gas (GHG) emissions, but this is to be accomplished largely through weak or unrealistic containment measures like carbon trading or technofixes like carbon sequestration and storage, not by reducing the economic growth rate or consumption, which remains the principal engine of greenhouse gas emissions.

The defense of high consumption by the North and the effort by the big emerging economies to reproduce the Northern consumption model lie at the root of the deadlock in the climate change negotiations – exemplified in the failure of the United Nations-sponsored talks in Copenhagen in 2009 and Durban in 2011 to agree on a successor agreement to the Kyoto Protocol. China, which is now the biggest contributor to greenhouse gas emissions, refuses to entertain mandatory reductions to its releases, while the United States, which has historically contributed so much more to accumulation of GHGs, also spurns demands for mandatory constraints. In this game of climate chicken, the Chinese at least recognize the necessity of mandatory cuts, while Washington's position is largely determined by a desire to accommodate climate skeptics in the US Congress who continue to believe, against all the evidence, that climate change is a figment of the liberal imagination.

With the world population reaching 7 billion in 2011, just twelve years after it reached 6 billion, population and its relation to poverty and ecological crisis have returned to the forefront. The issue of population has always been sensitive for progressives, who have traditionally upheld the view that inequality is the cause of human misery and viewed Malthus's 'law of diminishing returns' in the midst of a rise of population as leading a demographic crisis as a reactionary thesis. However, in the last few years, with agricultural productivity decreasing, soil quality worsening, food prices escalating, and extreme weather changes becoming more frequent, the role of global population increase in provoking ecological disequilibrium has become a central concern. This has occurred at the same time that effective population management has been associated with successful development in a number of countries, particularly in East Asia. Thus population has become less of a charged issue among progressives, though it has remained a hot button issue with the Catholic Church hierarchy and some religious fundamentalist groups.

The end of multilateralism?

The processes of globalization unfolded under the guidance of transnational institutions that legitimized them and set up rules and conventions that promoted and accelerated their spread. These multilateral institutions, which were sponsored and dominated by the United States, might be said to serve as the political canopy of globalization. Ernesto Zedillo, former president of Mexico and an advocate of globalization, has correctly called attention to the centrality of politics in the globalist project:

> Global integration has been driven by technological progress and economic incentives, but it would be inconceivable in its present form without the host of fundamental political decisions that have been taken at both the national and international levels. The global integration we have today results from political decisions taken by sovereign states – at the national level to liberalize domestic economies and foster the workings of the market – and at the international level – to sign on to agreements to liberalize foreign trade and investment. And the WTO, the European Union, and the NAFTA have not just happened, as the inescapable result of technological progress. They are above all the result of political vision and decisions by sovereign states.[45]

Aside from the United Nations system, the central multilateral institutions are the World Bank, the International Monetary Fund (IMF), and the World Trade Organization (WTO).

The WTO, established in 1995, was toasted by its former head Mike Moore as the 'jewel in the crown of multilateralism,'[46] an institution that would sweep away the barriers to trade and promote

---

45. Ernesto Zedillo, 'More, Not Less, Globalization is the Answer,' May 3, 2001, www.k-state.edu/media/newsreleases/landonlect/zedillotext501.html.

46. Mike Moore, *A World Without Walls* (Cambridge: Cambridge University Press, 2003), p. 109.

the accelerated integration of the world's economies. As the reality emerged that it was the interests of transnational corporations and the rich countries that were being advanced by the nineteen agreements that made up the WTO Agreement, developing-country governments and civil society movements worldwide began to resist newer WTO initiatives. This led to the collapse of two ministerial meetings, in Seattle in 1999 and Cancún in 2003.

Moreover, developing countries began to form alliances within the WTO framework, the most important of these being the Group of 20 and the Group of 33, two developing-country coalitions that resisted the European Union's and the United States' demand for greater access to the agricultural markets of developing countries. Agriculture became the Achilles heel of the WTO, and failure to reach agreement over massive subsidies given by the rich countries to their farming sectors and over market access to developing-country markets derailed the do-called Doha Round and crippled the WTO as a mechanism for further trade liberalization.

But it was not only the WTO that suffered reverses. The high failure rate of World Bank projects brought it severe criticism from the right, while the role of the Bank in imposing structural adjustment programs along with the IMF harmed its reputation throughout the South. In Africa and other parts of the South, China's loans, which were lacking neoliberal conditionalities, became an attractive alternative to World Bank loans.

The IMF, for its part, responded to the Asian financial crisis of 1997–98 by pushing governments to undertake austerity programs that worsened the crisis, which severely eroded its credibility, prompting a number of countries, including Thailand, Venezuela, and Argentina, to advance the repayment of rescue funds to the Fund so as to declare their 'independence' from the institution, as then prime minister Thaksin Shinawatra put it in 2003.[47] Another

---

47. Wayne Arnold, 'Thailand Sets Path to a Better Economy,' *New York Times*, October 24,

factor that alienated the global South was the continuing refusal of the North to increase significantly the quotas or shares of developing countries, particularly the more dynamic 'middle income' countries like China, Brazil, India, and Korea, which would have led to their having greater decision-making power. Also, the continuing feudal practice of having an American head the World Bank and a European to lead the Fund became increasingly unacceptable to a great number of member countries from the global South.

In short, even before the outbreak of the financial crisis in 2007, the multilateral system was already eroding. The WTO was in a stalemate while the World Bank was trying to reinvent itself as the 'Climate Bank.' As for the IMF, its leaders, notably managing director Dominique Strauss-Kahn and his successor Christine Lagarde, tried to shore up the Fund's position by rhetorically distancing themselves from the neoliberal approach of the past and putting a Keynesian gloss on the institution. The G20 also brought the Fund in as a mechanism to channel funds to Ireland, Greece, Iceland, and other European economies that were suffering from the financial crisis. However, its influence was very limited, as the European Commission, the European Central Bank, and national governments like Germany and France took the reins directly in dealing with the crisis, unlike during the Asian financial crisis, when the IMF played the central role.

The palpable loss of power and influence of the multilateral institutions was not unconnected to the crisis of globalization, which they had been structured to promote. In the early 1990s, globalization was said to be irreversible. But in the decade from the collapse of the Seattle ministerial meeting in 1999 to the outbreak of the financial crisis in 2008, the sense of inevitability disappeared. This was not only on account of the weak recovery in global economic activity and trade – which, incidentally, in 2009, led to the largest drop in the level of greenhouse gas emissions in forty years.[48]

According to *The Economist*, the 'integration of the world economy is in retreat on almost every front.' While the magazine said that corporations continued to believe in the efficiency of global supply chains, 'like any chain they are only as strong as their weakest link. A danger will come if firms decide that this way of organizing production has had its day.'[49] The fear that haunted many pro-globalist sectors was what happened after 1914, when the first era of globalization that began in 1815 – a period in which, in many ways, the global economy was more integrated than today – came to an end in war, national competition, and depression.

By the beginning of 2012, with indefinite economic stagnation in both the US and Europe a certainty, and with the BRICS slowing down, the retreat from globalization had become more of a certainty in many quarters. As Nader Mousavizadeh and George Kell wrote in the *International Herald Tribune*, 'we are entering a period of competitive sovereignty, replacing two decades of consensus around the universal benefits of globalization – however uneven and unequal its path.'[50]

Competing alternatives

With the deepening of the economic crisis, proposed solutions came from several quarters.

The neoliberal non-solution

After being on the defensive in the immediate aftermath of the crisis, the neoliberals bounced back in 2011 and 2012. The neo-

---

48. Fiona Harvey, 'Recession Results in Steep Fall in Emissions,' *Financial Times*, September 21, 2009.

49. 'Turning Their Backs on the World,' *The Economist*, February 19, 2009, www.economist.com/node/13145370?story_id=13145370.

50. Nader Mousavizadeh and George Kell, 'Getting Down to Business in Rio,' *International Herald Tribune*, June 15, 2002, p. 8.

liberal solution was no solution, however, inasmuch as it did not address the issue of ending unemployment and restarting growth. From the neoliberal perspective, a deepening of the crisis was, in fact, part of the natural order of things, whereby the 'excesses' and distortions created by government intervention were wrung out of the system. What the neoliberals managed to do was to change the narrative or the discourse, playing on the American middle class's traditional distrust of government, deficit spending, and taxes. Here they were supported by the propaganda machinery of Wall Street, which sought to move the public focus away from financial reform. Instead of unemployment and stagnation in the short and medium term, the real problem they pointed to was the debt and the deficit. Massive deficits financed by debt, they said, would ensure a future of debt slavery for future generations.

The limits of Keynesianism... and Marxism

The Keynesians saw unemployment as the problem, and it was to be banished by massive deficit spending, low interest rates, and loose money policies. Criticism of Keynesianism, however, came not only from the right but also from progressive quarters, which saw its focus on growth by stimulating consumption as simply a short-term solution bereft of a transformative vision for restructuring the economy along lines of greater equity and democracy. In the view of Marxists, Keynesianism's basic flaw was its adherence to the framework of monopoly capitalism, which rested fundamentally on deriving profit from the exploitative extraction of surplus value from labor, was driven from crisis to crisis by inherent tendencies toward overproduction, and tended to push the environment to its limits in its search for profitability.

In both the national and the global arena, the new Keynesianism promoted a new class compromise accompanied by new methods to contain or minimize capitalism's tendency toward crisis. Just as the old Keynesianism and the New Deal stabilized national capitalism, the historical function of the new Keynesianism was to iron out the contradictions of contemporary global capitalism and to relegitimize it after the crisis and chaos left by neoliberalism. In the view of many progressives, the new Keynesianism was, at root, about social management.

As for Marxists, while the analysis of capitalist crisis they offered was often very insightful, their alternative was often vague, being couched at times as 'post-capitalism,' a defensive paradigm and terminology that was a legacy, no doubt, of the collapse of central-ized bureaucratic socialism as an alternative during the latter half of the twentieth century.

The 'end-of-growth school'

Radical environmentalists located the crisis in the much broader context of a growth-oriented, fossil-fuel-addicted mode of produc-tion. To analysts like Richard Heinberg, the intersection of the financial collapse, economic stagnation, global warming, the steady depletion of fossil fuel reserves, and agriculture reaching its limits was a fatal one. It represented a far more profound crisis than a temporary setback on the road to growth. It portended not simply the end of a paradigm of global growth driven by the demand of the center economies. It meant the 'end of growth' as we know it. It was, in short, the Malthusian trap, though Heinberg understand-ably avoided using the term.

The gyrations of the finance economy, Heinberg said, did not simply stem from the dynamics of capital accumulation but from an all-encompassing ecological disequilibrium:

> Perhaps the meteoric rise of the finance economy in the past couple of decades resulted from semi-conscious strategy on the part of society's managerial elites to leverage the last possible increments of growth from a physical, resource based economy that was nearing its capacity. In any case, the implications of the current economic crisis cannot be captured by unemployment

statistics and real estate prices. Attempts to restart growth will inevitably collide with natural limits that simply don't respond to stimulus packages or bailouts. ... Burgeoning environmental problems require rapidly increasing amounts of efforts to fix them. In addition to facing limits on the amount of debt that can be accumulated in order to keep those problems at bay, we also face limits to the amounts of energy and materials we can devote to these purposes. Until now the dynamism of growth has enabled us to stay ahead of accumulating environmental costs. As growth ends, the environmental bills for the last two centuries of manic expansion may come due just as our bank account empties.[51]

The next few decades, Heinberg asserted, would be marked by a transition from expansion to contraction, a process 'characterized by an overall contraction of society until we are living within Earth's replenishable budget of renewable resources, while continually re-cycling most of the minerals and metals we continue to use.'[52] The future pointed in the direction of decentralized eco-communities marked by more manageable participatory decision-making, pow-ered by low-energy systems, reliant on co-operatives for production and other economic functions, dependent on organic farming for food, and using non-debt-based currencies for exchange.

Some of the proposals advanced by the 'End-of-Growth' school have been shared by other perspectives, such as the 'Food Sover-eignty' and 'Deglobalization' schools, though these do not endorse the former's view that radical economic contraction is inevitable and desirable. The Deglobalization perspective proposed by the author aims at enhancing ecological equilibrium, democracy, and equality while promoting the principle of subsidiarity or locat-ing the locus of production and decision-making at the lowest level, where it can be done with minimal economic cost. A more comprehensive discussion of Deglobalization is provided in the concluding chapter.

---

51. Richard Heinberg, *The End of Growth* (British Columbia: New Society, 2011), p. 152.
52. Ibid., p. 284.

Resistance and transformation

Articulating a vision and program for change is one thing; building a global mass movement is another. The power of mass movements was demonstrated in Seattle in November 1999, when 50,000 people on the streets opposing the WTO brought about the collapse of the Third Ministerial Meeting – an event which convinced many more people throughout the world about the wrong track that globalization was taking the world than a hundred studies documenting its failures. Seattle gave birth to the Anti-Globalization Movement, which introduced innovative organizing methods, as people confronted corporate capital and the multilateral institutions in different sites, in Prague in 2000, Genoa in 2001, and Cancún in 2003. The Anti-Globalization Movement was marked by non-hierarchical methods of organizing, by a horizontal process of coming together of networks, where struggles drew their strength from the non-centralized character of the movement, where there was no visible leadership structure, and where decisions were made via methods approximating direct democracy.

A central principle of the organizing approach of the new movement was that getting to the desired objective was not worth it if the methods violated democratic process, if democratic goals were reached via authoritarian means. Perhaps Subcomandante Marcos of the Zapatistas best expressed this fundamental philosophical bias of the new movements: 'The movement has no future if its future is military. If the EZLN [Zapatistas] perpetuates itself as an armed military structure, it is headed for failure. Failure as an alternative set of ideas, an alternative attitude to the world. The worst that could happen to it, apart from that, would be for it to come to power and install itself there as a revolutionary army.'[53]

---

53. 'Subcomandante Marcos: The Punch Card and the Hour Glass,' *New Left Review* 9 (May-June 2001), www.newleftreview.org/II/9/subcomandante-marcos-the-punch-card-and-the -hourglass.

One of the most important vehicles to emerge from the Anti-Globalization Movement was the World Social Forum (WSF), which was founded in 2000. The WSF was direct democracy in action. At its height in the mid-2000s, the WSF performed three critical functions for global civil society.

First, it represented a space – both physical and temporal – for a diverse movement to meet, to network, and, quite simply, to feel and affirm itself. Second, it was a retreat during which the movement gathered its energies and charted the directions of its continuing drive to confront and roll back the processes, institutions, and structures of global capitalism. Naomi Klein, author of *No Logo*, underlined this function when she told a Pôrto Alegre audience in January 2002 that the need of the moment was 'less civil society and more civil disobedience.' Third, the WSF provided a site and space for the movement to elaborate, discuss, and debate the vision, values, and institutions of an alternative world order built on a real community of interests.

Yet while the WSF and the Anti-Globalization Movement were significant and successful as resistance movements, they failed to move into the vacuum created by the collapse of the globalization paradigm. One reason was the lack of consensus on a common alternative vision, a key function that was played by the ideal of socialism from the late nineteenth to the late twentieth century. But the other key reason was just as important. This was articulated by Hugo Chávez during the World Social Forum assembly in Caracas in 2006, when he warned delegates in January 2006 about the danger of the WSF becoming simply a forum of ideas with no agenda for action. He told participants that they had no choice but to address the question of power: 'We must have a strategy of "counter-power." We, the social movements and political movements, must be able to move into spaces of power at the local, national, and regional level.'[54]

---

54. www.forumsocialmundial.org.br/noticias_textos.php?cd_news=395.

Developing a strategy of counter-power or counter-hegemony need not mean lapsing back into the old hierarchical and centralized modes of organizing characteristic of the old left. Such a strategy might, in fact, be best advanced through the multilevel and horizontal networking that the movements and organizations represented in the WSF excelled at in advancing their particular struggles. Articulating their struggles in action would mean forging a common strategy while drawing strength from and respecting diversity.

The Anti-Globalization Movement was at a crossroads when the financial collapse occurred in 2008, followed by the tumultuous political events in the Middle East in late 2010. Whether the 'Occupy Movement' and the 'Arab Spring,' two movements that emerged from these twin developments, will be successful where the Anti-Globalization Movement and the World Social Forum fell short remains to be seen.

PART I

THE DESTRUCTIVE DYNAMICS
OF FINANCE CAPITAL

CHAPTER I

WHY AND HOW
FINANCE BECAME DOMINANT

A primer on Wall Street meltdown

Written shortly after the Wall Street collapse in September 2008, this essay sought to capture the impact of the event on the American middle class while providing a primer on the causes and dynamics of the financial crisis. The central concept here is 'overproduction.' Rooted in the inherent tendency to create productive capacity that outstrips demand, capital's effort to surmount the crisis of overproduction is one of the central engines of globalization and financialization, which triggered the financial crisis. Deglobalization is thus, at bottom, a response to the crisis of capitalism.[1]

Flying into New York Tuesday, I had the same feeling I had when I arrived in Beirut two years ago, at the height of the Israeli bombing of that city – that of entering a war zone.

The immigration agent, upon learning I taught political economy, commented, 'Well, I guess you folks will now be revising all those textbooks?'

The bus driver welcomed passengers with the words, 'New York is still here, ladies and gentlemen, but Wall Street has disappeared, like the Twin Towers.'

---

1. Originally published in http://mrzine.monthlyreview.org/2008/bello031008p.html, reproduced with permission from Focus on the Global South.

Even the usually cheerful TV morning shows felt obligated to begin with the bad news, with one host attributing the bleak events to 'the fat cats of Wall Street who turned into pigs.'

This city is shell-shocked, and most people still have to digest the momentous events of the past two weeks:

- a trillion dollars' worth of capital going up in smoke in Wall Street's steep plunge of 778 points on Black Monday II, September 29, as investors reacted in panic to the US House of Representatives' rejection of President George W. Bush's gargantuan $700 billion bailout of financial institutions on the verge of bankruptcy;
- the collapse of one of the Street's most prominent investment banks, Lehman Brothers, followed by the largest bank failure in US history, that of Washington Mutual, the country's largest savings and loan institution;
- Wall Street's effective nationalization, with the Federal Reserve and the Department of Treasury making all the major strategic decisions in the financial sector and, with the rescue of the American International Group (AIG), the amazing fact that the US government now runs the world's biggest insurance company.

Over $5 trillion in total market capitalization has been wiped out since October of last year, with over a trillion of this accounted for by the unraveling of Wall Street's financial titans.

The usual explanations no longer suffice. Extraordinary events demand extraordinary explanations. But first...

Is the worst over?

No, if anything is clear from the contradictory moves of the last week – allowing Lehman Brothers and Washington Mutual to collapse while taking AIG over and engineering Bank of America's takeover of Merrill Lynch – there is no strategy to deal with the crisis, just tactical responses, like the fire department's response to a conflagration.

The proposed $700 billion buyout of banks' bad mortgaged-backed securities is not a strategy but mainly a desperate effort to shore up confidence in the system, to prevent the erosion of trust in the banks and other financial institutions and avoid a massive bank run such as the one that triggered the Great Depression of 1929.

Did greed cause the collapse of global capitalism's nerve center?

Good old-fashioned greed played a part. This is what Klaus Schwab, the organizer of the World Economic Forum, the yearly global elite jamboree in the Swiss Alps, meant when he told his clientele in Davos earlier this year: 'We have to pay for the sins of the past.'[2]

Was this a case of Wall Street outsmarting itself?

Definitely. Financial speculators outsmarted themselves by creating more and more complex financial contracts like derivatives that would securitize and make money from all forms of risk – including exotic futures instruments such as 'credit default swaps' that enable investors to bet on the odds that the banks' own corporate borrowers would not be able to pay their debts! This is the unregulated multi-trillion-dollar trade that brought AIG down.

On December 17, 2005, when International Financing Review (IFR) announced its 2005 Annual Awards – one of the securities industry's most prestigious awards – it had this to say:

> [Lehman Brothers] not only maintained its overall market presence, but also led the charge into the preferred space by ... developing new products and tailoring transactions to fit borrowers' needs. ... Lehman Brothers is the most innovative in the preferred space, just doing things you won't see elsewhere.[3]

---

2. www.theglobeandmail.com/report-on-business/turmoil-changes-mood-of-davos-summit/article666594.

3. http://www.ifre.com/section2.aspx?navCode=603.

No comment.

Was it lack of regulation?

Yes – everyone acknowledges by now that Wall Street's capacity to innovate and turn out more and more sophisticated financial instruments had run far ahead of government's regulatory capability, not because government was not capable of regulating but because the dominant neoliberal, laissez-faire attitude prevented government from devising effective mechanisms with which to regulate. The massive trading in derivatives helped precipitate this crisis, and the US Congress paved the way when it passed a law in 2000 excluding derivatives from being regulated by the Securities Exchange Commission.

But isn't something more happening, something systemic?

Well, George Soros, who saw this coming, says what we are going through is the crisis of the 'gigantic circulatory system' of a 'global capitalist system that is ... coming apart at the seams.'[4]

To elaborate on the arch-speculator's insight, what we are seeing is the intensification of one of the central crises or contradictions of global capitalism, which is the crisis of overproduction, also known as overaccumulation or overcapacity.

This is the tendency for capitalism to build up tremendous productive capacity that outruns the population's capacity to consume, owing to social inequalities that limit popular purchasing power. Profitability is thus eroded.

But what does the crisis of overproduction have to do with recent events?

Plenty. But to understand the connections, we must go back in time to the so-called Golden Age of Contemporary Capitalism, the period from 1945 to 1975.

---

4. http://news.bbc.co.uk/1/hi/business/172222.stm.

This was a period of rapid growth both in the center economies and in the underdeveloped economies – one that was partly triggered by the massive reconstruction of Europe and East Asia after the devastation of the Second World War, and partly by the new socioeconomic arrangements that were institutionalized under the new Keynesian state. Among the latter, key were strong state controls over market activity, aggressive use of fiscal and monetary policy to minimize inflation and recession, and a regime of relatively high wages to stimulate and maintain demand.

So what went wrong?

Well, this period of high growth came to an end in the mid-1970s, when the center economies were seized by stagflation, meaning the coexistence of low growth with high inflation, which was not supposed to happen under neoclassical economics.

Stagflation, however, was but a symptom of a deeper cause: the reconstruction of Germany and Japan and the rapid growth of industrializing economies like Brazil, Taiwan, and South Korea added tremendous new productive capacity and increased global competition, while social inequalities within countries and between countries worldwide limited the growth of purchasing power and demand, thus eroding profitability. This was aggravated by the massive oil price rises of the 1970s.

How did capitalism try to solve the crisis of overproduction?

Capital tried three escape routes from the conundrum of overproduction: neoliberal restructuring, globalization, and financialization.

What was neoliberal restructuring all about?

Neoliberal restructuring took the form of Reaganism and Thatcherism in the North and structural adjustment in the South. The aim was to invigorate capital accumulation, and this was to be done by (1) removing state constraints on the growth, use, and flow of capital and wealth, and (2) redistributing income from the poor and middle classes to the rich on the theory that the rich would then be motivated to invest and reignite economic growth.

The problem with this formula was that in redistributing income to the rich, they were gutting the incomes of the poor and middle classes, thus restricting demand, while not necessarily inducing the rich to invest more in production. In fact, what the rich did was to channel a large part of their redistributed wealth to speculation.

The truth is neoliberal restructuring, which was generalized in the North and South during the 1980s and 1990s, had a poor record in terms of growth: global growth averaged 1.1 percent in the 1990s and 1.4 percent in the 1980s, whereas it averaged 3.5 percent in the 1960s and 2.4 percent in the 1970s, when state interventionist policies were dominant. Neoliberal restructuring could not shake off stagnation.

How was globalization a response to the crisis?

The second escape route global capital took to counter stagnation was 'extensive accumulation' or globalization, or the rapid integration of semi-capitalist, non-capitalist, or pre-capitalist areas into the global market economy. Rosa Luxemburg, the famous German revolutionary economist, saw this long ago as necessary to shore up the rate of profit in the metropolitan economies. How? By gaining access to cheap labor; by gaining new, albeit limited, markets; by gaining new sources of cheap agricultural and raw material products; and by bringing into being new areas for investment in infrastructure. Integration is accomplished via trade liberalization, removing barriers to the mobility of global capital, and abolishing barriers to foreign investment.

China is, of course, the most prominent case of a non-capitalist area to be integrated into the global capitalist economy over the past twenty-five years.

To counter their declining profits, a sizable number of the Fortune 500 corporations have moved a significant part of their operations to China to take advantage of the so-called 'China Price' – the cost advantage deriving from China's seemingly inexhaustible cheap labor. By the middle of the first decade of the twenty-first century, roughly 40-50 percent of the profits of US corporations were derived from their operations and sales abroad, especially in China.

Why didn't globalization surmount the crisis?

The problem with this escape route from stagnation is that it exacerbates the problem of overproduction because it adds to productive capacity. A tremendous amount of manufacturing capacity has been added in China over the past twenty-five years, and this has had a depressing effect on prices and profits. Not surprisingly, by around 1997 the profits of US corporations stopped growing. According to another index, devised by economist Philip O'Hara, the profit rate of the Fortune 500 went from 7.15 in 1960-69 to 5.30 in 1980-90 to 4.02 in 1990-99 to 3.30 in 2000-02.[5]

What about financialization?

Given the limited gains in countering the depressive impact of overproduction via neoliberal restructuring and globalization, the third escape route became very critical for maintaining and raising profitability: financialization.

In the ideal world of neoclassical economics, the financial system is the mechanism by which the savers or those with surplus funds are joined with the entrepreneurs who have need of their funds to invest in production. In the real world of late capitalism, with investment in industry and agriculture yielding low profits owing to overcapacity, large amounts of surplus funds are circulating and being invested and reinvested in the financial sector – that is, the financial sector is turning in on itself.

---

5. Philip Anthony O'Hara, *Growth and Global Development in the Global Political Economy* (London: Routledge, 2006), p. 77.

The result is an increased bifurcation between a hyperactive financial economy and a stagnant real economy. As one financial executive notes, 'There has been an increasing disconnection between the real and financial economies in the last few years. The real economy has grown ... but nothing like that of the financial economy – until it imploded.'[6]

What this observer does not tell us is that the disconnect between the real and the financial economy is not accidental – that the financial economy imploded precisely to make up for the stagnation owing to overproduction of the real economy.

What were the problems with financialization?

The problem with investing in financial sector operations is that it is tantamount to squeezing value out of already created value. It may create profit, yes, but it does not create new value – only industry, agriculture, trade, and services create new value.

Because profit is not based on value that is created, investment operations become very volatile, and prices of stocks, bonds, and other forms of investment can depart very radically from their real value – for instance, the stock of Internet startups that keep on rising, driven mainly by upwardly spiraling financial valuations, and that then crash.

Profits then depend on taking advantage of upward price departures from the value of commodities, and then selling before reality enforces a 'correction' – that is, a crash back to real values.

The radical rise of prices of an asset far beyond real values is what is called the formation of a bubble.

Why is financialization so volatile?

Profitability being dependent on speculative coups, it is not surprising that the finance sector lurches from one bubble to another, or from one speculative mania to another.

---

6. www.ft.com/cms/s/0/93b9ccoc-d346-11dc-b861-0000779fd2ac.html.

Because it is driven by speculative mania, finance-driven capitalism has experienced about a hundred financial crises since capital markets were deregulated and liberalized in the 1980s.

Prior to the current Wall Street meltdown, the most explosive of these were the Mexican Financial Crisis of 1994-95, the Asian Financial Crisis of 1997-98, the Russian Financial Crisis of 1996, the Wall Street Stock Market Collapse of 2001, and the Argentine Financial Collapse of 2002.

Bill Clinton's treasury secretary, Wall Streeter Robert Rubin, predicted five years ago that 'future financial crises are almost surely inevitable and could be even more severe.'[7]

How do bubbles form, grow, and burst?

Let's first use the Asian financial crisis of 1997-98 as an example.

- First, capital account and financial liberalization at the urging of the IMF and the US Department of Treasury.
- Then entry of foreign funds seeking quick and high returns, meaning they went to real estate and the stock market.
- Overinvestment, leading to a fall in stock and real estate prices, leading to panicky withdrawal of funds – in 1997, $100 billion left the East Asian economies in a few weeks.
- Bailout of foreign speculators by the IMF.
- Collapse of the real economy – recession throughout East Asia in 1998.

Despite massive destabilization, efforts to impose both national and global regulation of the financial system were opposed on ideological grounds.

Let's go to the current bubble. How did it form?

The current Wall Street collapse has its roots in the Technology Bubble of the late 1990s, when the price of the stocks of Internet

---

7. www.nytimes.com/2003/11/30/books/the-man-behind-the-surplus-remember.html.

startups skyrocketed, then collapsed, resulting in the loss of $7 trillion worth of assets and the recession of 2001–02.

The loose money policies of the Fed under Alan Greenspan had encouraged the Technology Bubble. When the US fell into a recession, Greenspan, to try to counter a long recession, cut the prime rate to a 45-year low of 1.00 percent in June 2003 and kept it there for over a year. That had the effect of encouraging another bubble: the real estate bubble.

As early as 2002, progressive economists, such as Dean Baker of the Center for Economic Policy Research, were warning about the real estate bubble. However, as late as 2005, Ben Bernanke, then chairman of the Council of Economic Advisers and now chairman of the Federal Reserve, attributed the rise in US housing prices to 'strong economic fundamentals' instead of speculative activity. Is it any wonder that he was caught completely off guard when the subprime crisis broke in the summer of 2007?

And how did it grow?

Let's hear it from one key market player himself, George Soros: 'Mortgage institutions encouraged mortgage holders to refinance their mortgages and withdraw the excess equity. They lowered their lending standards and introduced new products, such as adjustable-rate mortgages (ARMs), "interest only" mortgages, and promotional "teaser rates." All this encouraged speculation in residential housing units. House prices started to rise in double-digit rates. This served to reinforce speculation, and the rise in house prices made the owners feel rich; the result was a consumption boom that has sustained the economy in recent years.'[8]

Looking at the process more closely, the subprime mortgage crisis was not a case of supply outrunning real demand. The 'demand' was largely fabricated by speculative mania among developers and

---

8. George Soros, *The Age of Fallibility: Consequences of the War on Terror* (New York: Public Affairs, 2007).

financiers that wanted to make great profits from their access to foreign money – lots of it from Asia – that flooded the US in the last decade. Big-ticket mortgages or loans were aggressively made to millions of people who could not normally afford them by offering low 'teaser' interest rates that would later be readjusted to jack up payments from the new homeowners.

But how could subprime mortgages going sour turn into such a big problem?

Because these assets were then 'securitized' with other assets into complex derivative products called 'collateralized debt obligations' (CDOs), by the mortgage originators working with different layers of middlemen who understated risk so as to offload them as quickly as possible to other banks and institutional investors. These institutions in turn offloaded these securities onto other banks and foreign financial institutions. The idea was to make a sale quickly, make a tidy profit, while foisting the risk on the suckers down the line.

When the interest rates were raised on the subprime loans, adjustable mortgages, and other housing loans, the game was up. There are about 6 million subprime mortgages outstanding, 40 percent of which will likely go into default in the next two years, according to Soros's estimates.

And 5 million more defaults from adjustable-rate mortgages and other 'flexible loans' will occur in the next several years. But securities whose values run in the trillions of dollars have already been injected, like a virus, into the global financial system. Global capitalism's gigantic circulatory system is fatally infected.

But how could Wall Street titans collapse like a house of cards?

For Lehman Brothers, Merrill Lynch, Fannie Mae, Freddie Mac, and Bear Stearns, the losses represented by these toxic securities simply overwhelmed their reserves and brought them down. And more are likely to fall once their books – since lots of these holdings are recorded 'off the balance sheet' – are corrected to reflect their actual holdings of these assets.

And many others will join them as other speculative operations, such as credit cards and different varieties of risk insurance, seize up. American International Group (AIG) was felled by its massive exposure in the unregulated area of credit default swaps, derivatives that make it possible for investors to bet on the possibility that companies will default on repaying loans. Such bets on credit defaults now make up a $45 trillion market that is entirely unregulated. It amounts to more than five times the total of the US government bond market. The mega-size of the assets that could go bad should AIG collapse was what made Washington change its mind and salvage it after it let Lehman Brothers collapse.

What's going to happen now?

We can safely say, then, that there will be more bankruptcies and government takeovers, with foreign banks and institutions joining their US counterparts; that Wall Street's collapse will deepen and prolong the US recession; and that in Asia and elsewhere a US recession will translate into a recession, if not worse.

The reason for that last point is that China's main foreign market is the US, and China in turn imports raw materials and intermediate goods that it uses for its exports to the US from Japan, South Korea, and Southeast Asia. Globalization has made 'decoupling' impossible. The US, China, and East Asia are like three prisoners bound together in a chain gang.

In a nutshell...?

The Wall Street meltdown is due not only to greed and the lack of government regulation of a hyperactive sector. It stems ultimately from the crisis of overproduction that has plagued global capitalism since the mid-1970s.

Financialization of investment activity has been one of the escape routes from stagnation, the other two being neoliberal restructuring and globalization. With neoliberal restructuring and globalization providing limited relief, financialization became attractive as a mechanism to shore up profitability. But financialization has proven to be a dangerous road, resulting in speculative bubbles that lead to the temporary prosperity of a few but end up in corporate collapse and in recession in the real economy.

The key questions now are these. How deep and long will this recession be? Does the US economy need another speculative bubble to drag itself out of this recession? And, if it does, where will the next bubble form? Some people say the military-industrial complex or the 'disaster capitalism complex' that Naomi Klein writes about is the next one, but that's another story.[9]

Recovery recedes, convulsion looms

By 2011, forecasts about recovery from the global economic crisis were fading, and long-term stagnation appeared to be the more likely prospect. Why the world should brace for long-term economic stagnation, with its portentous social and political consequences, was the subject of this essay. A key theme of the essay is that the accelerated integration of economies in the era of globalization is one of the key reasons for the failure of economies to recover. Thus a strategy that reverses globalization, or deglobalization, might be a precondition for a sustained recovery.[10]

The dominant mood in liberal economic circles as 2010 drew to a close, in contrast to the cautiously optimistic forecasts about a

---

9. Naomi Klein, *The Shock Doctrine: The Rise of Disaster Capitalism* (New York: Henry Holt, 2007).

10. Originally published as 'Recovery Recedes, Convulsion Looms,' www.fpif.org/articles/recovery_recedes_convulsion_looms.

sustained recovery at the end of 2009, was gloom, if not doom. Fiscal hawks have gained the upper hand in the policy struggle in the United States and Europe, to the alarm of spending advocates like Nobel laureate Paul Krugman and *Financial Times* columnist Martin Wolf, who see budgetary tightening as a surefire prescription for killing the hesitant recovery in the major economies.

But even as the United States and Europe appear to be headed for deeper crisis in the short term and stagnation in the long term, East Asia and other developing areas show signs of decoupling from the Western economies. This trend began in early 2009 on the strength of the massive Chinese stimulus program, which not only restored China to double-digit growth but swung several neighboring economies from Singapore to South Korea from recession to recovery. By 2010, Asia's industrial production had caught up with its historical trend, 'almost as if the Great Recession never happened,' as *The Economist* put it.[11]

The United States, Europe, and Asia seem to be going their separate ways. Or are they?

The triumph of austerity

In the major economies, outrage at the excesses of the financial institutions that precipitated the economic crisis has given way to concern about the massive deficits that governments incurred to stabilize the financial system, arrest the collapse of the real economy, and stave off unemployment. In the United States, the deficit stands at over 9 percent of gross domestic product. This is hardly a runaway deficit, but the American right managed the feat of making the fear of the deficit and federal debt a greater force in the mind of the public than the fear of deepening stagnation and rising unemployment. In Britain and the United States, fiscal

---

11. www.economist.com/node/17679675.

conservatives gained a clear electoral mandate in 2010, while in continental Europe a more assertive Germany put the rest of the eurozone on notice that it would no longer subsidize the deficits of the monetary union's weaker southern-tier economies such as Greece, Ireland, Spain, and Portugal.

In the United States, the logic of reason gave way to the logic of ideology. The Democrats' impeccable rationale that stimulus spending was necessary to save and create jobs was no match for the Republicans' heated message that more stimulus spending added to President Obama's $787 billion 2009 package would be one more step towards 'socialism' and the 'loss of individual freedom.' In Europe, Keynesians argued that fiscal loosening would help not only the troubled economies of southern Europe and Ireland but also the powerful German economic machine itself, since these economies absorbed German exports.

As in the United States, solid rationale lost out to provocative image, in this case the media-disseminated portrayal of thrifty Germans subsidizing hedonistic Mediterraneans and spendthrift Irishmen. Germany has grudgingly approved bailout packages for Greece and Ireland, but only on condition that the Greeks and Irish are subjected to savage austerity programs that have been described by no less than two former high-ranking German ministers, Frank-Walter Steinmeier and Peer Steinbrueck, writing in the *Financial Times*, as having a degree of social pain 'unheard of in modern history.'[12]

Decoupling revived

The triumph of austerity in the US and Europe will surely eliminate these two areas as engines of recovery for the global economy. But

---

12. 'Germany Must Lead Fightback,' *Financial Times*, December 14, 2010, www.ft.com/cms/s/0/effa001c-07ba-11e0-a568-00144feabdco.html.

is Asia indeed on a different track, one that would make it bear, like Atlas, the burden of global growth?

The idea that Asia's economic future had been decoupled from that of the center economies is not new. It was fashionable before the financial crisis dragged down the US economy in 2007-08. But it was shown to be a mirage as the recession in the United States, on which China and the other East Asian economies were dependent to absorb their exports, triggered a sudden and sharp downturn in Asia from late 2008 to mid-2009. This period produced television images of millions of Chinese migrant workers, laid off in coastal economic zones, heading back to the countryside.

To counter the contraction, a panicked China launched what Charles Dumas characterized as a 'violent domestic stimulus'[13] of 4 trillion yuan ($580 billion). This came to about 13 percent of gross domestic product in 2008 and constituted 'probably the largest such program in history, even including wars.' The stimulus not only pulled China back to double-digit growth; it also pushed the East Asian economies that had become dependent on it to a steep recovery even as Europe and the United States stagnated. This remarkable reversal led to the renaissance of the decoupling idea.

The ruling Communist Party of China has reinforced this notion by claiming a fundamental policy shift to prioritizing domestic consumption over export-led growth. But this contention is more rhetorical than real. In fact, export-led growth remains the strategic thrust, thus China's continuing refusal to let the yuan appreciate in order to keep its exports competitive. China, as Dumas notes, is 'in the process of shifting massively from the beneficial stimulation of domestic demand to something closely resembling business as usual, circa 2005-07: export-led growth with a bit of overheating.'[14]

---

13. *Globalisation Fractures: How Major Nations' Interests Are Now in Conflict* (London: Profile, 2010), p. 54.

14. Ibid., p. 113.

Not only Western analysts like Dumas have pointed to this return to export-led growth. Yu Yongding, an influential technocrat who served on the monetary committee of China's central bank, confirms that it is indeed back to business as usual:

> With China's trade-to-GDP ratio and exports-to-GDP ratio already respectively exceeding 60 percent and 30 percent, the economy cannot continue to depend on external demand to sustain growth. Unfortunately, with a large export sector that employs scores of millions of workers, this dependence has become structural. That means reducing China's trade dependency and trade surplus is much more than a matter of adjusting macroeconomic policy.[15]

The retreat back to export-led growth, rather than merely a case of structural dependency, reflects a set of interests from the reform period that, as Yu puts it, 'have morphed into vested interests, which are fighting hard to protect what they have.' The export lobby, which brings together private entrepreneurs, state enterprise managers, foreign investors, and government technocrats, is the strongest lobby in Beijing. If the justification for stimulus spending has been trumped by ideology in the United States, in China the equally impeccable rationale for domestic-market-centered growth has been trounced by material interests.

Global deflation

So decoupling is not a likely trend since China's leaders have chosen to stake the future of the Chinese economy on US and, to some extent, European demand. But the context has changed ever since the rupture in the pre-crisis 'partnership' between the American consumer and the Chinese producer. Not only are Americans deep in debt but the budgetary crunch pushed by the fiscal hawks will squeeze their incomes even further.

---

15. 'A Different Road Forward,' *China Daily*, www.chinadaily.com.cn/opinion/2010-12/23/content_11742757.htm.

Indeed, what analysts like Dumas refer to as China's 'reversion to type' as an export-oriented economy will clash with the efforts of the United States and Europe to speed recovery by adopting China's own formula: pushing exports while raising barriers to the inflow of imports. The likely result of the competitive promotion of this volatile mix of export push and domestic protection by all three leading sectors of the global economy at a time of stagnant world trade will not be global expansion but global deflation.

As Jeffrey Garten, former US undersecretary of commerce under Bill Clinton, has written:

> While so much attention has focused on consumer and industrial demand in the US and China, the deflationary policies enveloping the EU, the world's largest economic unit, could badly undermine global economic growth... The difficulties could cause Europe to redouble its focus on exports at the same time that the US, Asia, and Latin America are also betting their economies on selling more abroad, thereby exacerbating already-high currency tensions. It could lead to a resurgence of state-sponsored industrial policies, already growing around the world. And together, these factors could ignite the virulent protectionism that everyone fears.[16]

What is in store for us in 2011 and beyond, Garten warns, is 'exceptional turbulence as the waning days of the global economic order we have known plays [sic] out chaotically, possibly destructively.' He projects a pessimism that is increasingly capturing sections of a global elite that once heralded globalization but now sees it disintegrating before its eyes. This resigned *fin de siècle* mood is not a Western monopoly. Yu Yongding also claims that China's 'growth pattern has now almost exhausted its potential.' The economy that most successfully rode the globalization wave, China 'has reached a crucial juncture: without painful structural adjustments, the

---

16. 'Brace for Change as the Global Economic Order Crumbles,' *Yale Global Online*, http://yaleglobal.yale.edu/content/global-economic-order-crumbles.

momentum of its economic growth could suddenly be lost. China's rapid growth has been achieved at an extremely high cost. Only future generations will know the true price.'[17]

In contrast to the apprehension of establishment figures like Garten and Yu, many progressives see turbulence and conflict as necessary accompaniments of the birth of a new order. Workers have indeed been on the move in China, where strikes in selected foreign companies in 2010 resulted in significant wage gains. Protesters are indeed out in the streets in Ireland, Greece, France, and Britain.

Unlike in China, however, they are marching to preserve what rights they have left. And neither in China nor in the West nor elsewhere is this resistance accompanied by an alternative vision to the global capitalist order. A more far-reaching discussion of alternative economic arrangements should be ongoing as the global economic crisis enters its fourth year. But the debate continues to be trapped between the sterile spend-and-stimulate versus cut-the-deficit positions. The shape of things to come is simply not visible in the embers of the old. At least, not yet.

---

17. 'A Different Road Forward.'

CHAPTER 2

THE US:
CUTTING EDGE OF CRISIS

Capitalism in an apocalyptic mood

This essay, written as the US economy hurtled toward the abyss in 2008, focused on the evolution of the subprime housing bubble, linking it to increasingly byzantine financial innovations on Wall Street, seeing its roots in the dynamics of overproduction in the 'real economy,' and warning of the emergence of other bubbles. It contends that instability and crisis are the dominant features of global capitalism in the era of neoliberalism and globalization.[1]

Skyrocketing oil prices, a falling dollar, and collapsing financial markets are the key ingredients in an economic brew that could end up in more than just an ordinary recession. The falling dollar and rising oil prices have been rattling the global economy for some time. But it is the dramatic implosion of financial markets that is driving the financial elite to panic.

And panic there is. Even as it characterized Federal Reserve Board chairman Ben Bernanke's deep cuts, amounting to 1.25 points off the prime rate in late January, as a sign of panic, *The Economist* admitted that 'there is no doubt that this is a frightening

---

1. Originally published in *Foreign Policy in Focus*, www.fpif.org/articles/capitalism_in_an_apocalyptic_mood.

moment.'[2] The losses stemming from bad securities tied up with defaulted mortgage loans by 'subprime' borrowers are now estimated to be in the range of about $400 billion. But as the *Financial Times* warned, 'the big question is what else is out there' at a time that the global financial system 'is wide open to a catastrophic failure.'[3] In the last few weeks, for instance, several Swiss, Japanese, and Korean banks have owned up to billions of dollars in subprime-related losses. The globalization of finance was, from the beginning, the cutting edge of the globalization process, and it was always an illusion to think that the subprime crisis could be confined to US financial institutions, as some analysts had thought.

Some key movers and shakers sounded less panicky than resigned to some sort of apocalypse. At the global elite's annual week-long party at Davos in late January, George Soros sounded positively necrological, declaring to one and all that the world was witnessing 'the end of an era.' World Economic Forum host Klaus Schwab spoke of capitalism getting its just desserts, saying, 'We have to pay for the sins of the past.' He told the press, 'It's not that the pendulum is now swinging back to Marxist socialism, but people are asking themselves, "What are the boundaries of the capitalist system?" They think the market may not always be the best mechanism for providing solutions.'[4]

Ruined reputations and policy failures

While some appear to have lost their nerve, others have seen the financial collapse diminish their stature.

As chairman of President Bush's Council of Economic Advisers in 2005, Ben Bernanke attributed the rise in US housing prices

2. 'It's Rough Out There,' January 24, 2008, www.economist.com/node/10566731?story_id=10566731.

3. 'Future Shocks,' January 24, 2008.

4. 'Anxiety Crashes the Party at Davos,' *New York Times*, January 23, 2008, www.nytimes.com/2008/01/23/business/23davos.html?_r=2&pagewanted=print&oref=slogin&.

to 'strong economic fundamentals' instead of speculative activity. So is it any wonder why, as Federal Reserve chairman, he failed to anticipate the housing market's collapse stemming from the subprime mortgage crisis? His predecessor, Alan Greenspan, however, has suffered a bigger hit, moving from iconic status to villain in the eyes of some. They blame the bubble on his aggressively cutting the prime rate to get the United States out of recession in 2003 and restraining it at low levels for over a year. Others say he ignored warnings about aggressive and unscrupulous mortgage originators enticing 'subprime' borrowers with mortgage deals they could never afford.

The scrutiny of Greenspan's record and the failure of Bernanke's rate cuts so far to reignite bank lending have raised serious doubts about the effectiveness of monetary policy in warding off a recession that is now seen as all but inevitable. Nor will fiscal policy or putting money into the hands of consumers do the trick, according to some weighty voices. The $156 billion stimulus package recently approved by the White House and Congress consists largely of tax rebates, and most of these, according to *New York Times* columnist Paul Krugman, will go to those who don't really need them.[5] The tendency will thus be to save rather than spend the rebates in a period of uncertainty, defeating their purpose of stimulating the economy. The specter that now haunts the US economy is Japan's experience of virtually zero annual growth and deflation despite a succession of stimulus packages after Tokyo's great housing bubble deflated in the late 1980s.

The inevitable bubble

Even with the finger-pointing in progress, many analysts remind us that, if anything, the housing crisis should have been expected all

---

5. 'Stimulus Gone Bad,' *New York Times*, January 25, 2008, www.nytimes.com/2008/01/25/opinion/25krugman.html.

along. The only question was when it would break. As progressive economist Dean Baker of the Center for Economic Policy Research noted in an analysis several years ago, 'Like the stock bubble, the housing bubble will burst. Eventually, it must. When it does, the economy will be thrown into a severe recession, and tens of millions of homeowners, who never imagined that house prices could fall, likely will face serious hardship.'[6]

The subprime mortgage crisis was not a case of supply outrunning real demand. The 'demand' was largely fabricated by speculative mania on the part of developers and financiers who wanted to make great profits from their access to foreign money that flooded the United States in the last decade. Big-ticket mortgages were aggressively sold to millions who could not normally afford them by offering low 'teaser' interest rates that would later be readjusted to jack up payments from the new homeowners. These assets were then 'securitized' with other assets into complex derivative products called 'collateralized debt obligations' (CDOs) by the mortgage originators working with different layers of middlemen who understated risk so as to offload them as quickly as possible to other banks and institutional investors. The shooting up of interest rates triggered a wave of defaults, and many of the big-name banks and investors – including Merrill Lynch, Citigroup, and Wells Fargo – found themselves with billions of dollars' worth of bad assets that had been given the green light by their risk-assessment systems.

The failure of self-regulation

The housing bubble is only the latest of some hundred financial crises that have swiftly followed one another ever since the lifting of Depression-era capital controls at the onset of the neoliberal era

---

6. 'The Menace of an Unchecked Housing Bubble,' *The Economists' Voice*, March 30, 2006, www.cepr.net/index.php/op-eds-&-columns/op-eds-&-columns/the-menace-of-an-unchecked-housing-bubble.

in the early 1980s. The calls now coming from some quarters for curbs on speculative capital have an air of déjà vu. After the Asian Financial Crisis of 1997, in particular, there was a strong clamor for capital controls, for a 'new global financial architecture.' The more radical of these called for currency transactions taxes such as the famed Tobin Tax, which would have slowed down capital movements, or for the creation of some kind of global financial authority that would, among other things, regulate relations between northern creditors and indebted developing countries.

Global finance capital, however, resisted any return to state regulation. Nothing came of the proposals for Tobin taxes. The banks killed even a relatively weak 'sovereign debt restructuring mechanism' akin to the US Chapter Eleven to provide some maneuvering room to developing countries undergoing debt repayment problems, even though the proposal came from Ann Krueger, the conservative American deputy managing director of the IMF. Instead, finance capital promoted what came to be known as the Basel II process, described by political economist Robert Wade as steps toward global economic standardization that 'maximize [global financial firms'] freedom of geographical and sectoral maneuver while setting collective constraints on their competitive strategies.'[7] The emphasis was on private-sector self-surveillance and self-policing aimed at greater transparency of financial operations and new standards for capital. Despite the fact that it was finance capital from the industrialized countries that triggered the Asian crisis, the Basel process focused on making developing-country financial institutions and processes transparent and standardized along the lines of what Wade calls the 'Anglo-American' financial model.

---

7. Robert Wade, 'The Aftermath of the Asian Financial Crisis,' in Bhumika Muchhala, ed., *Ten Years After: Revisiting the Asian Financial Crisis* (Washington DC: Woodrow Wilson International Center for Scholars, 2007).

Calls to regulate the proliferation of these new, sophisticated financial instruments, such as derivatives placed on the market by developed-country financial institutions, went nowhere. Assessment and regulation of derivatives were left to market players who had access to sophisticated quantitative 'risk assessment' models.

Focused on disciplining developing countries, the Basel II process accomplished so little in the way of self-regulation of global financial from the North that even Wall Street banker Robert Rubin, former secretary of the treasury under President Clinton, warned in 2003 that 'future financial crises are almost surely inevitable and could be even more severe.'

As for risk assessment of derivatives such as the 'collaterized debt obligations' (CDOs) and 'structured investment vehicles' (SIVs) – the cutting edge of what the *Financial Times* has described as 'the vastly increased complexity of hyperfinance' – the process collapsed almost completely. The most sophisticated quantitative risk models were left in the dust. The sellers of securities priced risk by one rule only: underestimate the real risk and pass it on to the suckers down the line. In the end, it was difficult to distinguish what was fraudulent, what was poor judgment, what was plain foolish, and what was out of anybody's control. 'The U.S. subprime mortgage market was marked by poor underwriting standards and 'some fraudulent practices,'' as one report on the conclusions of a recent meeting of the Group of Seven's Financial Stability Forum put it.

> Investors didn't carry out sufficient due diligence when they
> bought mortgage-backed securities. Banks and other firms
> managed their financial risks poorly and failed to disclose to the
> public the dangers on and off their balance sheets. Credit-rating
> companies did an inadequate job of evaluating the risk of complex
> securities. And the financial institutions compensated their
> employees in ways that encouraged excessive risk-taking and
> insufficient regard to long-term risks.[8]

---

8. 'Global Financial Stability Report: GFSR Market Update,' January 29, 2008, www.imf.

The specter of overproduction

It is not surprising that the G7 report sounded very much like the post-mortems of the Asian financial crisis and the dot.com bubble. One financial corporation chief writing in the *Financial Times* captured the basic problem running through these speculative manias, perhaps unwittingly, when he claimed that 'there has been an increasing disconnection between the real and financial economies in the past few years. The real economy has grown ... but nothing like that of the financial economy, which grew even more rapidly – until it imploded.'[9] What his statement does not tell us is that the disconnect between the real and the financial is not accidental, that the financial economy expanded precisely to make up for the stagnation of the real economy.

The stagnation of the real economy is related to the condition of overproduction or overaccumulation that has plagued the international economy since the mid-1970s. Stemming from global productive capacity outstripping global demand as a result of deep inequalities, this condition has eroded profitability in the industrial sector. One escape route from this crisis has been 'financialization,' or the channeling of investment toward financial speculation, where greater profits could be had. This was, however, illusory in the long run since, unlike industry, speculative finance boiled down to an effort to squeeze out more 'value' from already created value, instead of creating new value.

The disconnect between the real economy and the virtual economy of finance was evident in the dotcom bubble of the 1990s. With profits in the real economy stagnating, the smart money flocked to the financial sector. The workings of this virtual economy were exemplified by the rapid rise in the stock values of Internet firms that, like Amazon, had yet to turn a profit. The dotcom phenom-

org/External/Pubs/FT/fmu/eng/2008/index.htm.

9. Francisco González, 'What Banks Can Learn from this Credit Crisis,' *Financial Times*, February 4, 2008, www.ft.com/cms/s/0/93b9ccoc-d346-11dc-b861-0000779fd2ac.html.

enon probably extended the boom of the 1990s by about two years. 'Never before in U.S. history,' Robert Brenner wrote, 'had the stock market played such a direct, and decisive, role in financing non-financial corporations, thereby powering the growth of capital expenditures and in this way the real economy. Never before had a US economic expansion become so dependent upon the stock market's ascent.'[10] But the divergence between momentary financial indicators like stock prices and real values could only proceed to a point before reality bit back and enforced a 'correction.' And the correction came savagely in the dotcom collapse of 2002, which wiped out $7 trillion in investor wealth.

A long recession was avoided, but only because another bubble, the housing bubble, took the place of the dotcom bubble. Here, Greenspan played a key role by cutting the prime rate to a 45-year low of 1 percent in June 2003, holding it there for a year, then raising it only gradually, in quarter-percentage increments. As Dean Baker put it, 'an unprecedented run-up in the stock market propelled the U.S. economy in the late nineties and now an unprecedented run-up in house prices is propelling the current recovery.'[11]

The result was that real estate prices rose by 50 percent in real terms, with the run-ups, according to Baker, being close to 80 percent in the key bubble areas of the West Coast, the East Coast north of Washington DC, and Florida. Baker estimates that the run-up in house prices

> created more than $5 trillion in real estate wealth compared to a scenario where prices follow their normal trend growth path. The wealth effect from house prices is conventionally estimated at five cents to the dollar, which means that annual consumption is approximately $250 billion (2 per cent of gross domestic product [GDP]) higher than it would be in the absence of the housing bubble.

---

10. *The Boom and the Bubble: The US in the World Economy* (London: Verso, 2003), p. 195.
11. 'The Menace of an Unchecked Housing Bubble.'

The China factor

The housing bubble fueled US growth, which was exceptional given the stagnation that has gripped most of the global economy in the last few years. During this period, the global economy has been marked by underinvestment and persistent tendencies toward stagnation in most key economic regions apart from the United States, China, India, and a few other places. Weak growth has marked most other regions, notably Japan, which was locked until very recently into a 1 percent GDP growth rate, and Europe, which grew annually by 1.45 percent in the last few years.

With stagnation in most other areas, the United States has pulled in some 70 percent of all global capital flows. A great deal of this has come from China. Indeed, what marks this current bubble period is the role of China as a source not only of goods for the US market but also capital for speculation. The relationship between the United States and Chinese economies is what I have characterized elsewhere as chain-gang economics.[12] On the one hand, China's economic growth has increasingly depended on the ability of American consumers to continue their debt-financed spending spree to absorb much of the output of China's production. On the other hand, this relationship depends on a massive financial reality: the dependence of US consumption on China's lending the US Treasury and private sector dollars from the reserves it accumulated from its yawning trade surplus with the United States: 1 trillion dollars so far, according to some estimates. Indeed, a great deal of the tremendous sums China – and other Asian countries – lent to American institutions went to finance middle-class spending on housing and other goods and services, prolonging the fragile US economic growth but only by raising consumer indebtedness to dangerous, record heights.

---

12. 'Chain-Gang Economics' in Chapter 4.

The China-US coupling has had major consequences for the global economy. The massive new productive capacity of American and other foreign investors moving to China has aggravated the persistent problem of overcapacity and overproduction. One indicator of persistent stagnation in the real economy is the aggregate annual global growth rate, which averaged 1.4 percent in the 1980s and 1.1 percent in the 1990s, compared to 3.5 percent in the 1960s and 2.4 percent in the 1970s. Moving to China to take advantage of low wages may shore up profit rates in the short term. But, as it adds to overcapacity in a world where a rise in global purchasing power is constrained by growing inequalities, such capital flight erodes profits in the long term. And, indeed, the profit rate of the largest 500 US transnational corporations fell from 7.15 in the period 1960-69 to 5.30 in 1980-90, to 4.02 in 1990-99, to 3.30 in 2000-2002. Behind these figures, notes Philip O'Hara, was the specter of overproduction: 'Oversupply of commodities and inadequate demand are the principal corporate anomalies inhibiting performance in the global economy.'[13]

The succession of speculative manias in the United States has had the function of absorbing investment that did not find profitable returns in the real economy and thus not only artificially propping up the US economy but also 'holding up the world economy,' as one IMF document put it.[14] Thus, with the bursting of the housing bubble and the seizing up of credit in almost the whole financial sector, the threat of a global downturn is very real.

13. Philip Anthony O'Hara, *Growth and Global Development in the Global Political Economy* (London: Routledge, 2006), p. 77.
14. Raghuram G. Rajan, 'Global Imbalances – An Assessment,' October 25, 2005, www.imf.org/external/np/speeches/2005/102505.htm.

Decoupling chain-gang economics?

In this regard, talk about a process of 'decoupling' regional economies, especially the Asian economic region, from the United States
has been without substance. True, most of the other economies in
East and Southeast Asia have been pulled along by the Chinese
locomotive. In the case of Japan, for instance, a decade-long stagnation was broken in 2003 by the country's first sustained recovery,
fueled by exports to slake China's thirst for capital and technology-intensive goods. Exports shot up by a record 44 percent, or
$60 billion. Indeed, China became the main destination for Asia's
exports, accounting for 31 percent, while Japan's share dropped
from 20 to 10 percent. As one account in the *Straits Times* in 2004
pointed out, 'In country-by-country profiles, China is now the
overwhelming driver of export growth in Taiwan and the Philippines, and the majority buyer of products from Japan, South Korea,
Malaysia, and Australia.'[15]

However, as research by C.P. Chandrasekhar and Jayati Ghosh
has underlined, China is indeed importing intermediate goods and
parts from these countries, but only to put them together mainly
for export as finished goods to the United States and Europe, not
for its domestic market. Thus, 'if demand for Chinese exports from
the United States and the EU slow down, as will be likely with a
U.S. recession, this will not only affect Chinese manufacturing
production, but also Chinese demand for imports from these Asian
developing countries.'[16] Perhaps the more accurate image is that
of a chain gang linking not only China and the United States but
a host of other satellite economies whose fates are all tied up with
the now-deflating balloon of debt-financed middle-class spending
in the United States.

---

15. 'China the Locomotive', *Straits Times*, February 23, 2004, p. 12.
16. 'Can China become the New Growth Pole for Asia?' *The Hindu Business Line*, www.
thehindubusinessline.com/todays-paper/can-china-become-the-new-growth-pole-for-
asia/article1614439.ece?ref=archive.

New bubbles to the rescue?

Do not overestimate the resiliency of capitalism. After the collapse of the dotcom boom and the housing boom, a third line of defense against stagnation owing to overcapacity may yet emerge. For instance, the US government might pull the economy out of the jaws of recession through military spending. And, indeed, the military economy did play a role in bringing the United States out of the 2002 recession, with defense spending in 2003 accounting for 14 percent of GDP growth while representing only 4 percent of the overall US GDP. According to estimates cited by Chalmers Johnson, defense-related expenditures will exceed $1 trillion for the first time in history in 2008.[17]

Stimulus could also come from the related 'disaster capitalism complex' so well studied by Naomi Klein: the 'full fledged new economy in homeland security, privatized war and disaster reconstruction tasked with nothing less than building and running a privatized security state both at home and abroad.' Klein says that, in fact, 'the economic stimulus of this sweeping initiative proved enough to pick up the slack where globalization and the dotcom booms had left off. Just as the Internet had launched the dotcom bubble, 9/11 launched the disaster capitalism bubble.'[18] This subsidiary bubble to the real estate bubble appears to have been relatively unharmed so far by the collapse of the latter.

It is not easy to track the sums circulating in the disaster capitalism complex. But one indication of the sums involved is that InVision, a General Electric affiliate producing high-tech bomb-detection devices used in airports and other public spaces, received an astounding $15 billion in homeland security contracts between 2001 and 2006.

---

17. 'Why the US Has Really Gone Broke,' *Le Monde Diplomatique*, http://mondediplo.com/2008/02/05military.

18. Naomi Klein, *The Shock Doctrine: The Rise of Disaster Capitalism* (New York: Henry Holt, 2007).

Whether or not 'military Keynesianism' and the disaster capitalism complex can in fact fill the role played by financial bubbles is open to question. To feed them, at least during the Republican administrations, has meant reducing social expenditures. A Dean Baker study, cited by Johnson, found that after an initial demand stimulus, by about the sixth year, the effect of increased military spending turns negative. After ten years of increased defense spending, there would be 464,000 fewer jobs than in a scenario of lower defense spending.

A more important limit to military Keynesianism and disaster capitalism is that the military engagements to which they are bound to lead are likely to create quagmires such as Iraq and Afghanistan. And these disasters could trigger a backlash both abroad and at home. Such a backlash would eventually erode the legitimacy of these enterprises, reduce their access to tax dollars, and erode their viability as sources of economic expansion in a contracting economy.

Yes, global capitalism may be resilient. But it looks like its options are increasingly limited. The forces making for the long-term stagnation of the global capitalist economy are now too heavy to be easily shaken off by the economic equivalent of mouth-to-mouth resuscitation.

The political consequences
of stagnation

With the Obama administration avoiding a decisive solution to the
crisis via massive fiscal spending in order to placate the right, the
way was opened up to the right to take the initiative and propose a
reinvigorated neoliberal solution to the crisis. This was not, the author
argues, a foreordained outcome. Timidity in the face of right-wing
pressure led not only to a tepid Keynesianism but to a dampening of
the economic imagination to pursue more innovative strategies such
as deglobalization.[19]

My apologies to T.S. Eliot, but September, not April, is the cruelest
month. Before 9/11/2001, there was 9/11/1973, when General
Pinochet toppled the Allende government in Chile and ushered
in a seventeen-year reign of terror. More recently, on 9/15/2008,
Lehman Brothers went bust and torpedoed the global economy,
turning what had been a Wall Street crisis into a near-death experience for the global financial system.

Two years later, the global economy remains very fragile. The
signs of recovery that desperate policymakers claimed to have
detected late in 2009 and early this year have proven to be mirages.
In Europe, 4 million people are unemployed and the austerity
programs imposed on highly indebted countries such as Greece,
Spain, Italy, and Ireland will add hundreds of thousands more to
the dole. Germany is an exception to the dismal rule.

Although technically the United States isn't in recession, recovery is a distant prospect in the world's biggest economy, which
contracted by 2.9 percent in 2009. This is the message of the
anemic second-quarter GDP growth rate of 1.6 percent and real
unemployment above the 9.6 percent official rate if one factors
in those who have given up looking for work. Firms continue to

---

19. Originally published in *Foreign Policy in Focus*, www.fpif.org/articles/the_
political_consequences_of_stagnation.

refrain from investing, banks continue not to lend, and consumers continue to refuse to spend. And the absence of a new stimulus program, as the impact of the $787 billion Washington injected into the economy in 2009 peters out, virtually ensures that the much-feared double-dip recession will become a reality.

That the American consumer does not spend has implications not only for the US economy, but for the global economy. The debt-fueled spending of Americans was the motor of the pre-crisis globalized economy, and nobody else has stepped in to replace them since the crisis began. Consumer spending in China, fueled by a government stimulus of $585 billion, has temporarily reversed contractionary trends in that country and East Asia. It has also had some impact in Africa and Latin America. But it has not been strong enough to pull the United States and Europe from stagnation. Moreover, in the absence of a new stimulus package in China, a relapse into low growth, stagnation, or recession is very real in East Asia.

To cut or to stimulate

Meanwhile, the debate in Western policy circles has divided into two camps. One group sees the threat of government default as a bigger problem than stagnation and refuses to countenance any more stimulus spending. The other thinks stagnation is the greater threat and demands more stimulus to counter it. At the G20 meeting in Toronto in June, the two sides collided. Germany's Angela Merkel advocated tightening, pointing to the threat of a default by Germany's debt-laden satellite economies in southern Europe, particularly Greece. President Obama, on the other hand, facing an intractably high unemployment rate, wanted to continue expansionary policies, though he lacked the political clout to sustain them.

To the pro-spending people, the anti-deficit people don't have much of an argument. At a time when deflation is the big threat, fear of government spending stoking inflation is misplaced. The idea of burdening future generations with debt is odd since the best way to benefit tomorrow's citizens is to ensure that they inherit healthy, growing economies. Deficit spending now is the means to achieve this growth. Moreover, government default is not a real threat for countries that borrow in currencies they control, like the United States, since, as a last option, they can repay their debts simply by having their central bank print more money.

Perhaps the most vocal pro-stimulus advocate is Paul Krugman, the Nobel laureate, who has become the bête noire of many on the right. For Krugman, the problem was that the original stimulus was not big enough. Yet how big is the extra stimulus needed, and what other anti-stagnation measures can the government take? On these questions Krugman betrays some unease, perhaps realizing that traditional Keynesianism has its limits: 'Nobody can be sure how well these measures would work, but it's better to try something that might not work than to make excuses while workers suffer.' The stark alternative to more aggressive deficit spending is 'permanent stagnation and high unemployment,' says Krugman.[20]

Krugman may have reason on his side, but reason has taken a backseat to ideology, interests, and politics. Despite high rates of unemployment, the anti-Big Government, anti-deficit forces have the initiative in three key Western countries: in Britain, where the Conservatives won on a platform of reducing government; in Germany, where the image of spendthrift Greeks and Spaniards financed with loans from hardworking Germans became the powerful horse Merkel's party rode to maintain power; and in the United States.

---

20. 'This is Not a Recovery,' *New York Times*, August 26, 2010, www.nytimes.com/2010/08/27/opinion/27krugman.html?_r=2&partner=rssnyt&emc=rss&.

The Obama debacle

The anti-deficit perspective has gained ascendancy in the United States despite high unemployment for a number of reasons. First of all, the anti-deficit stand appeals to the anti-Big Government senti-ments of the American middle class. Second, Wall Street has oppor-tunistically embraced anti-deficit policies to derail Washington's efforts to regulate it. Big Government is the problem, it screams, not the Big Banks. Third, and not to be underestimated, is the re-emergence of the ideological influence of doctrinaire neoliberals, including those who, as Martin Wolf puts it, 'believe a deep slump would purge past excesses, and so lead to healthier economies and societies.'[21] Fourth, the anti-spending economics has a mass base, the Tea Party movement. In contrast, the stimulus position is advocated by progressive intellectuals without a base or whose potential base has become disillusioned with Obama.

Still, the triumph of the hawks was not foreordained. According to Anatole Kaletsky, the economic commentator of *The Times* of London and someone not exactly sympathetic to the progressive point of view, the ascendancy of the anti-deficit forces stems from a major tactical mistake on the part of Obama coupled with the progressives' failure to offer a convincing narrative for the crisis. The blunder was Obama's taking responsibility for the crisis in a gesture of bipartisanship, in contrast to Ronald Reagan and Margaret Thatcher, who 'refused to take any blame for the eco-nomic hardships.' Reagan and Thatcher devoted 'the early years of their government to convincing voters that economic disaster was entirely the responsibility of previous left-wing governments, militant unions, and liberal progressive elites.'[22]

But even more problematic, says Kaletsky, was the Obama narrative, which was a contradictory one that put the blame on

---

21. 'Why the Battle Is Joined Over Tightening,' *Financial Times,* July 18, 2010, www.ft.com/cms/s/0/f3eb2596-9296-11df-9142-00144feab49a.html.

22. *Capitalism 4.0: The Birth of a New Economy* (London: Bloomsbury, 2011), p. 273.

greedy bankers while maintaining that the banks were too big to fail. 'With banks recovering from the crisis more profitably and quickly than voters had been led to expect,' he argues in his book *Capitalism 4.0*, 'politicians of all parties have been branded by public sentiment as stooges of the very bankers they tried to blame.'[23] Indeed, the Democrats' finance reform package that recently passed in Congress can only reinforce this public perception of their being co-opted or intimidated by the very people they denounce. It lacks provisions with teeth: a Glass–Steagall type of provision preventing commercial banks from doubling as investment banks; the banning of trading in derivatives, which Warren Buffett called 'weapons of mass destruction'; a global financial transactions tax or Tobin Tax; and a strong lid on executive pay, bonuses, and stock options.

For Kaletsky, Obama should have portrayed the economic crisis as one created 'by the polarized and oversimplified philosophy of market fundamentalism, not by bankers' and regulators' personality flaws. By offering such a systemic account of the crisis, politicians could capture the public imagination with a post-crisis narrative that is more constructive than the lynching of greedy bankers – and ultimately more dramatic.'[24] But with aides like treasury secretary Tim Geithner and National Economic Council director Larry Summers, neither of whom had broken completely with neoliberalism, such a systemic account was simply not in the cards.

Toward a progressive strategy

The right wing has the momentum now and will probably win big in the US elections in November. They will tie Obama and the Democrats so firmly to the crisis that people will forget it exploded during the reign of market fundamentalist George Bush. But with

23. Ibid.
24. Ibid., p. 274.

their primeval market economics, the fiscal hawks and Tea Partiers are unlikely to provide an alternative to what they have caricatured as Obama's 'socialism.' Allowing the economy to implode in order to be ideologically correct will invite an even greater repudiation from an economically insecure population.

But progressives should not take comfort from the dead end offered by Tea Party economics. They should try to understand what has led to the failure of Obama's pallid Keynesianism. Beyond the tactical mistake of taking responsibility for the crisis and the failure to advance an aggressive anti-neoliberal narrative to explain it, the central problem that has plagued Obama and his team is their failure to offer an inspiring alternative to neoliberalism.

The technical elements of a progressive solution to the crisis have been thrashed out by Keynesian and other progressive economists: a much bigger stimulus, tighter regulation of the banks, loose monetary policies, higher taxes on the rich, rebuilding the national infrastructure, an industrial policy promoting green industries, controls on speculative capital flows, controls on outward-bound foreign investment, a global currency, and a new global central bank.

The Obama administration has tried to enact some of these measures. But owing to its eagerness for bipartisanship, the ties of some of its prominent people to the economic elites, and the failure of key technocrats like Summers and Geithner to break with the neoliberal paradigm, it failed to present them as elements of a broader program of social reform aimed at democratizing control and management of the economy.

For progressives, the lesson to be derived from the stalling of Obamanomics is that technocratic management is not enough. Keynesian moves must be part of a broader vision and program. This strategy must have three key thrusts: democratic decision-making at all levels of the economy, from the enterprise to macroeconomic planning; greater equality in the distribution of wealth and income to make up for lower growth rates dictated by economic and environmental constraints; and a more cooperative, as opposed to competitive, ethic in production, distribution, and consumption.

Moreover, such a program cannot simply be dished out from above by a technocratic elite, as has been the fashion in this administration, one of whose greatest mistakes was to allow the mass movement that brought it to power to wither away. The people must be enlisted in the construction of the new economy, and here progressives have a lot to learn from the Tea Party movement that they must inevitably compete against in a life-and-death struggle for grassroots America.

Nature abhors a vacuum

Krugman predicts that the likely electoral results in November 'will paralyze policy for years to come.'[25] But nature abhors a vacuum, and the common failure of both market fundamentalists and technocratic Keynesians so far to address the fears of the unemployed, the about-to-be unemployed, and the vast numbers of economically insecure people will most likely produce social forces that would tackle their fears and problems head-on.

A failure of the left to fill this space innovatively will inevitably spawn a reinvigorated right with fewer apprehensions about state intervention, one that could combine technocratic Keynesian initiatives with a populist but reactionary social and cultural program. There is a term for such a regime: fascist. As Roger Bootle, author of *The Trouble with Markets*, reminds us, millions of Germans were disillusioned with the free market and capitalism during the Great Depression. But with the failure of the left to provide a viable alternative, they became vulnerable to the rhetoric of a party

---

25. 'This Is Not a Recovery.'

that, once it came to power, combined Keynesian pump-priming measures that brought unemployment down to 3 percent with a devastating counterrevolutionary social and cultural program.[26]

Fascism in the United States? It's not as far-fetched as you might think.

Lessons of the Obama debacle

This article discusses what progressives, in their effort to formulate a progressive economic platform, can learn from the failure of the Obama recovery plan, which might have contained more innovative elements, including some that could be part of a strategy of deglobalization.[27]

The problem with us progressives at this time of crisis is not that we lack an alternative paradigm to pit against the discredited neoliberal paradigm. No, the elements of the alternative based on the values of democracy, justice, equality, and environmental sustainability are there and have been there for some time, the product of collective intellectual and activist work over the last few decades.

The key problem is the failure of progressives to translate their vision and values into a program that is convincing and connects with the people trapped in the terrible existential conditions created by the global financial crisis. This fluid process is preeminently political. It requires translating a strategic perspective into a tactical program that takes advantage of the opportunities, ambiguities, and contradictions of the present moment to construct a critical mass for progressive change from diverse class and social forces.

---

26. Roger Bootle, *The Trouble with Markets: Saving Capitalism from Itself* (London: Nicholas Brealey, 2009).

27. Originally published in *Foreign Policy in Focus*, www.fpif.org/articles/lessons_of_the_obama_debacle.

We must look at the political experience of the global progressive movement in order to understand why our side has been derailed and how we can fight back to political relevance. The experience of the Obama presidency is rich in this regard. In the US political context, Obama is a social democrat, and the broad left supported his candidacy. Although he was no anti-capitalist, still we expected that he would initiate a program of recovery and reform similar in ambition to Roosevelt's New Deal. The electoral base that brought him to power, which cut across class, color, gender, and generational lines – was full of potential. Obama's ability to bring this base together on a message of change achieved what was then thought impossible – the election of an Afro-American as president of the United States – and showed how smart political leadership can shape social and political structures.

Two years after his spectacular electoral victory, President Obama and the Democrats face a rout in the US polls in early November. Indeed, Obama and his party are like a rabbit on the railroad track that is hypnotized by the light of an oncoming train. Whereas Obama seemed to do all the right things in his quest for the presidency, he seemed to make all the wrong moves as chief executive.

His prioritizing of healthcare reform, a massively complex task, has been identified as a key blunder. This decision certainly contributed to the debacle. But other important factors related mainly to his handling of the economic crisis, a primary concern of the electorate, were perhaps more critical.

Six reasons behind the debacle

Obama's first mistake was to take responsibility for the economic crisis. In his quixotic quest for a bipartisan solution, he made George W. Bush's problem his own. Margaret Thatcher and Ronald Reagan never made this mistake. They took no responsibility for the economic problems of the 1970s, heaping the blame entirely on their liberal predecessors and eschewing any bipartisan alliance with those they considered their ideological enemies. Roosevelt, too, slammed – and slammed hard – his ideological foes, those he termed 'economic royalists.'

Insofar as Obama and his lieutenants identified villains, this was Wall Street. Yet saying the financial elite brought on the crisis while bailing out key Wall Street financial institutions such as Citigroup and AIG on the grounds that they were 'to big to fail' involved Obama in a terrible contradiction. The least that he could have done was to remove the existing boards and top managers of these organizations as a condition for government funds. Instead, unlike in the case of General Motors, the top dogs stayed on board and continued to collect sky-high bonuses to boot.

The strong sense of disconnect between word and deed was exacerbated rather than alleviated by the Democrats' financial reform. The measure did not have the minimum conditions for a reform with real teeth: the banning of derivatives; a Glass–Steagall provision preventing commercial banks from doubling as investment banks; the imposition of a financial transactions or Tobin tax; and a strong lid on executive pay, bonuses, and stock options.

Third, Obama had a tremendous opportunity to educate and mobilize people against the neoliberal or market fundamentalist approach that deregulated the financial sector and caused the crisis. Although Obama did allude to unregulated financial markets as the key problem during the campaign, he refrained from demonizing neoliberalism after he took office, thus presenting an ideological vacuum that the resurgent neoliberals did not hesitate to fill. No doubt he failed to launch a full-scale ideological offensive because his key lieutenants for economic policy, National Economic Council head Larry Summers and treasury secretary Tim Geithner, had not broken with neoliberal thinking.

Fourth, the stimulus package of $787 billion was simply too small to bring down or hold the line on unemployment. Here, Obama cannot say he lacked good advice. Paul Krugman, the Nobel laureate, and a whole host of Keynesian economists were telling him this from the very start. For comparison, the Chinese stimulus package of $580 billion was much bigger relative to the size of the economy than the Obama package. For the White House now to say that the employment situation would be worse had it not been for the stimulus is, to say the least, politically naive. People operate not with wishful counterfactual scenarios but with the facts on the ground, and the facts have been rising unemployment with no relief in sight.

Politics in a time of crisis is not for the fainthearted. The middle-of-the-road approach represented by the size of the stimulus was the wrong response to a crisis that called for a political gamble: the deployment of the massive fiscal firepower of the government against the predictable howls of anger from the right.

Fifth, Obama and Federal Reserve Board chairman Ben Bernanke deployed mainly Keynesian technocratic tools – deficit spending and monetary easing – to deal with the consequences of the massive failure of market fundamentalism. During a normal downturn these countercyclical tools may suffice to reverse the downturn. But standard Keynesianism could address such a serious collapse only in a very limited way. Besides, people were looking not only for relief in the short term but for a new direction that would enable them to master their fears and insecurities and give them reason to hope.

In other words, Obama failed to locate his Keynesian technocratic initiatives within a larger political and economic agenda that could have fired up a fairly large section of American society. Such a larger agenda could have had three pillars: the democratization of economic decision-making, from the enterprise level to the heights of macro-policymaking; an income and asset redistribution strategy that went beyond increasing taxes on the top 2 percent of the population; and the promotion of a more cooperative rather than competitive approach to production, distribution, and the management of resources. This agenda of social transformation, which was not too left, could have been accommodated within a classical social-democratic framework. People were simply looking for an alternative to the Brave New Dog-Eat-Dog World that neoliberalism had bequeathed them. Instead, Obama offered a bloodless technocratic approach to cure a political and ideological debacle.

Related to this absence of a program of transformation was the sixth reason for the Obama debacle: his failure to mobilize the grassroots base that brought him to power. This base was diverse in terms of class, generation, and ethnicity. But it was united by palpable enthusiasm, which was so evident in Washington DC and the rest of the country on Inauguration Day in 2009. With his preference for a technocratic approach and a bipartisan solution to the crisis, Obama allowed this base to wither away instead of exploiting the explosive momentum it possessed in the aftermath of the elections.

At the eleventh hour, Obama and the Democrats are talking about firing up and resurrecting this base. But the dispirited and skeptical troops that have long been disbanded and left by the wayside rightfully ask: around what?

The right makes the right moves

In contrast to Obama, the right wing understood the demands and dynamics of politics at a time of crisis, as opposed to politics in normal times. While Obama persisted in his quest for bipartisanship, the Republicans adopted a posture of hard-line opposition to practically all of his initiatives.

Unlike Obama and the Democrats, the right posed the conflict in stark political and ideological terms: between left and right, between 'socialism' and 'freedom,' between the oppressive state and the liberating market. The Republican opposition used all the catchwords and mantras it could dredge up from bourgeois US ideology.

Finally, in contrast to Obama's neglect of the Democratic base, the right eschewed Republican interest-group politics. Fox News, Sarah Palin, and the Tea Party movement stirred up the right-wing base to challenge the Republican Party elite and drive a no-compromise, take-no-prisoners politics. To understand what has happened to the Republican Party in the last few weeks with the string of Tea Party successes in the primaries, historian Arno Mayer's distinction among conservatives, reactionaries, and counterrevolutionaries is useful. In Mayer's terms, the counterrevolutionaries, with their populist, anti-insider, and grassroots-driven politics are displacing the conservative elites that have long held sway in the Republican Party.

With their anti-spending platform, the Republicans and Tea Partiers that might capture the House and the Senate in November will probably bring about a worse situation than today. As such, Obama and the Democrats might repeat Bill Clinton's political trajectory when he scored a victory at the polls in 1996 because the Republicans led by Newt Gingrich overreached politically after their triumph in the midterm elections of 1994. But this is a desperate illusion. The current counterrevolutionaries and their backers are skilled in the politics of blame, and they will likely be successful in painting the worsening situation as a result of Obama's 'socialist policies,' not of drastic cuts in government spending.

Lessons for the left

The problem lies not so much in our lack of a strategic alternative as in our failure to translate our strategic vision or paradigm into a credible and viable political program. Politics in a period of crisis is different from politics in a period of normality, being more fluid and marked by the volatility of class, political, and intellectual attachments. We should remember that politics is the art of creating and sustaining a political movement from diverse class and social forces through a flexible but principled political program that can adapt to changing circumstances.

Finally, there is no such thing as an objectively determined situation. The art of politics is using the contradictions, spaces, and ambiguities of the current moment to shape structures and institutions and create a critical mass for change. Class, economic, and political structures may condition political outcomes; they do not determine them. Who will ultimately emerge the victor from this period of prolonged capitalist crisis will depend on smart and skilled political leadership.

CHAPTER 3

EUROPE'S TRAGIC SPIRAL

The Celtic Tiger follows the Asian Tigers to extinction

The 'Celtic Tiger' was Europe's miracle story of the 1980s and 1990s. With its receptivity to foreign capital and its export-oriented economy, Ireland became one of Europe's most globalized economies. Its spectacular economic collapse as the first decade of the twenty-first century drew to a close could have been avoided had its leaders learned from the earlier unraveling of the 'Asian Tigers' in 1997, which was brought about by the gyrations of unregulated global speculative capital.[1]

The financial collapse of Ireland, coming as the latest in a string of disasters, hardly shocks global public opinion. For people engaged in the development debate, however, it is resonant with meaning.

With the European Union and the International Monetary Fund now having to bail Ireland out to the tune of a whopping €85 billion, this is not the 'Celtic Tiger' of recent lore. The Irish economy that drew the admiration of a whole generation of neoliberal economists and technocrats successfully rode the wave of

---

1. Originally published in *Foreign Policy in Focus*, December 14, 2010, www.fpif. org/articles/the_celtic_tiger_follows_the_asian_tigers_to_extinction.

globalization to become Europe's fastest growing economy from the 1990s to the middle of this decade. In 1988, *The Economist* described Ireland as 'the poorest of the rich.' By 1997, it pitched Ireland as 'Europe's shining light.' By 2005, the country's per capita gross domestic product (GDP) was the second highest in the EU, after Luxembourg's.

After the Asian financial crisis brought down Asia's tiger economies in the late 1990s, Ireland remained, along with China, a star of export-oriented growth, seen by orthodox economists as the road to prosperity in the era of globalization. China learned the lessons of the Asian financial crisis and kept its financial sector on a tight leash. Ireland did not, and paid the price when the Western financial system unraveled in 2007.

The 'Irish miracle'

Like South Korea and the Southeast Asian tiger economies, the Irish economy passed through two phases. In the first phase of export-oriented growth, Ireland experienced real growth, especially in manufacturing and services. The growth was foreign-investment-driven, particularly in high-tech. As *Irish Times* economic columnist Fintan O'Toole notes, the country became the premier international location for US investment in information technology, with Intel leading the pack with 5,000 employees, Dell with 4,300, IBM with 3,500, Hewlett Packard with 2,500, and Microsoft with 1,200.[2] By the mid-2000s, tiny Ireland, whose population was no more than 4.5 million, had become the world's leading exporter of computer software and the source of a third of all personal computers sold in Europe.

Much of what has been written about the Celtic Tiger – a sobriquet thought up by Kevin Gardiner of the Wall Street investment

---

2. *Ship of Fools: How Stupidity and Corruption Sank the Celtic Tiger* (London: Faber & Faber, 2009).

bank Morgan Stanley – was hype. But not all. By the turn of the century, the boom in the real economy had brought down the country's chronically high unemployment rate to 5 percent and the poverty rate to the same figure as well.

At that fateful conjuncture in the early part of this decade, writes O'Toole, the Irish

> had an opportunity that was unique in Irish history. They had the resources to invest in the creation of a decent society, one that would be economically, socially, and environmentally sustainable. They had a population that was optimistic, self-confident, and ready for a challenge. They had incredibly favorable global conditions.[3]

Lessons not learned from Asia

Fifteen years earlier, the export-led economies of East Asia, then at their apogee, were at a similar crossroads ... and took the wrong turn. Tempted by foreign speculative capital knocking at the gate of the 'East Asian Miracle,' the economies of the region liberalized their financial sectors. Hot money came flooding in, for investment not in industry or in agriculture but in real estate and the stock market. Overinvestment in real estate led to a collapse in property prices, which led to dislocations in the rest of the economy, which in turn led to panicky flight by foreign investors. In summer 1997, some $100 billion that had flowed into the East Asian economies in the period 1994–97 flowed out of the region. The end result of this toxic cocktail of hot money and volatile property was a three-year recession that brought an end to the East Asian Miracle.

Had Ireland's leaders paid attention to the East Asian tragedy of the late 1990s, they would have been more careful about the dangers associated with financial liberalization and property development. They would have also avoided the second phase of the Asian growth

---

3. Ibid., p. 19.

process: illusory growth. How, instead, the Celtic Tiger followed in the footsteps of the Asian tigers is summed up cogently by the *New York Times*:

> Before Ireland joined the euro, its banks tended to do business the old-fashioned way, financing their lending through the deposits they took in. Once in the euro zone, banks were suddenly able to borrow huge sums of money inexpensively on international markets with nearly no exchange rate risk, an activity that was barely regulated by policy makers. With easy access to these funds, banks like Anglo Irish lent huge amounts to prominent Irish developers, leading to a frenzy of overdevelopment.[4]

Analyst David Smith points out that in the five years from 2003 to 2008 the net foreign borrowing of Irish banks increased from 10 to 60 percent of GDP. Lending standards were driven down to entice prospective homeowners, many with low or no credit history, much like the subprime phenomenon in the United States. And, as in the United States, regulators stood on the sidelines unwilling to take away the punch bowl, probably because so many of the top figures of the ruling party, Fianna Fáil, were tied to the bankers and developers.

Ireland's finances were already rotten when the global financial crisis blew in from Wall Street in 2007-08. The crisis simply exposed the decay. With Ireland's lenders becoming jittery, the country's finance minister guaranteed all debt and deposits in the six main Irish banks and financial institutions, effectively nationalizing the debt and bailing out the country's banking elites. But that move did not inspire confidence that the Irish state would be able to meet its financial obligations, should foreign creditors call in their loans. Smith points out that the spread between the interest rate on Irish government bonds and that on German government bonds, regarded as Europe's solid benchmark, rose from just 30

---

4. 'Europe Approves Irish Rescue and New Rules on Bailouts,' *New York Times*, November 28, 2010, www.nytimes.com/2010/11/29/business/global/29euro.html?pagewanted=all.

basis points in September 2008 to 284 basis points by March the following year.

The abrupt shut-off of the foreign financial tap triggered a disaster in the real economy. The GDP collapsed by 3 percent in 2008 and 10 percent in 2009. It is expected to shrink by 13.5 per cent in 2010. Unemployment, down to 5 percent in the middle of the decade, shot up to a Depression-level 13 percent. The amount of debt among Irish households and companies, according to Fintan O'Toole, is now the highest in the EU, with the average Irish citizen owing €37,000 at the start of 2010. That figure has risen several notches higher with the recent EU–IMF €85 billion bailout.

The global financial market that was once so enamored of the Irish has not been pacified by the bailout. Bond yields dropped insignificantly in the aftermath of the government's announcement that it would accept the EU–IMF offer. The *New York Times* characterized the quid pro quo for the bailout as the 'toughest austerity program in Europe,' involving 'the loss of about 25,000 public-sector jobs, equivalent to 10 percent of the government work force, as well as a four-year, $20 billion program of tax increases and spending cuts like sharp reductions in state pensions and minimum wage.'[5] The adjustment will be more savage than that imposed on Greece earlier this year. Yet this has not convinced the now merciless markets that, as *The Economist* put it, 'Ireland, having looked dodgy for so long ... would ever be able to repay its debts.'[6]

The end of the miracle era?

Given the East Asian Miracles' history, and with the Irish miracle having turned into a catastrophe, only one miracle of the era of export-oriented growth is left standing: China. Non-liberalization

---

5. 'Demonstrators in Ireland Protest Austerity Plan,' *New York Times*, November 27, 2010, www.nytimes.com/2010/11/28/world/europe/28dublin.html.

6. 'A Contagious Irish Disease?' *The Economist*, November 25 2010, www.economist.com/node/17577107.

of its financial sector is the key reason that China has so far escaped the fate of the smaller tigers. But is financial protectionism enough to stave off the global impact of the crisis of the real economy that is engulfing Europe and the United States, on which China has been severely dependent for its exports? Or does disaster await the biggest tiger of them all?

Greece: same tragedy, different scripts

This essay, published in the summer of 2010, traces the transformation of the narrative of the economic debacle from being a crisis triggered by the unregulated activities of finance capital to one allegedly brought about by irresponsible government borrowing and spending to build a 'welfare state.' The controversy over Greece was a battle over narratives, and the one supported by finance capital won, bringing with it the same solution that the International Monetary Fund promoted during the Asian financial crisis: massive cutbacks in government expenditures accompanied by rising unemployment, a rise in poverty, and social crisis all around. Driven to the wall, Greece is faced with the choice of drowning in austerity or striking it out in economic directions that would make it more independent of global capital and move in the direction of deglobalization.[7]

Cafés are full in Athens, and droves of tourists still visit the Parthenon and go island-hopping in the fabled Aegean. But beneath the summery surface, there is confusion, anger, and despair as this country plunges into its worst economic crisis in decades.

The global media have presented Greece, tiny Greece, as the epicenter of the second stage of the global financial crisis, much as it portrayed Wall Street as ground zero of the first stage.

Yet there is an interesting difference in the narratives surrounding these two episodes.

---

7. Originally published in *Foreign Policy in Focus*, July 14, 2010, www.fpif. org/articles/greece_same_tragedy_different_scripts.

Narratives in conflict

The unregulated activities of financial institutions, which created ever more complex instruments to magically multiply money, created the Wall Street crash that morphed into the global financial crisis.

With Greece, however, the narrative goes this way. The country piled up an unsustainable debt load to build a welfare state it could not afford, and is now the spendthrift that must tighten its belt. Brussels, Berlin, and the banks are the dour Puritans now exacting penance from the Mediterranean hedonists for living beyond their means and committing the sin of pride by hosting the costly 2004 Olympics.

This penance comes in the form of a European Union–International Monetary Fund program that will increase the country's value-added tax to 23 percent, raise the retirement age to 65 for both men and women, make deep cuts in pensions and public-sector wages, and eliminate practices promoting job security. The ostensible aim of the exercise is to radically slim down the welfare state and get the spoiled Greeks to live within their means.

Although the welfare-state narrative contains some nuggets of truth, it is fundamentally flawed. The Greek crisis essentially stems from the same frenzied drive of finance capital to draw profits from the massive indiscriminate extension of credit that led to the implosion of Wall Street. The Greek crisis falls into the pattern traced by Carmen Reinhart and Kenneth Rogoff in their book *This Time is Different: Eight Centuries of Financial Folly*: periods of frenzied speculative lending are inexorably followed by government or sovereign debt defaults, or near defaults.[8] Like the Third World debt crisis of the early 1980s and the Asian financial crisis of the late 1990s, the so-called sovereign debt problem of

---

8. *This Time Is Different: Eight Centuries of Financial Folly* (New Haven CT: Princeton University Press, 2011).

countries like Greece, Europe, Spain, and Portugal is principally a supply-driven crisis, not a demand-driven one.

In their drive to raise more and more profits from lending, Europe's banks poured an estimated $2.5 trillion into what are now the most troubled European economies: Ireland, Greece, Belgium, Portugal, and Spain. German and French banks hold 70 percent of Greece's $400 billion debt. German banks were great buyers of toxic subprime assets from US financial institutions, and they applied the same lack of discrimination to buying Greek government bonds. For their part, French banks, according to the Bank of International Settlements, increased their lending to Greece by 23 percent, to Spain by 11 percent, and to Portugal by 26 percent.[9]

The frenzied Greek credit scene featured not only European financial actors. Wall Street powerhouse Goldman Sachs showed Greek financial authorities how financial instruments known as derivatives could be used to make large chunks of Greek debt 'disappear,' thus making the national accounts look good to bankers eager to lend more. Then the very same agency turned around and, engaging in derivatives trading known as 'credit default swaps,' bet on the possibility that Greece would default, raising the country's cost of borrowing from the banks but making a tidy profit for itself.

If ever there was a crisis created by global finance, Greece is suffering from it right now.

Hijacking the narrative

There are two key reasons why the Greek narrative has become a time-worn cautionary tale of people living beyond their means, rather than a case of financial irresponsibility on the part of bankers and investors.

---

9. www.thedailybeast.com/newsweek/2010/07/02/worse-than-wall-street.html.

First of all, financial institutions successfully hijacked the narrative of crisis to serve their own ends. The Big Banks are now truly worried about the awful state of their balance sheets, impaired as they are by the toxic subprime assets they took on and realizing that they severely overextended their lending operations. The principal way they seek to rebuild their balance sheets is to generate fresh capital by using their debtors as pawns. As the centerpiece of this strategy, the banks seek to persuade the public authorities to bail them out once more, as the authorities did in the first stage of the crisis in the form of rescue funds and a low prime lending rate.

The banks were confident that the dominant eurozone governments would never allow Greece and the other highly indebted European countries to default because it would lead to the collapse of the euro. By having the markets bet against Greece and raising its cost of borrowing, the banks knew that the eurozone governments would come out with a bailout package, most of which would go toward servicing the Greek debt to them. Promoted as rescuing Greece, the massive €110 billion package, put together by the dominant eurozone governments and the IMF, will largely go toward rescuing the banks from their irresponsible, unregulated lending frenzy.

The banks and international financial institutions played this same old confidence game on developing-country debtors during the Third World debt crisis of the 1980s, and on Thailand and Indonesia during the Asian financial crisis of the 1990s. The same austerity measures – then known as structural adjustment – followed lending binges from northern banks and speculators. And the scenario played out the same way: pin the blame on the victims by characterizing them as living beyond their means, get public agencies to rescue you with money upfront, and stick the people with the terrible task of paying off the loan by committing a massive chunk of their present and future income streams as payments to the lending agencies.

No doubt the authorities are preparing similarly massive multi-billion-euro rescue packages for the banks that overextended themselves in Spain, Portugal, and Ireland.

Shifting the blame

The second reason for promoting the 'living beyond one's means' narrative in the case of Greece and the other severely indebted countries is to deflect the pressures for tighter financial regulation, which have come from citizens and governments since the start of the global crisis. The banks want to have their cake and eat it too. They secured bailout funds from governments in the first phase of the crisis, but don't want to honor what governments told their citizens was an essential part of the deal: the strengthening of financial regulation.

Governments, from the United States to China and Greece, had resorted to massive stimulus programs to keep the real economy from collapsing during the first phase of the financial crisis. By promoting a narrative that moves the spotlight from lack of financial regulation to this massive government spending as the key problem of the global economy, the banks seek to forestall the imposition of a tough regulatory regime.

But this is playing with fire. Nobel Prize laureate Paul Krugman and others have warned that if this narrative is successful, the lack of new stimulus programs and tough banking regulations will result in a double-dip recession, if not a full-blown depression. Unfortunately, as the recent G20 meeting in Toronto suggests, governments in Europe and the United States are caving in to the short-sighted agenda of the banks, which have the backing of unreconstructed neoliberal ideologues that continue to see the activist, interventionist state as the fundamental problem. These ideologues believe that a deep recession, even a depression, is the natural process by which an economy stabilizes itself, and that Keynesian spending to avert a collapse will only delay the inevitable.

Resistance: will it make a difference?

The Greeks are not taking all this lying down. Massive protests greeted the ratification of the EU–IMF package by the Greek parliament on July 8. In an earlier and much larger protest on May 5, 400,000 people turned out in Athens in the biggest demonstration since the fall of the military dictatorship in 1974. Yet street protests seem to do little to avert the social catastrophe that will unfold with the EU–IMF program. The economy is set to contract by 4 percent in 2010. According to Alexis Tsipras, president of the left parliamentary coalition Synaspismos, the unemployment rate will likely rise from 15 to 20 percent in two years, with the rate among young people expected to hit 30 percent.

As for poverty, a recent joint survey by Kapa Research and the London School of Economics found that even before the current crisis close to a third of Greece's 11 million people lived close to the poverty line. This process of creating a 'third world' within Greece will only be accelerated by the Brussels–IMF adjustment program.[10]

Ironically, this adjustment is being presided over by a Socialist government headed by George Papandreou voted into office last October to reverse the corruption of the previous conservative administration and the ill effects of its economic policies. There is resistance within Papandreou's party PASOK to the EU–IMF plan, admits the party's international secretary Paulina Lampsa. But the overwhelming sense among the party's parliamentary contingent is TINA, as Margaret Thatcher famously put it: 'there is no alternative.'

---

10. www.ipsnews.net/2007/11/greece-more-poverty-than-meets-the-eye.

The consequences of compliance

Faced with the program's savage consequences, an increasing number of Greeks are talking about adopting a strategy of threatening default or a radical unilateral reduction of debt. Such an approach could be coordinated, says Tsipras, with Europe's other debt-burdened countries, like Portugal and Spain. Here Argentina may provide a model: it gave its creditors a memorable haircut in 2003 by paying only 25 cents for every dollar it owed. Not only did Argentina get away with it, but the resources that would otherwise have left the country as debt service were channeled into the domestic economy, triggering an average annual economic growth rate of 10 percent between 2003 and 2008.

The 'Argentine Solution' is certainly fraught with risk. But the consequences of surrender are painfully clear, if we examine the records of countries that submitted to IMF adjustment. Forking over 25 to 30 percent of the government budget yearly to foreign creditors, the Philippines in the mid-1980s entered a decade of stagnation, from which it has never recovered and which condemned it to a permanent poverty rate of over 30 percent. Squeezed by draconian adjustment measures, Mexico was sucked into two decades of continuing economic crisis, with consequences such as the pervasive narcotics traffic that has brought it to the brink of being a failed state. The current state of virtual class war in Thailand can be traced partly to the political fallout of the economic sufferings of the IMF austerity program imposed on that country a decade ago.

The Brussels–IMF adjustment of Greece shows that finance capitalism in the throes of crisis no longer respects the North-South divide. The cynics would say, 'Welcome to the Third World, Greece.'

But this is no time for cynicism. Rather, it's a key moment for global solidarity. We're all in this together now.

Germany's Social Democrats and the European crisis

With Germany coming to center stage owing to its financial strength, the conservative German government's prioritization of the crisis countries' ability to repay the debt via austerity programs became the central solution to the European financial crisis. The problem was that this solution threatened to choke off growth, eventually making things worse. This essay explores what alternative policies the Social Democratic Party (SPD) would offer should they win the elections in 2013.[11]

Germany towers over Europe like a colossus. Its economy is the biggest in the European Union, accounting for 20 percent of the EU's gross domestic product. While most of Europe's economies are stagnating, Germany's will have grown by some 2.9 percent in 2011. It boasts the lowest unemployment rate, 5.5 percent, of Europe's major economies, compared to those of France (9.5 percent), the United Kingdom (8.3 percent), and Italy (8.1 percent).

In many ways, Germany is like Japan. Both countries were forced to give up armed expansion during the Second World War, only to have the national energy channeled into building formidable economies. But whereas Japan faltered in the 1990s, Germany has steadily plowed ahead, becoming the world's biggest exporter from 1992 to 2009, replaced by China only in 2010.

With the recent agreement by most EU countries to move toward tighter coordination of fiscal policies, the prime mover of which was Germany, Germans and other Europeans alike feel that a new era of German primacy has begun. Not only is Germany the strongest economy in Europe; it is also now writing the rules of economic governance.

---

11. Originally published in *Foreign Policy in Focus*, December 21, 2011, www.fpif. org/articles/germanys_social_democrats_and_the_european_crisis.

Unbalanced relationship?

This has brought a deep feeling of unease to other Europeans, who, as a BBC report puts it, now face a future 'of being told what to do by the Germans.'[12] Many Germans are also bothered by the turn of events, among them the country's opposition Social Democrats (SPD).

At the party's congress in Berlin earlier this month, Helmut Schmidt, the former prime minister and grand old man of the party, summed up the troubled relationship of Germany, which straddles the geographical center of Europe, with the rest of continent thus: 'When the center is weak, the periphery moves into the center. When the periphery is weak, the center expands to the periphery.' The key to a stable Europe is a balanced relationship.

That balance has been disrupted by recent developments, Schmidt implied. The center has become too strong, and nations now fear dictation of their economic governance by Germany and its preferences for fiscal and monetary tightness, strictures against debt, and obsession with inflation. Moreover, the fear of economic supervision by Germany is coupled with the fear that the austerity measures the Merkel government is promoting might provoke recession or depression – and Schmidt reminded his audience that it was deflation and depression, not inflation, that ended the Weimar Republic, the first attempt at democracy in Germany, and brought Hitler to power.

The SPD reforms

Schmidt's Social Democrats view Germany's condition with deep ambivalence. One wing of the party attributes Germany's ability to ride out the European recession to the labor and pension reforms carried out by the Social Democratic government of Gerhard

12. 'What is Germany's Vision for Europe?' www.bbc.co.uk/news/business-16030374.

Schröder from 1998 to 2005. In their view, the SPD did the dirty work, and Angela Merkel and her conservative coalition ate the Social Democrats' lunch.

The reforms, packaged as Agenda 2010, were a Thatcherite package that relied on cutting medical benefits, slashing pension and unemployment benefits, raising the age of retirement from 65 to 67, outsourcing health insurance, and abolishing craft requirements. Perry Anderson described this package as 'a more comprehensive bout of neoliberal legislation than [Britain's] New Labour, a much invoked model, was ever to do.'[13]

A conservative government could not have carried out the reforms without evoking massive resistance, say some activists. Only a labor government could discipline labor. But the price paid by the Social Democrats was high. Some 100,000 members, including former finance minister Oskar Lafontaine, split from the party, with many joining the former Communist Party of East Germany (renamed the Party of Democratic Socialism, or PDS) to form the 'Die Linke' party, 'The Left.' Trade-union members also withdrew their allegiance to the party en masse, and the loss of their support was a key factor in the party's rout in the 2009 elections, when it suffered the heaviest losses in its history and saw its seats in the Bundestag reduced to 23 percent. As Achim Post, head of the SPD's International Politics Department, put it, 'This was a case of the party doing something that was for good for society but not in the party's best interests.'

But for many members of the SPD, what orthodox economists see as a new resiliency in the German economy has to be balanced against the emergence of new social inequalities. An OECD study in 2008 discovered that inequality and poverty increased more rapidly in Germany in 2000–2005 than in any other OECD country. While unemployment stands at a relatively low 2.7 million at present, a

---

13. 'A New Germany?' *New Left Review* 57 (May-June 2009), http://newleftreview. org/II/57/perry-anderson-a-new-germany.

large number of the employed do not earn enough to meet their basic needs and must resort to state subsidies.

Indeed, some Social Democrats, like Thomas Meyer, author of a well-known book on social democracy, claim that a great deal of Europe's current troubles stem from the Schröder reforms. The fall in domestic demand owing to a sharp cutback in purchasing power forced German companies to step up their efforts to export their product to the rest of Europe, resulting in the trade imbalances between Germany and key European economies. This became one of the key factors forcing the latter to engage in massive foreign borrowing to cover their trade deficits.

Challenging Merkel

At the SPD Congress in Berlin, the party was in high spirits, having just come off a string of eight straight victories in regional elections, including the recapture of the old SPD stronghold of North Rhine-Westphalia in western Germany's industrial heartland. There was talk of 'putting the wild beast of capitalism back in its cage,' as one speaker put it, though the proposals for an electoral program were rather tame: among them, an increase in the rate of taxation of the wealthy from 42 to 49 percent, a wealth tax imposed on the very rich, a financial transactions tax, educational assistance for the less privileged, and an obligatory national minimum wage.

The Social Democrats know, however, that they are up against a formidable foe in Angela Merkel. Unlike Margaret Thatcher, Merkel is a pragmatist. She has absorbed the lessons of running an ideological campaign since her party's near defeat in the 2005 polls, when a weakened SPD nearly overtook the conservative coalition on election day as voters turned away from Merkel's anti-state, pro-market rhetoric. Of late, Merkel has been accused of stealing the Social Democrats' key proposals. Her government is now phasing out nuclear power plants, long a key element of the programs of the SPD and the Greens. She has also recently indicated that she is in favor of the minimum wage, another Social Democratic proposal. 'She keeps stealing our programs,' joked one activist at the Congress. 'Soon we'll be left with nothing.'

But Merkel is not the only obstacle to the SPD's coming back to power. An electoral coalition among the SPD, the Greens, and Die Linke for 2013 would be a strong contender in the elections. Unfortunately, there is no question of an alliance with Die Linke, which won nearly 12 percent of the vote in 2009. There is little enthusiasm in the SPD mainstream for an alliance with Die Linke, many of whose founders are seen as tied to outmoded class politics. And there is also little desire among the former SPD militants in Die Linke for a coalition with the SPD, whom they regard as having betrayed labor. Thomas Meyer, in fact, says that the former communists in Die Linke are more favorable to an alliance with the SPD than the former SPD members.

Being more than Europe's fiscal inspector

However, the 2013 elections will be about more than just domestic issues. The relationship between Germany and the EU will be a central concern of voters, and Merkel will try to present the recent fiscal pact as a case of creative German leadership in the European crisis. Indeed, the *New York Times* has described the recent agreement as a victory for Germany's 'favored remedy for the sovereign debt crisis that has shaken the Union for months: fiscal discipline, central oversight, and sanctions on countries that break the rules on debt limits, which will be written into national laws.'[14]

But the SPD paints the deal as too little too late. The SPD accuses Merkel of having irresponsibly catered to the Germans' strong populist aversion to bailing out the Greeks at the beginning of

---

14. 'Chronic Pain for the Euro,' *New York Times*, December 12, 2011, www.nytimes.com/2011/12/13/world/europe/european-debt-deal-may-not-be-a-cure.html?ref=david cameron.

the sovereign debt crisis in 2010, thus worsening the crisis. The deal on the Greek debt reached a few months ago, which involved writing off half the liability and the private banks taking losses in return for the Greeks implementing a draconian austerity program, came very late in the game. In the meantime, German and French indecisiveness contributed to the attack by the markets on the other weak economies of Southern Europe: Portugal, Italy, and Spain.

Rather than leading, Merkel, in the SPD's view, has put obstacles in the way of a truly comprehensive strategic plan to turn Europe's crisis around. Some Social Democrats have assailed the fiscal pact as a short-sighted remedy that has no vision except that of Germany looking over everyone else's shoulder, which, with its focus on fiscal discipline, might condemn the continent to a long period of little or no growth.

With the predominant German attitude of looking down on the crisis-ridden countries as profligate, hedonistic Mediterranean spenders, it will be a challenge for the Social Democrats to forge a more responsible German policy toward Europe and promote a more positive vision of Germany's relationship to Europe among Germans. But they have no choice but to go beyond the Merkel formula of Germany as economic disciplinarian.

As Helmut Schmidt told the party faithful at the congress, resurgent fears of domination by Germany had their basis in the past wrongs Germany had inflicted on its neighbors. Their fears were justified. More importantly, Germans had to relearn that their political and economic success in the last sixty years would not have been possible without the 'support and solidarity of others,' and that it was now Germany's turn to 'show solidarity with our neighbors.' Otherwise, Germany might 'risk isolation in Europe.'

CHAPTER 4

INVULNERABLE ASIA?

Chain-gang economics

Written before the onset of the financial crisis, this article detailed how the Chinese economy was contributing to global overcapacity at the same time that it had become intertwined irrevocably with the US economy, being dependent on the US market for its dynamic growth while at the same time being the indispensable source of financing for US consumption, on which the global economy increasingly depended for expansion. The US-China connection was probably the central engine of globalization.[1]

'The world is investing too little,' according to one prominent economist. 'The current situation has its roots in a series of crises over the last decade that were caused by excessive investment, such as the Japanese asset bubble, the crises in Emerging Asia and Latin America, and most recently, the IT bubble. Investment has fallen off sharply since, with only very cautious recovery.'[2]

These are not the words of a Marxist economist describing the crisis of overproduction but those of Raghuram Rajan, the new

---

1. Originally published in *Foreign Policy in Focus*, October 30, 2006, www.fpif. org/articles/chain-gang_economics.
2. Raghuram Rajan, 'Economic Ship Steady as She Goes,' *The Age*, September 23, 2005, www.imf.org/external/np/vc/2005/092305.htm.

chief economist of the International Monetary Fund (IMF). His analysis, now over a year old, continues to be accurate. Global overcapacity has made further investment simply unprofitable, which significantly dampens global economic growth. In Europe, for instance, GDP growth has averaged only 1.45 percent in the last few years. Global demand has not kept up with global productive capacity. And if countries are not investing in their economic futures, then growth will continue to stagnate and possibly lead to a global recession.

China and the United States, however, appear to be bucking the trend. But, rather than signs of health, growth in these two economies – and their ever more symbiotic relationship with each other – may actually be indicators of crisis. The centrality of the United States to both global growth and global crisis is well known. What is new is China's critical role. Once regarded as the greatest achievement of this era of globalization, China's integration into the global economy is, according to an excellent analysis by political economist Ho-Fung Hung, emerging as a central cause of global capitalism's crisis of overproduction.[3]

China and the crisis of overproduction

China's 8-10 percent annual growth rate has probably been the principal stimulus of growth in the world economy in the last decade. Chinese imports, for instance, helped to end Japan's decade-long stagnation in 2003. To satisfy China's thirst for capital and technology-intensive goods, Japanese exports shot up by a record 44 percent, or $60 billion. Indeed, China became the main destination for Asia's exports, accounting for 31 percent while Japan's share dropped from 20 percent to 10 percent. China is

---

3. Ho-Fung Hung, 'Rise of China and the Global Overaccumulation Crisis,' paper presented at the Global Division of the Annual Meeting of the Society for the Study of Social Problems, August 10-12, 2006, Montreal.

now the overwhelming driver of export growth in Taiwan and the Philippines, and the majority buyer of products from Japan, South Korea, Malaysia, and Australia.

At the same time, China became a central contributor to the crisis of global overcapacity. Even as investment declined sharply in many economies in response to the surfeit of productive capacity, particularly in Japan and other East Asian economies, it increased at a breakneck pace in China. Investment in China was not just the obverse of disinvestment elsewhere, although the shutting down of facilities and sloughing off of labor was significant not only in Japan and the United States but in the countries on China's periphery like the Philippines, Thailand, and Malaysia. China was significantly beefing up its industrial capacity and not simply absorbing capacity eliminated elsewhere. At the same time, the ability of the Chinese market to absorb its own industrial output was limited.

Agents of overinvestment

A major actor in overinvestment was transnational capital. In the late 1980s and 1990s, transnational corporations (TNCs) saw China as the last frontier, the unlimited market that could endlessly absorb investment and endlessly throw off profitable returns. However, China's restrictive rules on trade and investment forced TNCs to locate most of their production processes in the country instead of outsourcing only selected numbers of them. Analysts termed such TNC production activities 'excessive internalization.' By playing according to China's rules, TNCs ended up overinvesting in the country and building up a manufacturing base that produced more than China or even the rest of the world could consume.

By the turn of the millennium, the dream of exploiting a limitless market had vanished. Foreign companies headed for China not so much to sell to millions of newly prosperous Chinese customers but rather to make China a manufacturing base for global markets and take advantage of its inexhaustible supply of cheap labor. Typical of companies that found themselves in this quandary was Philips, the Dutch electronics manufacturer. Philips operates twenty-three factories in China and produces about $5 billion worth of goods, but two-thirds of their production is exported to other countries.

The other set of actors promoting overcapacity were local governments investing in and building up key industries. While these efforts are often 'well planned and executed at the local level,' notes Ho-Fung Hung, 'the totality of these efforts combined ... entail anarchic competition among localities, resulting in un-coordinated construction of redundant production capacity and infrastructure.'[4]

As a result, idle capacity in such key sectors as steel, automobile, cement, aluminum, and real estate has been soaring since the mid-1990s, with estimates that over 75 percent of China's industries are currently plagued by overcapacity and that fixed asset investments in industries already experiencing overinvestment accounted for 40–50 percent of China's GDP growth in 2005. China's State Development and Reform Commission projects that the automobile industry will produce double what the market can absorb by 2010. The impact on profitability is not to be underestimated if we are to believe government statistics: at the end of 2005, Hung points out, the average annual profit growth rate of all major enterprises had plunged by half and the total deficit of losing enterprises had increased sharply by 57.6 percent.

The low-wage strategy

The Chinese government can mitigate excess capacity by expanding people's purchasing power via a policy of income and asset redistribution. Doing so would probably mean slower growth but more

---

4. 'Rise of China and the Global Overaccumulation Crisis.'

domestic and global stability. This is what China's so-called New Left intellectuals and policy analysts have been advising. China's authorities, however, have apparently chosen to continue the old strategy of dominating world markets by exploiting the country's cheap labor. Although China's population is 1.3 billion, 700 million people – or over half – live in the countryside and earn an average of just $285 a year, according to some estimates. This reserve army of rural poor has enabled manufacturers, both foreign and local, to keep wages down.

Aside from the potentially destabilizing political effects of regressive income distribution, this low-wage strategy, as Hung points out, 'impedes the growth of consumption relative to the phenomenal economic expansion and great leap of investment.'[5] In other words, the global crisis of overproduction will worsen as China continues to dump its industrial production on global markets constrained by slow growth.

Vicious cycle

Chinese production and American consumption are like the pro-verbial prisoners who seek to break free from one another but can't because they're chained together. This relationship is increasingly taking the form of a vicious cycle. On the one hand, China's break-neck growth has increasingly depended on the ability of American consumers to continue their consumption of much of the output of China's production brought about by excessive investment. On the other hand, America's high consumption rate depends on Beijing lending the US private and public sectors a significant portion of the trillion-plus dollars it has accumulated over the last decade from its yawning trade surplus with Washington.

---

5. 'Rise of China and the Global Overaccumulation Crisis.'

This chain-gang relationship, says the IMF's Rajan, is 'unsustainable.'[6] Both the United States and the IMF have decried what they call 'global macroeconomic imbalances' and called on China to revalue the renminbi to reduce its trade surplus with the United States. Yet China can't really abandon its cheap currency policy. Along with cheap labor, cheap currency is part of China's successful formula of export-oriented production. And the United States really can't afford to be too tough on China since it depends on that open line of credit to Beijing to continue feeding the middle-class spending that sustains its own economic growth.

The IMF ascribes this state of affairs to 'macroeconomic imbalances.' But it's really a crisis of overproduction. Thanks to Chinese factories and American consumers, the crisis is likely to get worse.

China lassoes its neighbors

This essay details how China increasingly brought its Southeast Asian neighbors through unbalanced trade relations that were formalized in the China–ASEAN Free Trade Agreement. China's initial resilience at the outset of the crisis was due partly to its ability to fall back on this regional market it increasingly dominated, but this was eventually insufficient to balance its heavy dependence on the US and European markets. The perils of unequal integration to the Chinese economy provide a strong argument for more independent, deglobalized economic strategies.[7]

With the Doha Round of negotiations of the World Trade Organization in limbo, the heavy hitters of international trade have been engaged in a race to sew up trade agreements with smaller

---

6. 'Economic Ship Steady as She Goes.'
7. Originally published in *Foreign Policy in Focus*, March 8, 2010, www.fpif.org/articles/china_lassoes_its_neighbors.

partners. China has been among the most aggressive in this game, a fact underlined on January 1, 2010, when the China–ASEAN Free Trade Area (CAFTA) came into effect.

Touted as the world's biggest Free Trade Area, CAFTA will bring together 1.7 million consumers with a combined gross domestic product of $5.9 trillion and total trade of $1.3 trillion. Under the agreement, trade between China and Brunei, Indonesia, Malaysia, the Philippines, Thailand, and Singapore has become duty-free for more than 7,000 products. By 2015, the newer members of the Association of Southeast Asian Nations (ASEAN) – Vietnam, Laos, Cambodia, and Myanmar – will join the zero-tariff arrangement.

The propaganda mills, especially in Beijing, have been trumpeting the FTA as bringing 'mutual benefits' to China and ASEAN. In contrast, there has been an absence of triumphal rhetoric from ASEAN. In 2002, the year the agreement was signed, Philippines president Gloria Macapagal-Arroyo hailed the emergence of a 'formidable regional grouping' that would rival the United States and the European Union. ASEAN's leaders, it seems, have probably begun to realize the consequences of what they agreed to: that in this FTA most of the advantages will probably flow to China.

At first glance, it seems like the China–ASEAN relationship has been positive. After all, demand from a Chinese economy growing at a breakneck pace was a key factor in the Southeast Asian growth that began around 2003 after the low growth following the Asian financial crisis of 1997 and 1998. For Asia as a whole, in 2003 and the beginning of 2004, 'China was a major engine of growth for most of the economies in the region,' according to a UN report. 'The country's imports accelerated even more than its exports, with a large proportion of them coming from the rest of Asia.'[8] During the current international recession ASEAN governments, much like the United States, are counting on China – which registered

8. *Trade and Development Report 2004: Policy Coherence, Development Strategies and Integration into the World Economy* (New York: United Nations, 2004), p. 20.

an annualized growth rate of 10.7 percent in the last quarter of
2010 – to pull them out of the doldrums.

A more complex picture

But is the Chinese locomotive really pulling the rest of East Asia
along with it, on the fast track to economic nirvana? In fact, China's
growth has in part taken place at Southeast Asia's expense. Low
wages have encouraged local and foreign manufacturers to phase
out their operations in relatively high-wage Southeast Asia and
move them to China. China's devaluation of the yuan in 1994
had the effect of diverting some foreign direct investment away
from Southeast Asia. The trend of ASEAN losing ground to China
accelerated after the financial crisis of 1997. In 2000, foreign
direct investment in ASEAN shrank to 10 percent of all foreign
direct investment in developing Asia, down from 30 percent in
the mid-1990s.[9]

The decline continued in the rest of the decade, with the UN
World Investment Report attributing the trend partly to increased
competition from China. Since the Japanese have been the most
dynamic foreign investors in the region, much apprehension in
the ASEAN capitals greeted a Japanese government survey that
revealed that 57 percent of Japanese manufacturing transnational
corporations found China to be more attractive than the ASEAN-4
(Thailand, Malaysia, Indonesia, and the Philippines).

Snags in a trade relationship

Trade has been another and perhaps greater area of concern. Massive smuggling of goods from China has disrupted practically all

---

9. Karl Sauvant, 'Recent FDI Trends, Implications for Developing Countries, and Policy
Challenges,' paper delivered at OECD Forum on International Investment, Mexico City,
November 26–27, 2001, p. 2.

ASEAN economies. For instance, with some 70–80 percent of shoe shops in Vietnam selling smuggled Chinese shoes, the Vietnamese shoe industry has suffered badly. In the case of the Philippines, a recent paper by Joseph Francia and Errol Ramos of the Free Trade Alliance claims that the local shoe industry has also been hit hard by smuggling of Chinese goods. Indeed, the range of goods negatively affected is broad, including steel, paper, cement, petrochemicals, plastics, and ceramic tiles. 'Many Philippine companies, even those that are competitive globally, had to close shop or reduce production and employment, due to smuggling,' they write.[10]

Because of this massive smuggling, the official trade figures with China released by the Chinese embassy in Manila – which show the Philippines enjoying a positive trade balance in manufacturing and industrial commodities – are questionable.

CAFTA may simply legalize all this smuggling and worsen the already negative effects of Chinese imports on ASEAN industry.

The Thai 'early harvest' debacle

When it comes to agriculture, the trends are clearer. Even without the FTA, for instance, the Philippines already has a $370 million deficit with China. I recently visited Benguet, a key vegetable- and fruit-producing area of the country. The farmers were despondent, almost resigned to being destroyed by the expected deluge of Chinese goods. A national government official warned them that their only chance of survival lay in invoking trade restrictions, based on complaints that Chinese imports did not meet sanitary standards – a risky move that could invoke retaliatory measures. The governor of the province complained that the CAFTA sneaked up on them, with most farmers not knowing that the Philippines signed the agreement as far back as 2002.

---

10. www.philstar.com/balita/509130/nabuthag-granadang-polis-pasidunggan.

Similar bitter complaints have emerged in Thailand, where the impact of the 'early harvest' agreement with China under CAFTA has been better documented.

Under the agreement, Thailand and China agreed to eliminate immediately tariffs on more than 200 items of vegetables and fruit. Thailand would export tropical fruits to China, while winter fruits from China would be eligible for the zero-tariff deal. The expectations of mutual benefit evaporated after a few months, however. Thailand got the bad end of the deal. As one assessment put it, 'despite the limited scope of the Thailand–China early harvest agreement, it has had an appreciable impact in the sectors covered. The "appreciable impact" has been to wipe out northern Thai producers of garlic and red onions and to cripple the sale of temperate fruit and vegetables from the Royal projects.'[11] Thai newspapers pointed to officials in Southern China refusing to bring down tariffs as stipulated in the agreement, while the Thai government brought down the barriers to Chinese products.

Resentment at the results of the China–Thai early harvest agreement among Thai fruit and vegetable growers contributed to widespread disillusionment with the broader free-trade agenda of the Thaksin government. Opposition to free trade was a prominent feature of the popular mobilizations that culminated in a military coup that ousted that regime in September 2006.

The Thai early harvest experience created consternation not just in Thailand but throughout Southeast Asia. It stoked fears of ASEAN becoming a dumping ground for China's extremely competitive industrial and agricultural sectors, which could drive down prices because of China's cheap urban labor and even cheaper labor coming to the cities from the countryside. These fears at the grassroots have, however, fallen on deaf ears as ASEAN governments have been extremely reluctant to displease Beijing.

---

11. Chanida Chanyapate, 'Dangerous Advice on Free Trade Pacts,' *Bangkok Post*, September 2005, www.bangkokpost.com/News/20Sep2005_opin24.php.

The Chinese view

For Chinese officials, the benefits to China of an FTA with ASEAN are clear. The aim of the strategy, according to Chinese economist Angang Hu, is to more fully integrate China into the global economy as the 'center of the world's manufacturing industry.'[12] A central part of the plan was to open up ASEAN markets to Chinese manufactured products. China views Southeast Asia, which absorbs only around 8 percent of China's exports, as an important market with tremendous potential to absorb even more goods, which is particularly important given the growing popularity of protectionist sentiments in the United States and European Union.

China's trade strategy is a 'half open model,' argues Hu: It's 'open or free trade on the export side and protectionism on the import side.'

ASEAN: a beneficiary?

Despite the brave words from Arroyo and other ASEAN leaders in 2002, when the agreement was signed, it's much less clear how ASEAN will benefit from the ASEAN–China relationship. The benefits will certainly not come in labor-intensive manufacturing, where China enjoys an unbeatable edge because of its cheap labor. Nor would benefits come from high-tech, since even the United States and Japan are scared of China's remarkable ability to move very quickly into high-tech industries even as it consolidates its edge in labor-intensive production.

In agriculture will ASEAN also not be net beneficiary? As the early harvest experience with the Philippines and Thailand has shown, China is clearly super-competitive in a vast array of agricultural products from temperate crops to semi-tropical produce,

---

12. In H. Hirakawa and Y.-H. Kim (eds), *Co-Design for a New East Asia After the Crisis* (New York: Springer, 2004).

as well as in agricultural processing. Vietnam and Thailand might be able to hold their own in rice production, Indonesia and Vietnam in coffee, and the Philippines in coconut and coconut products, but there may not be many more products to add to the list.

Moreover, even if, under CAFTA, ASEAN were to gain or retain competitiveness in some areas of manufacturing and trade, China will not likely depart from what Hu calls its 'half open' model of international trade. The Thai early harvest experience underlines the effectiveness of administrative obstacles that can act as non-tariff barriers in China.

In terms of raw materials, Indonesia and Malaysia have oil that is in scarce supply in China, Malaysia has rubber and tin, and the Philippines has palm oil and metals. China, however, is largely reproducing the old colonial division of labor, whereby it receives low-value-added natural resources and agricultural products and sends to the Southeast Asian economies high-value-added manufactures.

With multilateral trade negotiations stuck at the WTO, the big trading countries have been engaged in a race to sew up trade agreements with weaker partners. China is turning out to be the most successful at this game, having managed to create the world's largest free-trade area. For China, the benefits are clear. For its Southeast Asian partners, the benefits are less clear. Indeed, with the likely erosion of local industry and agriculture, Southeast Asia will be paying a big price for a bad deal.

Will China save the world from depression?

In this essay, I make the case that China, which was probably the main beneficiary of globalization, is too dependent on export-oriented production to serve as an alternative pole of global growth to stagnant Europe and the United States despite the massive $585 billion stimulus program it launched in 2009.[13]

This question has become a favorite topic as the heroic American middle-class consumer, weighed down by massive debt, ceases to be the key stimulus for global production.

Although China's GDP growth rate fell to 6.1 percent in the first quarter – the lowest in almost a decade – optimists see 'shoots of recovery' in a 30 percent surge in urban fixed-asset investment and a jump in industrial output in March. These indicators are proof, some say, that China's stimulus program of $586 billion – which, in relation to GDP, is much larger proportionally than the Obama administration's $787 billion package – is working.

Countryside as launching pad for recovery?

With China's export-oriented urban coastal areas suffering from the collapse of global demand, many inside and outside China are pinning their hopes for global recovery on the Chinese countryside. A significant portion of Beijing's stimulus package is destined for infrastructure and social spending in the rural areas. The government is allocating 20 billion yuan ($3 billion) in subsidies to help rural residents buy televisions, refrigerators, and other electrical appliances.

---

13. First published in *Foreign Policy in Focus*, May 19, 2009, www.fpif.org/articles/will_china_save_the_world_from_depression.

But with export demand down, will this strategy of propping up rural demand work as an engine for the country's massive industrial machine?

There are grounds for skepticism. For one, even when export demand was high, 75 percent of China's industries were already plagued with overcapacity.[14] Before the crisis, for instance, the automobile industry's installed capacity was projected to turn out 100 percent more vehicles than could be absorbed by a growing market. In the last few years, overcapacity problems have resulted in the halving of the annual profit growth rate for all major enterprises.

There is another, greater, problem with the strategy of making rural demand a substitute for export markets. Even if Beijing throws in another hundred billion dollars, the stimulus package is not likely to counteract in any significant way the depressive impact of a 25-year policy of sacrificing the countryside for export-oriented urban-based industrial growth. The implications for the global economy are considerable.

Subordinating agriculture to industry

Ironically, China's ascent during the last thirty years began with the rural reforms Deng Xiaoping initiated in 1978. The peasants wanted an end to the Mao-era communes, and Deng and his reformers obliged them by introducing the 'household-contract responsibility system.' Under this scheme, each household received a piece of land to farm. The household was allowed to retain what was left over of the produce after selling to the state a fixed proportion at a state-determined price, or by simply paying a tax in cash. The rest it could consume or sell on the market. These were the halcyon years of the peasantry. Rural income grew by over 15 percent a year on

---

14. Ho-fung Hung, 'Rise of China and the Global Overaccumulation Crisis,' *Review of International Political Economy* 15(2), 2008.

average, and rural poverty declined from 33 percent to 11 percent of the population.

This golden age of the peasantry came to an end, however, when the government adopted a strategy of coast-based, export-oriented industrialization premissed on rapid integration into the global capitalist economy. This strategy, which was launched at the 12th National Party Congress in 1984, essentially built the urban industrial economy on 'the shoulders of peasants,' as rural specialists Chen Guidi and Wu Chantao put it.[15] The government pursued primitive capital accumulation mainly through policies that cut heavily into the peasant surplus.

The consequences of this urban-oriented industrial development strategy were stark. Peasant income, which had grown by 15.2 percent a year from 1978 to 1984, dropped to 2.8 percent a year from 1986 to 1991. Some recovery occurred in the early 1990s, but stagnation of rural income marked the latter part of the decade. In contrast, urban income, already higher than that of peasants in the mid-1980s, was on average six times the income of peasants by 2000.

The stagnation of rural income was caused by policies promoting rising costs of industrial inputs into agriculture, falling prices for agricultural products, and increased taxes, all of which combined to transfer income from the countryside to the city. But the main mechanism for the extraction of surplus from the peasantry was taxation. By 1991, central state agencies levied taxes on peasants for 149 agricultural products, but this proved to be but part of a much bigger bite, as the lower levels of government began to levy their own taxes, fees, and charges. Currently, the various tiers of rural government impose a total of 269 types of tax, along with all sorts of often arbitrarily imposed administrative charges. Taxes and fees are not supposed to exceed 5 percent of a farmer's income,

15. *Will the Boat Sink the Water? The Life of China's Peasants* (New York: Public Affairs, 2006).

but the actual amount is often much greater. Some Ministry of Agriculture surveys have reported that the peasant tax burden is 15 percent – three times the official national limit.

Expanded taxation would perhaps have been bearable had peasants experienced returns such as improved public health and education and more agricultural infrastructure. In the absence of such tangible benefits, the peasants saw their incomes as subsidizing what Chen and Wu describe as the 'monstrous growth of the bureaucracy and the metastasizing number of officials,'[16] who seemed to have no other function than to extract more and more from them.

Aside from being subjected to higher input prices, lower prices for their goods, and more intensive taxation, peasants have borne the brunt of the urban-industrial focus of economic strategy in other ways. According to one report, '40 million peasants have been forced off their land to make way for roads, airports, dams, factories, and other public and private investments, with an additional two million to be displaced each year.'[17] Other researchers cite a much higher figure of 70 million households, meaning that, calculating 4.5 persons per household, by 2004, land grabs have displaced as many as 315 million people.

Impact of trade liberalization

China's commitment to eliminate agricultural quotas and reduce tariffs, made when it joined the World Trade Organization in 2001, may yet dwarf the impact of all the previous changes experienced by peasants. The cost of admission for China is proving to be huge and disproportionate. The government slashed the average agricultural tariff from 54 percent to 15.3 percent, compared with the world average of 62 percent, prompting the commerce minister to boast

---

16. Ibid., p. 172.
17. *China's Rise: Challenges and Opportunities*, China Balance Sheet.

(or complain): 'Not a single member in the WTO history has made such a huge cut [in tariffs] in such a short period of time.'[18]

The WTO deal reflects China's current priorities. If the government has chosen to put at risk large sections of its agriculture, such as soybeans and cotton, it has done so to open up or keep open global markets for its industrial exports. The social consequences of this trade-off are still to be fully felt, but the immediate effects have been alarming. In 2004, after years of being a net food exporter, China registered a deficit in its agricultural trade. Cotton imports skyrocketed from 11,300 tons in 2001 to 1.98 million tons in 2004, a 175-fold increase. Chinese sugarcane, soybean and, most of all, cotton farmers were devastated. In 2005, according to Oxfam Hong Kong, imports of cheap US cotton resulted in a loss of $208 million in income for Chinese peasants, along with 720,000 jobs. Trade liberalization is also likely to have contributed to the dramatic slowdown in poverty reduction between 2000 and 2004.

Loosening the property regime

In the past few years, the priority placed on a capitalist transformation of the countryside to support export-oriented industrialization has moved the Party to promote not only agricultural trade liberalization but the loosening of a semi-socialist property regime that favors peasants and small farmers. This involves easing public controls over land in order to move toward a full-fledged private property regime. The idea is to allow the sale of land rights (the creation of a land market) so that the most 'efficient' producers can expand their holdings. In the euphemistic words of a US Department of Agriculture publication, 'China is strengthening farmers' rights – although stopping short of allowing full ownership of land

---

18. www.atimes.com/atimes/China_Business/GL2oCbo4.html.

– so farmers can rent land, consolidate their holdings, and achieve efficiencies in size and scale.'[19]

This liberalization of land rights included the passage of the Agricultural Lease Law in 2003, which curtailed the village authorities' ability to reallocate land and gave farmers the right to inherit and sell leaseholds for arable land for thirty years. With the buying and selling of rights to use land, the government essentially re-established private property in land in China. In talking about 'family farms' and 'large-scale farmers,' the Chinese Communist Party was, in fact, endorsing a capitalist development path to supplant one that had been based on small-scale peasant agriculture. As one partisan of the new policy argued, 'The reform would create both an economy of scale – raising efficiency and lowering agricultural production costs – but also resolve the problem of idle land left by migrants to the cities.'[20]

Despite the Party's assurance that it was institutionalizing the peasants' rights to land, many feared that the new policy would legalize the process of illegal land grabbing that had been occurring on a wide scale. This would, they warned, 'create a few landlords and many landless farmers who will have no means of living.'[21] Given the turbulent transformation of the countryside by the full-scale unleashing of capitalist relations of production in other countries, these fears were not misplaced.

In sum, simply allocating money to boost rural demand is unlikely to counteract the powerful economic and social structures created by subordinating the development of the countryside to export-oriented industrialization. These policies have contributed to greater inequality between urban and rural incomes and stalled the reduction of poverty in the rural areas. To enable the rural areas of China to serve as the launching pad for national and

---

19. *Amber Waves*, June 2008, www.ers.usda.gov/Amber Waves.
20. www.ipsnews.net/2008/10/economy-china-flirting-with-land-tenure-reforms.
21. http://news.xinhuanet.com/english/2008-10/19/content_10218172.htm.

global recovery would entail a fundamental policy shift, and the government would have to go against the interests, both local and foreign, that have congealed around the strategy of foreign-capital-dependent, export-oriented industrialization.

Beijing has talked a lot about a 'New Deal' for the countryside over the last few years. But there are few signs that it has the political will to adopt policies that would translate its rhetoric into reality. So don't expect Beijing to save the global economy any time soon.

PART II

GLOBALIZATION IN CRISIS

CHAPTER 5

THE REAL ECONOMY OF THE GLOBAL ECONOMY

Capital is a fickle lover

Even as financial institutions ran aground in Europe and the United States, transnational corporations continued to expand their investments in selected developing countries. Labor cost is, however, no longer the only consideration. Indeed, other factors, such as systems of governance, come to the forefront. This article suggests that in the calculations of global capital formal democratic systems might present advantages over authoritarian systems in assuring a stable polity for capitalist production. In the wake of the economic crisis, however, global supply chains may be losing their luster for corporations and 'deglobalize' their operations. As *The Economist* put it, one of the consequences of the current global crisis might be transnational corporations 'turning their backs' on the world in favor of more domestic or region-based strategies of production.[1]

'China is today the ideal capitalist state: freedom for capital, with the state doing the "dirty job" of controlling the workers,' writes the prominent Slovenian philosopher Slavoj Žižek. 'China as the emerging power of the twenty first century ... seems to embody a new kind of capitalism: disregard for ecological consequences,

---

1. Originally published in *Foreign Policy in Focus*, June 22, 2011, www.fpif.org/articles/capitals_new_crushes.

disdain for workers' rights, everything subordinated to the ruthless drive to develop and become the new world force.'[2]

Capital, however, is a fickle lover.

Recently, a growing number of corporate leaders are having second thoughts about the 'Chinese model' that has been so central in the globalization of production and markets over the last three decades.

Labor rises up

The relief in corporate circles that greeted the East Asian recovery, powered by the massive $580 billion Chinese stimulus program in 2009, has been replaced by concern over the bursting of the real estate bubble, powerful inflationary pressures, and massive over-capacity owing to uncontrolled investment. There is also a sense that China's leadership is fighting a losing battle against entrenched interests and structures in its drive to move from a strategy of export-led growth to one that is domestic-market-led – a move that many consider urgent as China's traditional markets in the United States and Europe are in the vise of long-term stagnation.

But it is the worry that the key source of corporate profitability – Chinese labor – may not be docile and cheap for much longer that mainly nags at the country's corporate guests as well as its rising capitalist class. And many fear that the very ruthlessness that Žižek talks about – the iron fist that the Chinese state has deployed over the last three decades in order to achieve the unbeatable 'China price' – has become a central part of the problem.

The worry first became palpable last year, when workers at several transnational corporations based in Southeastern China, like Honda and Toyota, went on strike and succeeded in winning substantial wage increases. To the surprise of foreign investors, the

---

2. *In Defense of Lost Causes* (London: Verso, 2008), p. 191.

government did not oppose the workers' demands for higher wages, prompting some to speculate that the regime saw the strikes as complementary to its effort to reorient the economy from export-led growth to one based on rising domestic consumption.

The strike wave receded, but a second wave of protest since May of this year, this time taking a violent riot form, has both government and the capitalist elites worried. The mass base of the current protests is not the relatively educated, higher-paid workers at big Japanese subsidiaries, but the low-paid migrant workers that work for small and medium-sized Chinese-owned enterprises that turn out goods for foreign buyers. Zengcheng, one of the centers of protest, is home to hundreds of subcontractors specializing in mass-producing brand blue jeans that end up, under different brand names, in retailers like Target and Walmart in the United States.

Guangdong province, where most of the protests have occurred, accounts for about a third of China's exports, prompting the authorities to respond in force. But police repression will not buy stability, says a report of a government think tank, the State Council Development Research Center. 'Rural migrant workers are marginalized in the cities,' it says, 'treated as mere cheap labor, not absorbed by the cities but even neglected, discriminated against and harmed.' The report warns: 'If they are not absorbed into urban society, and do not enjoy the rights that are their due, many conflicts will accumulate... If mishandled, this will create a major destabilizing threat.'[3]

But the problem is fundamental, and there seems no easy way out. The seemingly inexhaustible reserves of rural labor from China's hinterland kept wages low and worker organization minimal over the last three decades. Now the supply of labor to the export-oriented coastal provinces may be drying up, resulting in steadily rising wages, greater worker militancy, and the end of the 'China price.'

---

3. www.ft.com/cms/s/0/b2239ad8-9a9e-11e0-bab2-00144feab49a.html.

Brazil takes off?

'South–South cooperation' was what was on the mind of many observers when, at the conclusion of her trip to China in April, Brazil's new president, Dilma Rousseff, announced that Foxconn International Holdings, the world's largest electronics contract manufacturer, was shifting some of its operations from China to Brazil, and was expected to spend $12 billion building factories in her country. But there was apparently more to the move than BRIC solidarity. Foxconn, the maker of iPhones and iPads for Apple, computers for Dell, and many other devices for well-known high-tech customers around the world, reported a loss for 2010 because of higher labor costs in China.

It is not only Foxconn that is voting with its feet and going to Brazil. The key reason investors are flocking to Brazil seems to be that the country under Lula not only became friendly to capital, having attractive foreign investment laws and following conservative macroeconomic policies, but also had social policies that promoted stability. One of Brazil's most enthusiastic boosters, *The Economist*, compared Brazil with China and other 'emerging markets' for investment:

> Unlike China, it is a democracy. Unlike India, it has no insurgents, no ethnic and religious conflicts nor hostile neighbors. Unlike Russia, it exports more than oil and arms, and treats foreign investors with respect. Under the presidency of Luiz Inácio Lula da Silva, a former trade-union leader born in poverty, its government has moved to reduce the searing inequalities that have long disfigured it. Indeed, when it comes to smart social policy and boosting consumption at home, the developing world has much more to learn from Brazil than from China.[4]

Continuing its paean to Lula's Brazil, the magazine says:

---

4. 'Brazil Takes Off,' *The Economist*, November 12, 2009, www.economist.com/node/14845197.

Foreign investment is pouring in, attracted by a market boosted by falling poverty and a swelling lower-middle class. The country has established some strong political institutions. A free and vigorous press uncovers corruption – though there is plenty of it, and it mostly goes unpunished.

It concludes: 'Its take-off is all the more admirable because it has been achieved through reform and democratic consensus-building. If only China could say the same.'

Lula seems to have squared the circle. Is this for real? The progressive analyst Perry Anderson believes it is. In a long, illuminating article in the *London Review of Books*, he says that Lula's innovation was to combine conservative macroeconomic policy and foreign-investment-friendly policies with an anti-poverty program, the Bolsa de Familia, that cost relatively little in terms of government outlays but produced socially and politically significant impacts.[5] Bolsa, a program of cash transfers conditioned on parents keeping the family children in school and subjecting them to periodic health checkups, by some estimates, has contributed to the reduction in the number of poor people from 50 million to 30 million – and made Lula one of the few contemporary political leaders who is more popular at the end of his reign than at the beginning. As for organized labor, which accounts for 17 percent of the Brazilian workforce, it has largely been content to follow the leadership of Lula, who rose from the ranks to become the country's top union leader before he launched his political career.

Indonesia's moment?

Much the same boosterism now marks the business press's commentaries on Indonesia. Brazil and Indonesia are roughly comparable population-wise and in terms of geographic spread. While Brazil

---

5. 'Lula's Brazil,' *London Review of Books*, March 31, 2011.

is the world's eighth largest economy, Indonesia is the eighteenth largest. Both were barely touched by the global economic crisis, being primarily domestic-market-driven instead of export-driven, though they have strong export sectors. While the rest of its export-oriented neighbors in Southeast Asia suffered significant declines in economic growth at the height of the global economic crisis in 2009, Indonesia managed an impressive 4.6 percent.

In recent years, according to Mari Pangestu, Indonesia's minister of trade, the country has been the recipient of 'a lot of displacements' from China, brought about by 'the [appreciating] yuan, the increase in salaries, the strict regulation of work and all the problems China had to face.'[6] With average wages now lower in Indonesia than in China in many sectors, such as information technology, the country is becoming a choice relocation site for firms worried about double-digit wage increases in China and Vietnam. Foreign investment was approximately $15 billion in 2008, fell to $10 billion in 2009, recovered to $12.5 billion in 2011, and is expected to hit $14.5 billion in 2011.

This year's site for the World Economic Forum for East Asia on June 12-13 was Jakarta, and with it came a glowing endorsement from global capital's chief promotions agency. In its report on Indonesia's 'competitiveness,' the WEF noted, 'Among Indonesia's strengths, the macroeconomic environment stands out... Fast growth and sound fiscal management have put the country on a strong fiscal footing. The debt burden has been drastically reduced, and Indonesia's credit rating has been upgraded.' It pointed out that 'as one of the world's 20 largest economies, Indonesia boasts a large pool of potential consumers, as well as a rapidly growing middle class, of great interest to both local and foreign investors.'[7] Infrastructure is still insufficient, but providing it is also what

6. 'Indonesia – A Model for Economic Growth,' September 27, 2010, www.metrolic.com/indonesia-a-model-for-economic-growth-133104.
7. *The Indonesia Competitiveness Report 2011*, www.weforum.org/reports/indonesia-competitiveness-report-2011?fo=1.

makes foreign capital salivate, with the *Wall Street Journal*, in an otherwise laudatory editorial, warning the government to surrender infrastructure provision to the private sector and foreign capital.

But it is Indonesia's governance that makes it most attractive to foreign capital. Corruption is still a pervasive problem and some foreign capital investors complain that the revised labor code is more favorable to labor than to capital. But Indonesia is said to have traversed the fall of the Suharto dictatorship, the Asian financial crisis, and a chaotic period of democratic experimentation with flying colors. Thirteen years after the overthrow of Suharto, the country's unique advantage is said to be its offering global capital 'rapid growth with democratic stability.' While there is no one program like the Bolsa in Brazil, Indonesia's poverty reduction is trumpeted by the United Nations and the World Bank as being among the most impressive in the world, with the number of those living in poverty estimated at 13 percent of the population. Contributing to this has been what many regard as one of the Suharto regime's few enduring positive legacies: a successful population management program.

Lula's Indonesian counterpart is President Susilo Bambang Yudhoyono, a former general under Suharto, who is credited with stabilizing the economy while consolidating democratic governance during his first term in office from 2004 to 2009. Like Lula, Yudhoyono is popular not only with global capital, but with the people: in his run for a second term in 2009, he coasted to a commanding victory. And like Lula, who did not behave as labor's representative in power, Yudhoyono – 'SBY' to most Indonesians – has not ruled in the top-down fashion expected from an ex-military man.

For many on the left in both countries, however, the social situation is far from ideal, and they see Lula and SBY's formula of friendship with capital cum poverty mitigation as the wrong formula to address their countries' massive problems. Their skepticism is not unjustified: according to the Institute for Applied Economic Research, social inequality has not changed in twenty-five years. Half the total income in Brazil is held by the richest 10 percent, and only 10 percent of the national wealth is shared by the poorest 50 percent.[8] Owing to continuing plunder by powerful logging interests with friends in high places, Indonesia's rate of deforestation is among the ten quickest on earth, the main reason it has become the third largest emitter of greenhouse gases.[9] For the moment, however, these dissenters are a subdued minority.

Does global capital need more liberal regimes?

It will take some time before China is displaced from its premier position as global capital's preferred investment site, but the latter's fears are increasingly coming to the fore. Žižek is right, and wrong: it seems that while iron-fisted authoritarian rule served global capital's interests well for the last two decades, it also – in the view of China's corporate guests – produced a polity with deep fissures that now regularly erupt. Their great worry about China is that it is becoming a pressure cooker with few safety valves, as the Communist Party comes down harder on labor and becomes even more resistant to democratic initiatives.

It seems that for the stable reproduction of capitalist relations during the current phase of the global economy, more open political systems that allow conflicts to be settled via elections and possess more liberal labor regimes are a better bet, from the perspective of capital. The irony of the situation is that even Chinese corporations may eventually find the social regimes of Brazil and Indonesia more favorable for their profitability and stable growth than China itself.

8. www.hart-brasilientexte.de/2010/09/19/social-inequality-in-brazil-brasiliens-wicht igster-befreiungstheologe-frei-betto-lula-regierungsresultat.

9. www.treehugger.com/natural-sciences/illegal-logging-makes-indonesia-worlds-third-largest-emitter-of-greenhouses-gases.html.

The Apple connection

While financial institutions were the focus of mass anger, transnational corporations were largely exempted from criticism at the outset of the current global crisis, with some information technology stars like Apple enjoying high ratings in public opinion. Yet, as this essay argues, the deindustrialization promoted by these corporations was a key contributor to the crisis since the loss of jobs and lower wages it created had to be compensated by looser lending to consumers to keep up effective demand and maintain political stability. Apple has been a key practitioner of subcontracting, one of the key methods corporations have used to globalize their production structures. As worker rights' violations in subcontractors like Foxconn in China were exposed, Apple found it increasingly difficult to maintain its clean image, one that was associated mainly with it being a technological innovator.[10]

Ever since the beginning of the current global economic crisis, the focus of both critical analysis and public odium has been speculative capital. In the populist narrative, it was the breathtaking shenanigans of the banks in an atmosphere of deregulation that led to the economic collapse. The 'financial economy,' characterized as parasitic and bad, was contrasted to the 'real economy,' which was said to produce real goods and real value. Resources flowed into speculative activities in finance, resulting in a loss of dynamism in the real economy and eventually leading to credit cutoff at the height of the crisis, causing bankruptcies and massive layoffs.

Vampire squid versus corporate Galahad?

The principal villain in this narrative is Goldman Sachs. The image of this Wall Street denizen has been etched in the public mind by Matt Taibbi's description of it as 'a great vampire squid wrapped

---

10. Originally published in *Foreign Policy in Focus*, February 1, 2012, www.fpif. org/articles/the_apple_connection.

around the face of humanity, relentlessly jamming its blood funnel into anything that smells like money.'[11]

In this account, the old nemesis of the progressive analysts, the transnational corporation (TNC), slips quietly into the background. Indeed, it is seen as part of the real economy, as the commonly used term 'non-financial corporation' implies. In contrast to the investment banks that create fictitious products like derivatives, TNCs are said to create real products like Apple's nifty iPads and iPhones. While Goldman Sachs is pictured as a vampire squid, Apple is depicted as a corporate Galahad that can be relied on to deliver the consumer's wildest desires. In one survey, 56 percent of Americans associated nothing negative with Apple.

A recent two-part series in the *New York Times* on Apple, however, reminds us that transnational corporations and their practice of outsourcing jobs are front and center when it comes to the current economic crisis.[12] And it is not only 'smokestack' corporations like GM and Boeing that have massively shifted work from the United States to cheap labor havens abroad, but also those involved in the knowledge industry. Indeed, the highest proportion of firms with an offshoring strategy belongs to the information technology and software development industries. But while HP and Dell have become associated with outsourcing, Apple's prowess at turning out products that capture the popular imagination has kept it from being tainted with the image of being a labor exporter.

Apple and outsourcing

Apple earned over $400,000 in profit per employee in 2011, more than Goldman Sachs or Exxon. Yet in the last few years, it has

---

11. 'The Great American Bubble Machine,' *Rolling Stone*, July 9, 2009, www.rollingstone.com/politics/news/the-great-american-bubble-machine-20100405.

12. Charles Duhigg and Keith Bradsher, 'How the U.S. Lost Out on iPhone Work' and 'In China, Human Costs Are Built Into an iPad,' *New York Times*, January 21 and 25, 2012, www.nytimes.com/interactive/business/ieconomy.html.

created few jobs in its home base and prime market, the United States. According to the *New York Times* account,

> Apple employs 43,000 people in the United States and 20,000 overseas, a small fraction of the over 400,000 American workers at General Motors in the 1950s, or the hundreds of thousands at General Electric in the 1980s. Many more people work for Apple's contractors: an additional 700,000 people engineer, build and assemble iPads, iPhones and Apple's other products. But almost none of them work in the United States. Instead, they work for foreign companies in Asia, Europe and elsewhere, at factories that almost all electronics designers rely upon to build their wares.

The genesis of the financial crisis, in fact, cannot be separated from the strategic moves of 'real economy' actors like Apple. Their readiness to leave their home base and home market was one of the central causes of the crisis. The creation of credit was the central link between this trend in the real economy and the dynamics of finance. Before we examine this link, however, it is important to review some facts about outsourcing.

It is estimated that 8 million US manufacturing jobs were eliminated between June 1979 and December 2009. One report describes the grim process of deindustrialization:

> Long before the banking collapse of 2008, such important U.S. industries as machine tools, consumer electronics, auto parts, appliances, furniture, telecommunications equipment, and many others that had once dominated the global marketplace suffered their own economic collapse. Manufacturing employment dropped to 11.7 million in October 2009, a loss of 5.5 million or 32 percent of all manufacturing jobs since October 2000. The last time fewer than 12 million people worked in the manufacturing sector was in 1941. In October 2009, more people were officially unemployed (15.7 million) than were working in manufacturing.[13]

---

13. Richard McCormack, 'The Plight of American Manufacturing,' *The American Prospect*, http://prospect.org/article/plight-american-manufacturing.

Outsourcing and stagnation in the real economy

This decimation of the manufacturing sector, which involved the elimination of a massive number of well-paying manufacturing jobs, played a central role in the stagnation of income, wages, and purchasing power in the United States. In the three decades prior to the crash of 2008, Robert Reich notes, the wages of the typical American hardly increased, and actually dropped in the 2000s.[14]

This stagnation of income posed a threat to both business and the state. To the first, the slow growth of demand would translate into overproduction and, thus, diminished profits in the corporations' key market. To the state, it posed the specter of rising social conflict and instability.

The threat of a stagnant market was thwarted – temporarily – by the private sector via a massive increase in credit creation by banks, which lowered lending standards and hooked millions of consumers into multiple credit cards, with a great deal of the funds lent sourced from China and other capital-exporting Asian economies. Credit kept consumption up and fueled the booms in the 1990s and the middle of the first decade of the twenty-first century.

Washington tried to ward off political resentment by adopting a strategy of 'populist credit expansion' – that is, making easy credit for housing available for low-income groups via Freddie Mac and Fannie Mae. Political stability was not the only outcome of this approach; it was accompanied by greater profitability for speculative capital. As Raghuram Rajan writes,

> As more money from the government flooded into financing or supporting low income housing, the private sector joined the party. After all, they could do the math, and they understood that the political compulsions behind government actions would not disappear quickly. With agency support, subprime mortgages would be liquid, and low-cost housing would increase

---

14. In *Aftershock: The Next Economy and America's Future* (New York: Vintage, 2011).

in price. Low risk and high return – what more could the private
sector desire?[15]

The Apple–China connection

Co-opting the masses with credit expansion collapsed with the
financial implosion of 2008. Today, millions of Americans are
both without jobs and in terrible debt. But, as the continuing
high unemployment rate indicates, the export of jobs continues
unabated, and China remains the favored destination.

Part of the reason South China retains its primacy as an investment site is that Chinese suppliers, with subsidies from the
state, have established an unbeatable supply chain of contiguous
factories, radically bringing down transport costs, enabling rapid
assembly of an iPad or iPhone, and thus satisfying customers in a
highly competitive market in record time.

Steve Jobs, the legendary founder of Apple, played a key role in
creating this system. Apple executives recount his wanting a glass
screen for the iPhone that could not be scratched, and his wanting
it in 'six weeks.' After one executive left that meeting, says the
New York Times, he booked a flight to China. 'If Mr. Jobs wanted
perfect,' he recalled, 'there was nowhere else to go.'[16]

Mastery of the economics of the supply chain is, however, only
one of the reasons Jobs and Apple favored China. The central
reason continued to be cheap labor that is disciplined by the state.
What emerges in the *Times* account about Apple's practices is that,
despite its protestations about being a socially responsible firm,
Apple bargains hard, allowing its contractors 'only the slimmest of
profits.' Thus, 'suppliers often try to cut corners, replace expensive
chemicals with less costly alternatives, or push their employees to

---

15. *Fault Lines: How Hidden Fractures Still Threaten the World Economy* (New Haven
CT: Princeton University Press, 2011), p. 38.
16. 'How the U.S. Lost Out on iPhone Work.'

work faster and longer.' 'The only way you make money working for Apple is figuring out how to do things more efficiently or cheaper,' said an executive at one company that helped bring the iPad to market. 'And then they'll come back the next year, and force a 10 percent price cut.' Not surprisingly, a number of Apple suppliers have been plagued with accidents, including explosions, since, as one former Apple executive put it, 'If you squeeze margins, you're forcing them to cut safety.'

The consequences of severe cost-cutting have been not only accidents but also protests by workers. Some of them took the tragic route of suicide, such as those that occurred in 2009 and 2010 at Foxconn, a notorious, gigantic corporate contractor, while others resorted to spontaneous labor actions that were put down forcefully by management and the state.

Apple's products are top of the line, distinguished by their superior design, engineering, and personality or 'soul.' But the company's march to market supremacy has been accomplished at tremendous cost to both American and Chinese workers. The iPad and iPhone are engineering masterpieces. But these commodities are not simply material. They also incarnate the social relations of production. They are the expression of the marriage between a demanding enterprise that has become the cutting edge corporation of our time and what Slavoj Žižek has called today's 'ideal capitalist state.'[17] China, with the freedom it offers capital along with its unparalleled capacity to discipline labor. One cannot but agree with Jared Bernstein, a former White House economic adviser, when he told the *Times*, 'If it's [the Apple system] the pinnacle of capitalism, we should be worried.'[18]

17. 'Mao Zedong: The Marxist Lord of Misrule,' www.lacan.com/zizmaozedong.htm.
18. 'How the U.S. Lost Out on iPhone Work.'

Labor trafficking:
modern-day slave trade

This essay contends that, like early capitalism in the sixteenth century, contemporary globalization promotes the spread of unfree labor, a system that is especially notable in the newer centers of global accumulation like the Gulf States in the Middle East. Clearly, economic strategies, like deglobalization, that would focus more on enhancing the domestic economy and creating inside rather than outside the country would have a dampening effect on the new slave trade.[19]

The freer flow of commodities and capital has been one of the features of the contemporary process of globalization. Unlike in the earlier phase of globalization in the nineteenth century, however, the freer flow of commodities and capital has not been accompanied by a freer movement of labor globally. The dynamic centers of the global economy, after all, have imposed ever tighter restrictions on migration from the poorer countries. Yet the demand for cheap labor in the richer parts of the world continues to grow, even as more and more people in developing countries seek to escape conditions of economic stagnation and poverty that are often the result of the same dynamics of a system of global capitalism that have created prosperity in the developed world.

The number of migrants worldwide has grown from 36 million in 1991 to 191 million in 2005, according to Guy Arnold, author of *Migration: Changing the World*,[20] one of the most exhaustive studies of the phenomenon. The aggregate numbers do not, however, begin to tell the critical role that migrant labor plays in the prosperous economies. For instance, the booming economies in the Persian Gulf and Saudi peninsula are relatively lightly populated in terms of their local Arab population, but they host a substantial

19. Originally published in *Foreign Policy in Focus*, May 11, 2012, www.fpif.org/articles/labor_trafficking_modern-day_slave_trade.
20. *Migration: Changing the World* (London: Pluto, 2011).

number of foreign migrant workers, many of whom come from South Asia and Southeast Asia. Indeed, foreign migrant workers are a disproportionate part of the populations of the Persian Gulf states– ranging from 25 percent in Saudi Arabia to 66 percent in Kuwait, to over 90 percent in the United Arab Emirates and Qatar.

This gap between increasing demand and restricted supply has created an explosive situation, one that has been filled by a global system of trafficking in human beings that can in many respects be compared to the slave trade of the sixteenth century.

The dynamics of the current system of trade in repressed labor is illustrated in the case of the Philippines. This country is one of the great labor exporters of the world. Some 10 percent of its total population and 22 percent of its working-age population are now migrant workers in other countries. With transfers totaling some $20 billion a year, the Philippines places fourth as a recipient of remittances, after China, India, and Mexico.

Labor export and structural adjustment

The role of the Philippines as a labor exporter cannot be divorced from the dynamics of neoliberal capitalism. The labor export program began in the mid-1970s as a temporary program under the Marcos dictatorship, with a relatively small number of workers involved – about 50,000. The ballooning of the program to encompass 9 million workers owes much to the devastation of the economy and jobs by the structural adjustment policies imposed by the World Bank and the International Monetary Fund beginning in 1980, trade liberalization under the World Trade Organization, and the prioritization of debt repayment by the post-Marcos governments in national economic policy since 1986.

Structural adjustment resulted in deindustrialization and the loss of many manufacturing jobs; trade liberalization pushed many peasants out of agriculture, a great number directly to overseas employment; and prioritization of debt repayments robbed the government of resources for capital expenditures that could act as an engine of economic growth since 20–40 percent of the budget went every year to servicing the debt. In the role that structural adjustment and trade liberalization played in creating pressures for labor migration, the experience of the Philippines parallels that of Mexico, another key labor-exporting country.

For the governments of the two countries, massive labor export has served another function: as a safety valve for the release of social pressures that would otherwise have been channeled into radical movements for political and social change internally. Those who migrate are often among the most intrepid, the most nimble, and the most acute people in the lower and middle classes, the kind of people who would make excellent cadres and members of progressive movements for change. Along with the crisis of socialization of children owing to the absence of the mother, this is one of the most damaging legacies of the massive labor migration in the Philippines: that it has allowed our elites to ignore overdue structural reforms.

Unfree labor: the case of the Middle East

Labor export is big business, having spawned a host of parasitic institutions that now have a vested interest in maintaining and expanding it. The transnational labor export network includes labor recruiters, government agencies and officials, labor smugglers, and big corporate service providers like the US multinational service provider Aramark. Labor trafficking is expanding to become just as big and profitable as sex trafficking and the drug trade. The spread of free wage labor has often been associated with the expansion of capitalism. But what is currently occurring is the expansion and institutionalization of a system of unfree labor under contemporary neoliberal capitalism, a process not unlike the expansion of slave labor and repressed labor in the early phase of global capitalist expansion in the sixteenth century, as elaborated in the work of sociologists like Immanuel Wallerstein.

This expansive system that creates, maintains, and expands unfree labor is best illustrated in the case of the Middle East. As Atiya Ahmad writes,

> With the booming of the Gulf states' petrodollar-driven economies from the early 1970s onwards, a vast and consolidated assemblage of government policies, social and political institutions, and public discourse developed to manage and police the region's foreign resident population. Anchored by the kefala or sponsorship and guarantorship system, this assemblage both constructs and disciplines foreign residents into 'temporary labor migrants.'[21]

This elite-promoted construction of migrant identity promotes an internalization of the migrants' role as social subordinates and an emasculation of their status as political agents. They are expected to remain and so far have largely behaved as non-participants in the politics of their so-called host societies, even as these societies are swept by the winds of political change.

In 2009, 64 percent of the more than 1 million Filipino workers who left to work abroad went to the Middle East. Most of these workers were women and the biggest occupational category was household service workers or maids.

Here is how the labor trafficking system works in the states in the Arabian peninsula along the Persian Gulf. A recruiter from a Gulf state contacts his man in the Philippines. The Filipino contact goes to the remote provinces to recruit a young woman promising a wage of $400 a month, which is the minimum amount set by the Philippine government. When she departs, the recruitment agency

---

21. In *Migrant Labor in the Gulf*, www12.georgetown.edu/sfs/qatar/cirs/MigrantLabor-SummaryReport1.pdf.

gives her another contract at the airport, one that is often written in Arabic, saying she will be paid only half or less than that amount. On arrival at the destination, she receives from the Gulf recruiter a temporary residence permit or *iqama*, but this is taken from her along with her passport by the recruiter or by her employer.

The migrant worker is then turned over to a family where she labors under slave-like conditions for 18 to 20 hours a day. She is isolated from other Filipino domestic workers, making her communication with the outside world dependent on her employer. She cannot leave the employer because her temporary residence certificate and passport are with him. If she runs away, however, and goes to the labor recruiter, she is 'sold' to another family, sometimes at an even lower rate than that paid by the original employer.

Unable to leave the country since she has no documents, the runaway most often ends up being sold from one family to another by the labor recruiter. If she is lucky, she might find her way to the Philippine embassy, which operates a shelter for runaways, but it will take months if not years for the Philippine embassy to obtain the necessary permits to enable her to return home.

How regulation is subverted

In its effort to curb this free market in virtual slavery or to prevent workers from going into countries where their physical security would be in great danger, like Afghanistan or Iraq, the Philippine government requires government-issued permits for workers to be able to leave or it has imposed deployment bans to some countries. However, labor recruiters, who are often in cahoots not only with Middle East employers but also with the US Defense Department and US private contractors, have found ways of getting around these regulations.

Clandestine networks have developed to smuggle workers from the southern Philippines to destinations in the Middle East. A number of women domestics interviewed in Damascus a few weeks ago told of being smuggled out of the southern Philippine city of Zamboanga by small boat to the Malaysian state of Sabah. From there they were transported in the hold of a bigger boat going to Singapore, where they were then offloaded and brought by land transport to a site near Kuala Lumpur. In Kuala Lumpur they were forced to work for their subsistence for six weeks. Only after two months were they finally transported by plane from Kuala Lumpur to Dubai, then to Damascus.

With such illegal transnational human smuggling networks in operation, the Philippine embassy estimated that 90 percent of the 9,000 domestic workers in Syria were there illegally – that is, they had no valid exit papers from the Philippines. Among other things, this has made locating and contacting them very difficult after Manila issued orders to the embassy last January to evacuate all Filipino workers from Syria.

The situation is similar in Afghanistan and Iraq. For much the same reason, we do not have an accurate figure of how many Filipinos have been illegally recruited to be service workers at the US bases by the Pentagon and US military contractors, but 10,000 is probably a conservative number. In the case of Afghanistan, the collusion between illegal labor traffickers, the US government, and US private contractors poses a gargantuan challenge to the weak Philippine state.

Sexual abuse: the ever-present menace

The predominance of women among the workers being trafficked to the Middle East has created a situation rife with sexual abuse. In this system labor trafficking and sexual trafficking are increasingly intersecting. Here is an excerpt from a report of the House Committee on Overseas Workers of the Philippines following the visit of some members to Saudi Arabia in January 2011:

Rape is the ever-present specter that haunts Filipino domestic
workers in Saudi Arabia. ... Rape and sexual abuse is more
frequent than the raw Embassy statistics reveal, probably coming
to 15 to 20 per cent of cases reported for domestics in distress. If
one takes these indicators as roughly representative of unreported
cases of abuse of domestic workers throughout the kingdom, then
one cannot but come to the conclusion that rape and sexual abuse
is common.[22]

One could go further and say that there is a strong element of
sex trafficking in the trafficking of Filipino women into the Middle
East given that many Gulf households expect that providing sex to
the master of the household is one of the domestic worker's tasks.
What results is an unbearable situation, not only because refusal
often brings a beating but also because this brings the domestic
into conflict with the wife. Indeed, in many instances, domestic
workers are 'lent' to relatives not only to have them clean up the
their homes but also to serve as sexual playthings to male brothers
or in-laws.

Slavery is said to be a thing of the past. However, the dynamics
of global capitalism have reproduced a system of repressive labor
globally that is serviced and maintained by legal and illegal labor
trafficking. Female domestic workers are at the bottom of the
migrant social hierarchy in places like the Middle East. Their conditions of work, which often include rape and sexual abuse, constitute
a condition virtually indistinguishable from slavery. As was the case
with traditional slavery in the eighteenth and nineteenth centuries,
abolition of this system of repressed, unfree labor must be high on
the agenda of the twenty-first century.

---

22. Committee on Overseas Workers Affairs, 'The Dark Kingdom? The Condition of
Overseas Filipino Workers in Saudi Arabia,' Final Report of the Investigating Mission of the
Committee on Overseas Workers (COWA) to Saudi Arabia, January 9-13, 2011, pp. 10-11.

Destroying African agriculture

The food price crisis shocked the world in 2006–08, serving as the precursor of the massive financial collapse in the fall of 2008. Along with financial speculation and the channeling of corn production from food to fuel, an important cause of the crisis was the erosion of the productive capacity of agriculture in many developing economies owing to the imposition of structural adjustment programs by the World Bank and the International Monetary Fund, which paved the way for the creation of a global agricultural market serving mainly the upper and middle classes and dominated by transnational agribusiness. This essay suggests that a deglobalized, small-farmer-based agriculture ultimately provides the solution to the deepening crisis of agriculture.[23]

Biofuel production is certainly one of the culprits in the current global food crisis. But while the diversion of corn from food to biofuel feedstock has been a factor in food prices shooting up, the more primordial problem has been the conversion of economies that are largely food-self-sufficient into chronic food importers. Here the World Bank, the International Monetary Fund (IMF), and the World Trade Organization (WTO) figure as much more important villains.

Whether in Latin America, Asia, or Africa, the story has been the same: the destabilization of peasant producers by a one–two punch of IMF–World Bank structural adjustment programs that gutted government investment in the countryside followed by the massive influx of subsidized US and European Union agricultural imports after the WTO's Agreement on Agriculture pried open markets.

African agriculture is a case study of how doctrinaire economics serving corporate interests can destroy a whole continent's productive base.

---

23. Originally published in *Foreign Policy in Focus*, June 3, 2008, www.fpif.org/ articles/destroying_african_agriculture.

From exporter to importer

At the time of decolonization in the 1960s, Africa was not just self-sufficient in food but was actually a net food exporter, its exports averaging 1.3 million tons a year between 1966 and 1970.[24] Today, the continent imports 25 percent of its food, with almost every country being a net food importer. Hunger and famine have become recurrent phenomena, with the last three years alone seeing food emergencies break out in the Horn of Africa, the Sahel, Southern Africa, and Central Africa.

Agriculture is in deep crisis, and the causes are many, including civil wars and the spread of HIV/AIDS. However, a very important part of the explanation was the phasing out of government controls and support mechanisms under the structural adjustment programs to which most African countries were subjected as the price for getting IMF and World Bank assistance to service their external debt.

Instead of triggering a virtuous spiral of growth and prosperity, structural adjustment saddled Africa with low investment, increased unemployment, reduced social spending, reduced consumption, and low output, all combining to create a vicious cycle of stagnation and decline.

Lifting price controls on fertilizers while simultaneously cutting back on agricultural credit systems simply led to reduced applications, lower yields, and lower investment. One would have expected the non-economist to predict this outcome, which was screened out by the Bank and Fund's free-market paradigm. Moreover, reality refused to conform to the doctrinal expectation that the withdrawal of the state would pave the way for the market and private sector to dynamize agriculture. Instead, the private sector believed that reducing state expenditures created more risk and failed to step into the breach. In country after country, the predictions of neoliberal

24. http://news.bbc.co.uk/1/hi/world/africa/4662232.stm.

doctrine yielded precisely the opposite: the departure of the state 'crowded out' rather than 'crowded in' private investment. In those instances where private traders did come in to replace the state, an Oxfam report noted, 'they have sometimes done so on highly unfavorable terms for poor farmers,' leaving 'farmers more food insecure, and governments reliant on unpredictable aid flows.'[25] The usually pro-private sector *Economist* agreed, admitting that 'many of the private firms brought in to replace state researchers turned out to be rent-seeking monopolists.'[26]

What support the government was allowed to muster was channeled by the Bank to export agriculture – to generate the foreign exchange earnings that the state needed to service its debt to the Bank and the Fund. But, as in Ethiopia during the famine of the early 1980s, this led to the dedication of good land to export crops, with food crops forced into more and more unsuitable soil, thus exacerbating food insecurity. Moreover, the Bank's encouraging several economies undergoing adjustment to focus on export production of the same crops simultaneously often led to overproduction that then triggered a price collapse in international markets. For instance, the very success of Ghana's program to expand cocoa production triggered a 48 percent drop in the international price of cocoa between 1986 and 1989, threatening, as one account put it, 'to increase the vulnerability of the entire economy to the vagaries of the cocoa market.'[27] In 2002-03, a collapse in coffee prices contributed to another food emergency in Ethiopia.

As in many other regions, structural adjustment in Africa was not simply underinvestment but state divestment. But there was one major difference. In Latin America and Asia, the Bank and Fund

25. Oxfam International, *Causing Hunger: An Overview of the Food Crisis in Africa* (Oxford: Oxfam, July 2006), p. 18.

26. Samake Bakary, 'Food and the Poor: The New Face of Hunger,' *The Economist*, April 17, 2008, www.economist.com/node/11049284?story_id=11049284.

27. Charles Abugre, *Behind Crowded Shelves: An Assessment of Ghana's Structural Adjustment Experiences, 1983–1991* (San Francisco: Food First, 1993), p. 87.

confined themselves for the most part to macromanagement, or supervising the dismantling of the state's economic role from above. These institutions left the dirty details of implementation to the state bureaucracies. In Africa, where they dealt with much weaker governments, the Bank and Fund micromanaged such decisions as how fast subsidies should be phased out, how many civil servants had to be fired, or even, as in the case of Malawi, how much of the country's grain reserve should be sold and to whom. In other words, Bank and IMF resident proconsuls reached into the very innards of the state's involvement in the agricultural economy to rip it up.

The role of trade

Compounding the negative impact of adjustment were unfair trade practices on the part of the EU and the United States. Trade liberalization allowed low-priced subsidized EU beef to enter and drive many West African and South African cattle raisers to ruin. With their subsidies legitimized by the WTO's Agreement on Agriculture, US cotton growers offloaded their cotton on world markets at 20-55 percent of the cost of production, bankrupting West African and Central African cotton farmers in the process.[28]

These dismal outcomes were not accidental. As then-US agriculture secretary John Block put it at the start of the Uruguay Round of trade negotiations in 1986, 'the idea that developing countries should feed themselves is an anachronism from a bygone era. They could better ensure their food security by relying on U.S. agricultural products, which are available, in most cases, at lower cost.'[29]

What Block did not say was that the lower cost of US products stemmed from subsidies that were becoming more massive each year, despite the fact that the WTO was supposed to phase out

---

28. 'Trade Talks Round Going Nowhere sans Progress in Farm Reform,' *Business World*, September 8, 2003, p. 15.
29. Quoted in 'Cakes and Caviar: The Dunkel Draft and Third World Agriculture,' *Ecologist* 23(6), 1993, p. 220.

all forms of subsidy. From $367 billion in 1995, the first year of the WTO, the total amount of agricultural subsidies provided by developed-country governments rose to $388 billion in 2004. Subsidies now account for 40 percent of the value of agricultural production in the European Union (EU) and 25 percent in the United States.

The social consequences of structural adjustment cum agricultural dumping were predictable. According to Oxfam, the number of Africans living on less than a dollar a day more than doubled to 313 million people between 1981 and 2001 – or 46 percent of the whole continent. The role of structural adjustment in creating poverty, as well as severely weakening the continent's agricultural base and consolidating import dependency, was hard to deny. As the World Bank's chief economist for Africa admitted, 'We did not think that the human costs of these programs could be so great, and the economic gains would be so slow in coming.'[30]

That was, however, a rare moment of candor. What was especially disturbing was that, as Oxford University political economist Ngaire Woods pointed out, the 'seeming blindness of the Fund and Bank to the failure of their approach to sub-Saharan Africa persisted even as the studies of the IMF and the World Bank themselves failed to elicit positive investment effects.'[31]

The case of Malawi

This stubbornness led to tragedy in Malawi.

It was a tragedy preceded by success. In 1998 and 1999, the government initiated a program to give each smallholder family a 'starter pack' of free fertilizers and seeds. This followed several years of successful experimentation in which the packs were

---

30. Morris Miller, *Debt and the Environment: Converging Crisis* (New York: UN, 1991), p. 70.
31. Ngaire Woods, *The Globalizers: the IMF, the World Bank, and Their Borrowers* (Ithaca NY: Cornell University Press, 2006), p. 158.

provided only to the poorest families. The result was a national surplus of corn. What came after, however, is a story that will be enshrined as a classic case study in a future book on the ten greatest blunders of neoliberal economics.

The World Bank and other aid donors forced the drastic scaling down and eventual scrapping of the program, arguing that the subsidy distorted trade. Without the free packs, food output plummeted. In the meantime, the IMF insisted that the government sell off a large portion of its strategic grain reserves to enable the food reserve agency to settle its commercial debts. The government complied. When the crisis in food production turned into a famine in 2001-02, there were hardly any reserves left to rush to the countryside. Some 1,500 people perished. The IMF, however, was unrepentant; in fact, it suspended its disbursements on an adjustment program with the government on the grounds that 'the parastatal sector will continue to pose risks to the successful implementation of the 2002/03 budget. Government interventions in the food and other agricultural markets ... crowd out more productive spending.'[32]

When an even worse food crisis developed in 2005, the government finally had enough of the Bank and IMF's institutionalized stupidity. A new president reintroduced the fertilizer subsidy program, enabling 2 million households to buy fertilizer at a third of the retail price and seeds at a discount. The results: bumper harvests for two years in a row, a surplus of 1 million tons of maize, and the country transformed into a supplier of corn to other countries in Southern Africa.

But the World Bank, like its sister agency, still stubbornly clung to the discredited doctrine. As the Bank's country director told the *Toronto Globe and Mail*, 'All those farmers who begged, borrowed, and stole to buy extra fertilizer last year are now looking at that

---

32. www.imf.org/external/np/ms/2002/051402.htm.

decision and rethinking it. The lower the maize price, the better for food security but worse for market development.'[33]

Fleeing failure

Malawi's defiance of the World Bank would probably have been an act of heroic but futile resistance a decade ago. The environment is different today. Owing to the absence of any clear case of success, structural adjustment has been widely discredited throughout Africa. Even some donor governments that once subscribed to it have distanced themselves from the Bank, the most prominent case being the official British aid agency that co-funded the latest subsidized fertilizer program in Malawi.[34] Perhaps the motivation of these institutions is to prevent the further erosion of their diminishing influence in the continent through association with a failed approach and unpopular institutions. At the same time, they are certainly aware that Chinese aid is emerging as an alternative to the conditionalities of the World Bank, the IMF, and Western government aid programs.

Beyond Africa, even former supporters of adjustment, like the International Food Policy Research Institute (IFPRI) in Washington and the rabidly neoliberal *Economist* acknowledged that the state's abdication from agriculture was a mistake. In a recent commentary on the rise of food prices, for instance, IFPRI asserted that 'rural investments have been sorely neglected in recent decades,' and said that it is time for 'developing country governments [to] increase their medium- and long-term investments in agricultural research and extension, rural infrastructure, and market access for small

---

33. 'How Malawi Went from a Nation of Famine to a Nation of Feast,' *Toronto Globe and Mail*, October 12, 2007, www.theglobeandmail.com/news/world/how-malawi-went-from-a-nation-of-famine-to-a-nation-of-feast/article1084092/?page=all.
34. http://webarchive.nationalarchives.gov.uk/+/http://www.dfid.gov.uk/casestudies/files/africa/malawi-harvest.asp.

farmers.'[35] At the same time, the Bank and IMF's espousal of free trade came under attack from the heart of the economics establishment itself, with a panel of luminaries headed by Princeton's Angus Deaton accusing the Bank's research department of being biased and 'selective' in its research and presentation of data.[36] As the old saying goes, success has a thousand parents and failure is an orphan.

Unable to deny the obvious, the Bank has finally acknowledged that the whole structural adjustment enterprise was a mistake, though it smuggled this concession into the middle of the 2008 *World Development Report*, perhaps in the hope that it would not attract too much attention. Nevertheless, it was a damning admission:

> Structural adjustment in the 1980s dismantled the elaborate system of public agencies that provided farmers with access to land, credit, insurance inputs, and cooperative organizations. The expectation was that removing the state would free the market for private actors to take over these functions – reducing their costs, improving their quality, and eliminating their regressive bias. Too often, that didn't happen. In some places, the state's withdrawal was tentative at best, limiting private entry. Elsewhere, the private sector emerged only slowly and partially – mainly serving commercial farmers but leaving smallholders exposed to extensive market failures, high transaction costs and risks, and service gaps. Incomplete markets and institutional gaps impose huge costs in forgone growth and welfare losses for smallholders, threatening their competitiveness and, in many cases, their survival.[37]

---

35. Joachim von Braun, 'Rising Food Prices: What Should Be Done?' http://www.ifpri.org/publication/rising-food-prices.

36. http://econ.worldbank.org/wbsite/external/extdec/o,,contentMDK:21165468~pagePK:64165401~piPK:64165026~theSitePK:469372,00.html.

37. *World Development Report 2008: Agriculture for Development* (Washington DC: World Bank, 2008), p. 138.

In sum, biofuel production did not create but only exacerbated the global food crisis. The crisis had been building up for years, as policies promoted by the World Bank, the IMF, and the WTO systematically discouraged food self-sufficiency and encouraged food importation by destroying the local productive base of small-holder agriculture. Throughout Africa and the global South, these institutions and the policies they promoted are today thoroughly discredited. But whether the damage they have caused can be undone in time to avert more catastrophic consequences than we are now experiencing remains to be seen.

CHAPTER 6

CAPITALISM AND
THE ENVIRONMENT

Climate and capitalism in Copenhagen

At the end of 2009, two international meetings that were of great significance to the climate took place: representatives to the United Nations Climate Conference in Copenhagen met to tackle the challenge of climate change, while delegates to the World Trade Organization's Seventh Ministerial Conference in Geneva came together in another effort to bring to a conclusion the nine-year-old Doha Round of trade negotiations. As this essay written at the time argued, the two meetings were at cross-purposes and their juxtaposition highlighted a profound reality: the world has to choose between globalization and effective climate management.[1]

The global downturn: relief for the climate

The last twelve months have seen the unraveling of a particular type of international economy: export-oriented and marked by the accelerated integration of production and markets. This globalized economy has been transportation-intensive, greatly dependent on the ever-increasing long-distance transportation of goods. For instance, a plate of food consumed in the United States travels an

---

1. Originally published in *Foreign Policy in Focus*, December 1, 2009, www.fpif.org/articles/climate_and_capitalism_in_copenhagen.

average of 1,500 miles from source to table.[2] Transportation, in turn, is fossil-fuel-intensive, accounting in 2006 for 13 percent of global greenhouse gas (GHG) emissions and 23 percent of global carbon dioxide emissions.

A downturn in the export-dependent global economy thus brings about a significant downturn in carbon emissions as well. It spells relief for the climate. In 2009, the drop in the level of greenhouse gas emissions was the largest in the last forty years.[3] The thousands of ships marooned by lack of global demand in ports such as New York, Singapore, Rio de Janeiro, and Seoul means a significant reduction in the use of high-carbon Bunker C oil, which is used in 80 percent of ocean shipping. The cutback in air freight has meant a significant reduction in the use of aviation fuel, which has been the fastest growing source of GHG emissions in recent years.

Deglobalization as opportunity

In response to the collapse of the export-oriented global economy, many governments have fallen back on their domestic markets, revving them up via stimulus programs that put spending money in the hands of consumers. This move has been accompanied by a retreat from globalized production structures, or 'deglobalization.' 'The integration of the world economy is in retreat on almost every front,' writes *The Economist*.[4] While the magazine says that corporations continue to believe in the efficiency of global supply chains, 'like any chain, these are only as strong as their weakest link. A danger point will come if firms decide that this way of organizing production has had its day.'

For many environmentalists and ecological economists in the South and the North, the unraveling of the export-oriented global

---

2. www.leopold.iastate.edu/pubs-and-papers/2001-06-food-fuel-freeways.
3. www.ft.com/cms/s/0/a0f0331c-a611-11de-8c92-00144feabdco.html.
4. 'Turning Their Backs on the World,' February 19, 2009, www.economist.com/node/13145370?story_id=13145370.

economy spells opportunity. It opens up the transition to more climate-friendly and ecologically sensitive ways of organizing economic life. But the fossil-fuel-intensiveness of global transport and freight is merely one dimension of the problem. Environmentalists insist there must be a change in the reigning economic model itself. The global economy must make a transition from being driven fundamentally by overproduction and overconsumption to being geared to real needs, marked by moderate or low consumption, and based on sustainable and decentralized production processes.

Accordingly, the assumption of most policymakers in the North that consumption trends can continue – and that the only challenge is the transformation of the energy mix and the adoption of technofixes such as biofuels, 'clean coal,' nuclear power, carbon sequestration and storage, and carbon trading – is not only based on illusions but positively dangerous. Indeed, the climate problem cannot be addressed strategically without addressing the inherently environmentally destabilizing dynamics of capitalism – its incessant drive, motivated by the search for profit, to transform living nature into dead commodities.

Instead of heralding this transition to a much less fossil-fuel-intensive and ecologically sustainable production, most technocrats and economists see only a temporary retreat from export-led growth until global demand makes the latter viable again. The policy debate in establishment circles focuses on who will replace the bankrupt American consumer as the engine of global demand. With Europe stagnant and Japan in almost permanent recession, the hope is that China's growth will be the basis of global reflation. This is a mirage. China's 8.9 percent annualized growth in the last quarter is due to their current stimulus, a $585 billion program that has been funneled mainly to the countryside. Domestic demand will likely cease to grow once the money is spent. A limited spurt of cash will not transform Chinese peasants into the saviors of the global economy. After all, because they bore the costs of the country's export-oriented economy, these peasants have seen their incomes and welfare severely erode over the last quarter of a century.

The Doha dead end

But however this debate over the global consumer of last resort is resolved, the World Trade Organization and its most influential members, from both the North and the South, hope that completing the Doha Round at the Seventh Ministerial Meeting in Geneva will bring about a resumption of the carbon-intensive march toward globally integrated production and markets.

The preoccupation of economists and policymakers with the export engine to revive the global economy, which often excludes concerns about the negative impact of export-led globalization on the climate, is a dangerous divide leading up to Copenhagen. Says John Cavanagh, director of the Institute for Policy Studies: 'We have economic policymakers concerned with reversing recession and ecological economists concerned with strategic ways of reversing climate change talking past one another.'[5]

The climate negotiations have their own share of problems, even without the WTO threat. In the lead-up to Copenhagen, the focus of the climate discussions has been on two issues: mitigation and adaptation. Both are stymied, largely owing to the positions of the industrialized (Annex 1) countries. On mitigation, pivotal developed countries have so far resisted offering legally binding cuts. And what voluntary cuts they have offered are slight. In the case of the United States, President Obama's nonbinding commitment is to reduce greenhouse gas emissions by 17 percent from 2005 levels. This translates into an insignificant 4 percent reduction from 1990 levels, which serve as the benchmark for serious cuts.

---

5. Personal communication, August 2009.

The Intergovernmental Panel on Climate Change has asserted that a 25-40 percent cut in GHGs by 2020 is the minimum figure that would keep global mean temperature from rising above 2 degrees Celsius during this century. And already this is said to be an underestimate.

In the area of adaptation – assisting the poorer countries to prepare themselves for the consequences of climate change – the negotiations have been held up by the rich countries' reluctance to come up with the minimum amounts of aid necessary, to transfer technology unconditionally, and to channel the sums to the developing world through institutions apart from the World Bank, which they control.

The challenges in these two areas are daunting enough. And yet, unless the question of which economic model or strategy the countries of the world should move toward is front and center in Copenhagen, even the most ambitious agreements arrived at on mitigation and adaptation will be simply a Band-Aid. Unless the negotiators in Copenhagen dethrone the Doha model, the fundamental driver of climate change – an export-oriented globalized capitalist economy based on perpetually rising consumption – will continue to reign.

Can capitalism survive climate change?

Are capitalism and the environment at odds with each other? This is the question posed by this essay, written shortly after the UN-sponsored Climate Change Conference in Bali in December 2007. The dynamics of global capitalism are inherently ecologically disruptive, says the essay, and therefore, while it does not assert it explicitly, deglobalized non-capitalist economic arrangements appear to be a key part of the solution to the challenge of climate change and other forms of environmental degradation.[6]

There is now a solid consensus in the scientific community that if the change in global mean temperature in the twenty-first century exceeds 2.4 degrees Celsius, changes in the planet's climate will be large-scale, irreversible, and disastrous. Moreover, the window of opportunity for action that will make a difference is narrow – that is, the next ten to fifteen years.

Throughout the North, however, there is strong resistance to changing the systems of consumption and production that have created the problem in the first place. Alongside this resistance is a preference for 'techno-fixes,' such as 'clean' coal, carbon sequestration and storage, industrial-scale biofuels, and nuclear energy.

Globally, transnational corporations and other private actors resist government-imposed measures such as mandatory caps. They have preferred to use market mechanisms like the buying and selling of 'carbon credits,' which largely amount to a license for corporate polluters to keep on polluting.

In the global South, elites have shown little willingness to depart from the high-growth, high-consumption model inherited from the North. They maintain a self-interested conviction that the North must first adjust and bear the brunt of adjustment before

---

6. Originally published in *Foreign Policy in Focus*, April 1, 2008, www.fpif.org/articles/can_capitalism_survive_climate_change.

the South takes any serious step toward limiting its greenhouse gas emissions.

Contours of the challenge

In the climate change discussions, all parties recognize the principle of 'common but differentiated responsibility.' In other words, the global North must shoulder the brunt of the adjustment to the climate crisis since it is responsible for the economic trajectory that has brought the world to the edge of catastrophe. Also, the global response should not compromise the right of the countries of the global South to develop.

The devil, however, is in the detail. As analysts like Martin Khor of the Third World Network have pointed out, the global reduction of 80 percent in greenhouse gas emissions from 1990 levels by 2050 that many now recognize as necessary translates into reductions of at least 150-200 percent on the part of the global North in order to adhere to these two principles: 'common but differentiated responsibility' and recognition of the right of the countries of the South to development.[7]

Psychologically and politically, however, the North at this point does not likely have what it takes to meet the problem head-on.

The prevailing assumption is that the affluent societies can take on commitments to reduce their greenhouse gas emissions but still grow and enjoy their high standards of living if they shift to non-fossil-fuel energy sources. This assumption extends to the method of reduction, namely that the mandatory cuts agreed to multilaterally by governments will be implemented within the country according to a market-based system – that is, the trading of emission permits. The subtext is: techno-fixes and the carbon

---

7. Martin Khor, 'Paradignm Clash,' *Our Planet*, February 2007, 222.unep.org/our-planet/2007/feb/en/toc.asp.

market will make the transition relatively painless and – why not? – profitable, too.

But many of these technologies are decades away from viable use. In the short and medium term, relying on a shift in energy dependence to non-fossil-fuel alternatives will not be able to support current rates of economic growth. Also, the trade-off for more crop land devoted to biofuel production means less land on which to grow food and therefore greater food insecurity globally.

Clearly, the dominant paradigm of economic growth is one of the most significant obstacles to a serious global effort to deal with climate change. But this destabilizing, fundamentalist growth-consumption paradigm is itself more effect than cause.

The central problem is a mode of production whose main dynamic is the transformation of living nature into dead commodities, creating tremendous waste in the process. The driver of this process is consumption – or, more appropriately, overconsumption – and the motivation is profit or capital accumulation: capitalism, in short.

It has been the generalization of this mode of production in the North and its spread from the North to the South over the last 300 years that have caused the accelerated burning of fossil fuels and rapid deforestation, two of the key man-made processes behind global warming.

The South's dilemma

One way of viewing global warning is as a key manifestation of the latest stage of a wrenching historical process: the privatization of the global commons by capital. The climate crisis must thus be seen as the expropriation by the advanced capitalist societies of the ecological space of less developed or marginalized societies.

This leads us to the dilemma of the South. Before the full extent of the ecological destabilization brought about by capitalism, the

South was expected simply to follow the 'stages of growth' of the North. But now, the South can't do so without bringing about ecological Armageddon. Already, China is on track to overtake the United States as the biggest emitter of greenhouse gases, and yet the elite of China as well as those of India and other rapidly developing countries are intent on reproducing American-type overconsumption-driven capitalism.

Thus, for the South, the implications of an effective global response to global warming include several necessary but insufficient conditions. First, countries like China can no longer opt out of a mandatory regime on the grounds that it is a developing country. Second, developing countries must push the North to transfer technology to mitigate global warming and provide funds to assist in adapting the new technology.

These steps are important, but they are only the initial steps in a broader, global reorientation of the paradigm for achieving economic well-being.

While this adjustment will need to be much, much greater and faster in the North, the adjustment for the South will essentially be the same: a break with the high-growth, high-consumption model in favor of another model of achieving the common welfare.

The strategy of Northern elites has been to try to decouple growth from energy use. In contrast, a progressive comprehensive climate strategy in both the North and the South must reduce growth and energy use while raising the quality of life of the broad masses of people. This will mean placing economic justice and equality at the center of the new paradigm.

The transition must be one not only from a fossil-fuel-based economy but also from an overconsumption-driven economy.

The goal must be the adoption of a low-consumption, low-growth, high-equity development model that results in an improvement in people's welfare, a better quality of life for all, and greater democratic control of production.

The elites of the North and the South will not likely agree to such a comprehensive response. The farthest they can be expected to go is for techno-fixes and a market-based cap-and-trade system. Growth will be sacrosanct, as will the system of global capitalism.

Yet, confronted with apocalypse, humanity cannot self-destruct. It may be a difficult road, but the vast majority will not commit social and ecological suicide to enable the minority to preserve its privileges.

Threat and opportunity

Climate change is both a threat and an opportunity to bring about the long postponed social and economic reforms that had been derailed or sabotaged in previous eras by elites seeking to preserve or increase their privileges.

The difference is that today the very existence of humanity and the planet depend on the institutionalization of economic systems based not on feudal rent extraction or capital accumulation or class exploitation, but on justice and equality. I am hopeful that a thorough reorganization of production, consumption, and distribution will be the end result of humanity's response to the climate emergency and the broader environmental crisis.

In the social and economic system that will be collectively crafted, there will be room for the market. However, the more interesting question is: will such a system have room for capitalism? Will capitalism as a system of production, consumption, and distribution survive the challenge of coming up with an effective solution to the climate crisis?

Breaking the climate stalemate

In this essay, I argue that the biggest con game being played on the world in the United Nations climate meetings is the seeming conflict between China and the US, which actually serves the interests of both in maintaining a weak climate regime.[8]

The Bangkok intersessional meeting of the United Nations Framework Convention on Climate Change (UNFCCC) ended this week, with no progress among countries to commit to increasing the level of emission reductions for this decade. Why are the climate talks stalemated and what should be done to break the deadlock?

Alarming developments

Over the last year alone, the Greenland ice sheet has virtually vanished. This July was the hottest July ever recorded in the United States. A normally dry Beijing had the worst flooding since 1951. Long-delayed monsoon rains in India resulted in the second drought in four years. The ensuing bad harvest and the worst power outages in the country's history could cause a 5 percent decrease in GDP growth. Last month, a protracted 'rainstorm with no name,' as many Filipinos termed it, persisted for over a week in the Philippines and plunged Manila into a watery disaster that is probably the worst in recent history. And, of course, Thailand itself was a water world for over a month last year due to floods.

Climate change is triggered by the accumulation of carbon dioxide (CO_2) and other greenhouse gases in the atmosphere. The developed countries, termed in UNFCCC parlance 'Annex 1' countries, contributed 70 percent of the world's greenhouse gas emissions from 1890 to 2007. Yet these countries have also been the most difficult to persuade to address global warming seriously

8. Co-written with Pablo Solon; originally published in *Foreign Policy in Focus*, September 7, 2012, www.fpif.org/articles/breaking_the_climate_statelmate.

by curbing their emissions, limiting consumption, and providing finance and technology for developing countries to deal with
climate change.

The stalemate

The US Congress is populated by Republican climate skeptics who
continue to believe, against all evidence, that climate change is a
figment of the liberal imagination and have prevented the passage
of any meaningful legislation on the climate. The European Union's
false face in climate diplomacy was clearly seen here in Bangkok
too, as it insisted on a pledge of 20 percent emission cuts instead
of 25 percent, calling the latter 'wishful thinking' and unrealistic.
The EU's commitment will be accomplished largely through weak
or unrealistic containment measures like carbon trading or techno-
fixes like carbon sequestration and storage, not by moderating
economic growth or reducing consumption.

The North–South dimension has added a deadly dynamic to
this process, as the so-called emerging capitalist economies of the
South – notably China, India, Brazil, and South Africa – make
claims to their share of ecological space to grow, even as the North
continues to refuse to give up any of the vast ecological space it now
occupies and exploits. China is now the world's biggest producer of
greenhouse gases, but the basis of its refusal to entertain mandatory
limits is that its accumulated emissions have been quite low, about
9 percent of the historical total.

The refusal of the North to curb high consumption and the
intention of big emerging economies to reproduce the Northern
consumption model lies at the root of the deadlock in the climate
change negotiations – one symbolized by the failure of the talks in
Copenhagen in 2009, Cancún in 2010, and Durban in 2011 to agree
on the contours of a successor agreement to the Kyoto Protocol.
What was agreed in Durban is a 'laissez faire' regime where only

'voluntary pledges' for emission reductions will be made until 2020. The tragedy is that these nonbinding pledges are going to represent only a 13 percent reduction of greenhouse gas emissions from 1990 levels, which will lead to an increase in the global mean temperature of at least 4-6 degrees Celsius this century. Leading climate scientists have said that any increase must be limited to 2 degrees Celsius at most.

Reflecting what many see as the incomprehensibly rigid attitude of Washington, US climate official Todd Stern recently urged governments to be 'more flexible' with the 2 degrees Celsius target. This can only provide the governments of Annex 1 countries with an excuse to postpone making commitments, if not junk mandatory reductions altogether.

In reality, both the United States and China want a weaker climate agreement. In the United States, influential politicians and corporations are not committed to real deep cuts. And China's leaders realize that the longer they can put off a legally binding agreement the better, since China will be far ahead in GHG emissions in a few years and a weak agreement will be in its interest.

The climate talks stalemate is not therefore the result of a disagreement between the two biggest powers, but rather of a common desire not to be obliged to change their policies of consumption, production, and gaining control of natural resources around the world.

The position of the US and Chinese delegations, as well as those from many other countries, reflects more the concerns of their elites than of their people. In China, there are massive protests against environmentally destructive development projects. In the United States and Canada, the movement against the exploitation of tar sands is the expression of a civil society that wants to stop polluting our planet.

The elites of emerging economies are using the just demand of 'historical responsibility' or 'common but differentiated responsibility' in order to steal time and secure a weak binding agreement. The deliberate prolonging of the stalemate means allowing business as usual. Given that this strategy has led to a dead end, it is imperative that civil society regain its independent voice and articulate a position distinct from that of the Group of 77 and China.

Forging a new approach

We must demand that Annex 1 countries make legally binding commitments to real deep cuts (40-50 percent by 2020 without offsets) and commit to them in the coming Conference of Parties in Doha. They must commit substantial new funds immediately to the Green Climate Fund and guarantee transfer of technology as part of their historical responsibility.

At the same time, we should demand that China, India, Brazil, and South Africa also agree to mandatory cuts without offsets, although of course these should be lower than those for the Annex 1 countries, in line with the United Nations Framework Convention on Climate Change (UNFCCC) principles. Big emerging economies – which are launched into high-speed, consumption-dependent, and greenhouse-gas-intensive growth paths – can no longer hide behind the rubric of the Group of 77 to avoid making mandatory greenhouse gas reduction commitments.

Even as we demand that both Annex 1 and the emerging economies make mandatory commitments, other governments, though they may not be significant greenhouse gas emitters, must be encouraged to make binding commitments. This will send a very strong message to both the Annex 1 and the emerging economies that a real binding agreement is needed now. Many developing countries have the capacity to commit to reducing their emissions now. Mitigation must be a collective effort, and developing countries can't be seen demanding cuts while increasing their own emissions, in many cases for the benefit of their upper classes.

We can no longer tolerate a situation in which the United States and China portray themselves as opponents but actually provide each other with the rationale to pursue their environmentally destabilizing trajectories.

Seven billion ... and rising

Written on the occasion of the world's population passing the 7 billion mark in late 2011, this essay poses the issue of whether the interaction of declining agricultural capacity, climate change, and continuing high population growth poses the Malthusian specter for the world. The intersection of the ecological and economic crisis raises the issue of the unsustainability of global capitalism and the necessity of moving towards deglobalized, more locally oriented economic alternatives.[9]

The world's population surpassed 7 billion on October 31, 2011. But, except for perhaps the anti-family-planning lobby, this was a milestone that few were in a mood to celebrate.

Concerns about overpopulation were present when the world hit the 6 billion mark in 1999, but they were subdued in that era of growth and – at least in the North – optimism. There was a sense then that, although there would be major hurdles along the way, the world's future could only get brighter.

Globalization, according to its apostles – foremost among them then-US president Bill Clinton – was inevitable, and could only bring about a better life for all. The Kyoto Protocol had just been adopted, and, although it had its flaws, seemed to be the first step in an increasingly coordinated global effort to cut greenhouse gas emissions.

---

9. Originally published in *Foreign Policy in Focus*, November 3, 2011, www.fpif.org/articles/seven_billion_and_rising.

The Earth Policy Institute valiantly issued its 'State of the World' warnings against overfishing, desertification, and an emerging water crisis. But many were persuaded by corporate agribusiness's propaganda that it had developed the technological capacity to more than feed the world, and that the only remaining problem was the distribution of food, a logistical as well as a political matter.

Malthus's specter?

Today's mood could not be more different, and it's not only because of unease over the speed with which we added another billion people since 1999.

Global capitalism is in a deep, deep funk, with the center economies caught indefinitely in the iron grip of stagnation and high unemployment. Extreme weather events have become a fact of life, yet any move towards a successor to the Kyoto Protocol continues to elude the world's governments. Agriculture seems to be at the limits of its productive capacity, prompting many to ask, have we walked into the Malthusian trap?

Malthus, that enigmatic Victorian figure, predicted that population growth would outstrip the capacity of the soil to produce food, leading to a demographic cataclysm that would eventually result in a smaller population in equilibrium with the soil's productive capacity. While Malthus's views were adopted – uneasily – by many ecologists and environmentalists, he became the bête noire of both progressive and neoclassical economists. Progressives saw his theory as an elitist, conservative effort to blame the poor for their misfortunes, while some neoclassical economists, most notably Julian Simon, saw him and his followers as underestimating the human capacity to innovate to surmount limits to production and economic growth.

The food price crisis of 2008 was, to many, a wake-up call that agriculture might be reaching its productive limits – that the problem in agriculture was no longer just distribution, but production. That crisis saw the food import bills of the least developed countries rise by 37 percent in 2008, adding 75 million to the ranks of the hungry and driving an estimated 125 million into extreme poverty.

In accounting for the causes of the rapid rise in the price of food, analysts pointed to the convergence of a number of developments to create the perfect storm: among them, World Bank- and IMF-imposed structural adjustment programs in developing countries, which severely cut government support for agriculture and reduced agricultural production; the subsidized diversion of vast amounts of corn land, especially in the United States, to feedstock for biofuels rather than food production; speculation in food commodities in financial markets; and the growing resistance of insects to pesticides and the refusal of soils to respond to more applications of fertilizer.

Food crisis redux

After registering lower increases for two years, prices began again to rise markedly over the last year, underlining that the 2006-08 crisis was no fluke. In July, the average price of wheat was 45 percent higher than it was earlier, while that of corn was 89 percent higher.

This time around, though, extreme weather events caused by climate change were the central factor, reminding people how extremely fragile the links are between the soil and the atmosphere. In the last year, massive wildfires in Russia devastated hundreds of thousands of acres of farmland, forcing the government to impose a ban on grain exports; a stubborn drought in China ravaged 14 million hectares and left 14 million people short of water; unremitting rains in Pakistan devastated the country's croplands for the second year in a row; practically the whole Australian state of Queensland, including its capital Brisbane, was submerged by floods, with billions of dollars' worth of grain, vegetables, and livestock swept away; and, in the last few months, the Horn of Africa has been paralyzed by a drought that has placed some 12.4 million people at risk of famine.

In the last few weeks, it has been the turn of Southeast Asia's rice bowls to suffer nature's revenge for human beings' inordinate carbon consumption. Some 1.5 million hectares of rice land have been inundated in Cambodia, Laos, Vietnam, and Thailand, with 1 million hectares in Thailand, the world's leading rice exporter, alone. An estimated 1.3 million metric tons of rice in Thailand have been lost, while in the Philippines more than 103,000 metric tons of the standing rice crop were wiped out by the recent typhoons. Already the price of Thai rice in the international market is 26 percent higher than it was in May, and is expected to rise even more steeply.

Things can only get worse over the next few years, say climate experts.

Progressives and population

The crisis of agricultural production has led many to take a fresh look at the population issue. Among them are people on the left. In the past, progressives tended to be lumped together with the Catholic hierarchy and Christian fundamentalists as population skeptics, though for different reasons. Some of them saw family planning as a US plot to keep developing countries under its thumb, while others argued that the main problem lay in the concentration of wealth and the means of production in the hands of a few. Ending this stranglehold, they asserted, would open the way to egalitarian redistribution, which would address the problems brought about by the rise in population.

At the global level, progressives argued that overconsumption by the 20 percent that lived in the North, not population pressure from the 80 percent that lived in the South, constituted the main social and environmental challenge.

Once in power, however, progressives acknowledged that even without class inequalities, unrestrained population growth would foreclose the possibility of economic growth and development. Thus, concern over population growth outstripping food production and economic growth led China in the 1980s to institute its one-child policy, which, for all the abuses connected to it, has appeared largely positive on balance – resulting in as many as 300 million fewer births and providing the breathing space to channel significant resources from consumption to investment.

Vietnam followed suit, promoting a two-child policy that, unlike in China, was implemented non-coercively. The results have been equally positive. The country's population growth rate is down to 1.2 percent per annum. The total fertility rate (TFR), or the average number of children per woman of reproductive age, has dropped from over 6 in 1961, when the program first began, to 2.1, a figure that demographers tag as 'replacement-level fertility.' Vietnam has 88.2 million people; had there been no family-planning program, it would now have 104 million people.

18.6 million fewer births has meant that Vietnam could devote more resources to upgrading the quality of education, alleviating poverty, and increasing investment. The country registered a growth rate of 7.2 percent per annum in the period from 2000 to 2010. By 2010, average per capita income in the country had tripled, reflecting economic growth outpacing the population growth rate.

Population management and the East Asian 'miracle'

In adopting family planning, the post-revolutionary societies of China and Vietnam most likely drew inspiration from their East Asian capitalist neighbors. Thailand, Indonesia, South Korea,

Japan, and Taiwan had found it necessary to implement strong pre-emptive family-planning programs to create the space for economic takeoff. Although effective family planning was not the only factor explaining their rapid growth, it was a major one.

By providing access to contraceptives, state-supported family planning programs in these countries enabled women to have greater control over reproduction. The proportion of women using contraceptives in East Asia is four times the rate in Africa, and surveys have shown that the difference is largely explained by the state provision of contraceptives in East Asia. And when access to contraceptives was joined to greater access to education, the trend was for women to limit their births in order to accumulate the resources to improve their families' living standards. Such were the dynamics of the demographic revolution in East Asia.

The end of growth?

Yet the success of these societies in achieving high growth by managing their populations may be wiped out if the era of growth is over, as some analysts contend.

Most of the East Asian economies, and some other developing economies in Latin America and Africa, followed export-oriented development strategies that were dependent on continuing growth in the North. Yet the Northern economies, bludgeoned by the current crisis of capitalism, now face a future of stagnation or low growth. For the advanced developing economies to now shift and follow an alternative strategy of achieving growth by relying on domestic consumption seems logical, but this is easier said than done. The social classes and enterprises that formed around a thirty-year-old strategy can stymie an effective transition, as has been the case in China. This is not surprising since a shift in development strategy is not simply a change in policy, but also involves a redistribution of income and economic power if the rural and urban lower classes are to be equipped with the purchasing power to be the new sources of demand.

But the bigger question faced by all developing economies, whether export- or domestic-market-oriented, is whether it is still possible to follow the traditional growth strategy. To analysts like Richard Heinberg, the intersection of the financial collapse, economic stagnation, global warming, the steady depletion of fossil fuel reserves, and agriculture reaching its limits is a fatal one. It represents a far more profound crisis than a temporary setback on the road to growth. It portends not simply the end of a paradigm of global growth driven by the demand of the center economies. It means the 'end of growth' as we know it. It is, in short, the Malthusian trap, though Heinberg understandably avoids using the term.

Paradoxically, the so-called least-developed countries in Africa and South Asia may have an easier time making the transition to a post-growth global economy. They are less integrated into the global economy, and many maintain agricultural sectors that have not been totally damaged by structural adjustment and liberalization. They have also been far behind in the institutionalization of the high-growth-dependent Western consumption model, owing to widespread poverty. If they can combine effective family-planning programs with successful redistribution initiatives and economic strategies emphasizing improvement in the quality of life, they may well pioneer the forging of a post-growth, post-globalization development strategy.

It will not be easy though.

Dilemmas

The current dilemmas of our planet of 7 billion are well summed up by Richard Heinberg in his latest book, *The End of Growth*:

Perhaps the meteoric rise of the finance economy in the past couple of decades resulted from semi-conscious strategy on the part of society's managerial elites to leverage the last possible increments of growth from a physical, resource-based economy that was nearing its capacity. In any case, the implications of the current economic crisis cannot be captured by unemployment statistics and real estate prices. Attempts to restart growth will inevitably collide with natural limits that simply don't respond to stimulus packages or bailouts. ... Burgeoning environmental problems require rapidly increasing amounts of effort to fix them. In addition to facing limits on the amount of debt that can be accumulated in order to keep those problems at bay, we also face limits to the amounts of energy and materials we can devote to these purposes. Until now the dynamism of growth has enabled us to stay ahead of accumulating environmental costs. As growth ends, the environmental bills for the last two centuries of manic expansion may come due just as our bank account empties.[10]

---

10. Richard Heinberg, *The End of Growth* (British Columbia: New Society Publishers, 2011), p. 152.

CHAPTER 7

THE END OF MULTILATERALISM?

The crisis of multilateralism

The first decade of the twenty-first century was not kind to the International Monetary Fund and the World Bank, two of the three agencies of global economic governance in the era of globalization. On the eve of the IMF-World Bank annual meeting in Singapore in 2006, I wrote this essay that sought to provide an explanation for the crisis of legitimacy that the two institutions were undergoing. This analysis remains valid today, although the World Bank has attempted to reinvent itself as the 'climate bank' allegedly supporting developing countries to adapt to climate change and the Fund has tried to become an actor in the European financial crisis by taking on an old role: bailing out irresponsible banks.[1]

Already buffeted by institutional crisis and policy conflicts, the International Monetary Fund (IMF) and the World Bank are heading into their fall meeting – scheduled to begin on September 13 in Singapore – with yet one more problem. Desperate to win credibility among civil society groups, the Bank and the Fund had given official accreditation to representatives of four civil society organizations. The Singapore government had a different idea. It banned the

---

1. Originally published in *Foreign Policy in Focus*, September 12, 2006, www.fpif.org/articles/the_crisis_of_multilateralism.

groups 'for security reasons.' This commentator was among those specifically named and banned as a 'security threat.'

The two institutions have formally protested the government's action. But they are simply reaping the consequences of their decision to hold the fall meeting in the authoritarian island-state in order to avoid street protests like those that have attended WTO ministerial meetings. Angry at the banning of their colleagues, many civil society representatives are now asking the Bank and Fund to cancel the annual meeting, demanding that the two agencies be consistent with their declared support for practices of 'good governance.'

Controversial reforms

Prior to the controversy over the banning of the NGOs, the IMF's Executive Board was trying to steer through two reforms intended to 'safeguard and enhance the Fund's credibility.' The first involved reallocating the voting power of IMF member countries according to the current size of their gross domestic product. This proposal was ostensibly intended to increase the voting power of a selected number of big developing countries – Korea, Turkey, China, and Mexico – while laying the ground for eventually expanding the decision-making power of other developing countries. The other initiative the IMF leadership was trying to get off the ground would give the Fund the new role of solving 'global macroeconomic imbalances' – a euphemism for disciplining countries with large trade surpluses like China. Both reforms are mired in controversy.

A bloc of around fifty developing countries object to the proposed GDP-based formula. These countries see the move as dividing developing countries while producing only one real winner: the United States, which would increase its voting power under the new system. The second initiative has generated opposition for attempting to get the Fund to do Washington's dirty work of pressuring

China to revalue its currency to reduce the massive US trade deficit with Beijing.

These troubles are the latest in a string of crises to plague the two agencies, also known as the 'Bretton Woods institutions' after the site of the July 1944 conference where they were founded. The Fund, in particular, is in a state of demoralization. 'Ten years ago, the IMF was flying high, arrogant in its belief that it knew what was the best for developing countries,' notes one civil society policy paper. 'Today, it is an institution under siege, hiding behind its four walls in Washington, DC, unable to mount an effective response to its growing numbers of critics.'[2]

The IMF's Stalingrad

The IMF's equivalent of Stalingrad – where the defeat of the German Sixth Army marked the turning point of World War II – was the Asian financial crisis, where it 'lost its legitimacy and never recovered it,' according to Dennis de Tray, a former IMF and World Bank official who is now vice president of the Washington-based Center for Global Development.[3]

The Fund was blamed for pushing policies of capital account liberalization that made the Asian economies vulnerable to the volatile movements of speculative capital; assembling multi-billion-dollar rescue programs that rescued creditors at the expense of the debtors; imposing expenditure-cutting programs that merely worsened the downspin of the economy; and opposing the formation of an Asian Monetary Fund that could have provided the crisis countries with financial reserves to save their currencies from speculative attacks.

2. 'The IMF: Shrink it or Sink it: A Consensus Declaration and Strategy Paper,' 2006, www.stwr.org/imf-world-bank-trade/the-imf-shrink-it-or-sink-it-a-consensus-declaration-and-strategy-paper.html.
3. Comments at lunch seminar on the IMF and World Bank, Carnegie Endowment for International Peace, Washington, DC, April 21, 2006.

The Fund went from one financial disaster to another. The Russian financial collapse in 1998 was attributed to its policies, as was Argentina's economic unraveling in 2002.

Resistance was not long in coming. In the midst of the Asian financial crisis, Prime Minister Mahathir bin Mohamad of Malaysia broke with the IMF approach and imposed capital controls, saving the country from the worst effects of the crisis. Mahathir's defiance of the IMF was not lost on Thaksin Shinawatra, who ran for prime minister of Thailand on an anti-IMF platform and won. He went on to push for large government expenditures, which stimulated the consumer demand that brought Thailand out of recession. Nestor Kirchner completed the humbling of the IMF when, upon being elected president of Argentina in 2003, he declared that his government would pay its private creditors only 25 cents for every dollar owed. Enraged creditors told the IMF to discipline Kirchner. But, with its reputation in tatters and its leverage eroded, the Fund backed off from confronting the Argentine president, who got away with the radical debt write-down.

By 2006, underscoring the crisis of legitimacy of the institution, the governor of the Bank of England described the IMF as having 'lost its way.'

From crisis of legitimacy to budget crisis

The crisis of legitimacy has had financial consequences. In 2003, the Thai government declared it had paid off most of its debt to the IMF and would soon be financially independent of the organization. Indonesia ended its loan agreement with the Fund in 2003 and recently announced its intention to repay its multibillion-dollar debt in two years. A number of other big borrowers in Asia, mindful of the devastating consequences of IMF-imposed policies, have refrained from new borrowings from the Fund. These include the Philippines, India, and China. Now, this trend has been reinforced

by the move of Brazil and Argentina earlier this year to pay off all
their debts to the Fund and declare financial sovereignty.

What is, in effect, a boycott by its biggest borrowers is translating into a budget crisis for the IMF. Over the last two decades the
IMF's operations have been increasingly funded from the loan
repayments of its developing-country clients rather than from the
contributions of wealthy Northern governments. The burden of
sustaining the institution has shifted to the borrowers. The upshot
of these developments is that payments of charges and interests,
according to Fund projections, will be cut by more than half, from
$3.19 billion in 2005 to $1.39 billion in 2006, and again by half, to
$635 million, in 2009. These reductions have created what Ngaire
Woods, an Oxford University specialist on the Fund, describes as
'a huge squeeze on the budget of the organization.'[4]

Role crisis

The erosion of the Fund's role as a disciplinarian of debt-ridden
countries and an enforcer of structural adjustment has been accompanied by a futile search to find a new role.

The Group of Seven tried to make the Fund a central piece of
a new 'global financial architecture' by putting it in charge of
a 'contingency credit line' to which countries about to enter a
financial crisis would have access if they fulfilled IMF-approved
macroeconomic conditions. But the prospect of a government seeking access to a credit line that could trigger the very financial panic
that it sought to avert doomed the project.

Another proposal envisioned an IMF-managed 'Sovereign Debt
Restructuring Mechanism' – an international version of a Chapter
11 bankruptcy mechanism that would provide countries protection
from creditors while they came out with a restructuring plan. But

---

4. 'The Globalizers in Search of a Future,' www.cgdev.org/content/publications/ detail/
7371?print=1&id=7371&datatype=5.

when Southern countries objected that the mechanism was too weak and the United States opposed the proposal for fear it would curtail the freedom of operations of US banks, this new prospect also collapsed.

The role of righting 'global macroeconomic imbalances' assigned to the Fund during the spring meetings of the IMF leadership earlier this year is part of this increasingly desperate effort by the G7 governments to find a task for an international economic bureaucracy that has become obsolete and irrelevant.

Hiding the World Bank's crisis

While it does not have the aura of controversy and failure that surrounds the IMF, the World Bank is also in crisis, say informed observers. A budget crisis is also overtaking the Bank, according to Ngaire Woods. Income from borrowers' fees and charges dropped from US$8.1 billion in 2001 to US$4.4 billion in 2004, while income from the Bank's investments fell from US$1.5 billion in 2001 to US$304 million in 2004. China, Indonesia, Mexico, Brazil, and many of the more advanced developing countries are going elsewhere for their loans.

The budgetary crisis is, however, only one aspect of the overall crisis of the institution. The policy prescriptions offered by Bank economists are increasingly seen as irrelevant to the problems faced by developing countries, says de Tray, who served as the IMF's resident officer in Hanoi and the World Bank's representative in Jakarta. The problem, he says, lies in the emphasis at the Bank's research department on producing 'cutting edge' technical economic work geared to the Western academic world rather than coming out with knowledge to support practical policy prescriptions. The Bank is currently staffed by some 10,000 professionals, most of them economists, and de Tray claims that 'there is nothing wrong at the World Bank that a 40% staff reduction would not fix.'

American university professor Robin Broad, an expert on the Bank, claims that the Bank is, in fact, in more of a crisis than the IMF but that this is less visible to the public. 'The IMF's response has been to withdraw behind its four walls, thus reinforcing the public perception of its being besieged,' she notes. 'The Bank's response, however, has been to engage the world to hide its mounting crisis.'[5]

Broad identifies three elements in the Bank's offensive:

> First, it goes out and tells donors that it is the institution best positioned to do lending to end poverty, for the environment, for addressing HIV–AIDS, you name it ... when in fact its record proves that it's not. Second, it has the world's largest 'development' research department – funded to the tune of about $50 million – whose *raison d'être* is to produce research to back up predetermined conclusions. Third, it has this huge external affairs department, with a budget of some $30 million – a PR unit that feeds these so-called objective research findings to the press and fosters the image of an all-knowing Bank.

But, she concludes, 'This can't last. Inside the Bank, they know they're in crisis and are scrambling. And sooner or later, if we do our work, the truth will come out.'

Multilateralism in disarray

The crisis of the Bretton Woods institutions must be seen as part of the same phenomenon that has overtaken the World Trade Organization, whose latest round of trade liberalization negotiations fell apart in July. Noting that 'trade liberalization has stalled, aid is less coherent than it should be, and the next financial conflagration will be managed by an injured fireman,' the *Washington Post*'s Sebastian Mallaby contends that 'the great powers of today are simply not interested in creating a resilient multilateral system.'[6]

---

5. Comments at lunch seminar on the IMF and World Bank, April 21, 2006.
6. 'Why Globalization Has Stalled,' *Washington Post*, April 24, 2006, www.washington-

What is troubling for people like Mallaby, however, offers an opportunity for those who have long regarded the current multilateral system of global economic governance as mainly concerned with ensuring the hegemony of the developed countries, particularly the United States. Proposals for alternative institutions for global finance have been circulating for some time. The current crisis may be the break in the system that will make governments, especially those in the South, willing to seriously consider the alternatives.

The Dracula round

In August 2008, Pascal Lamy, director general of the World Trade Organization (WTO), assembled the member countries of the trading body in Geneva in a major effort to finish what were known as the 'Doha Round' of trade negotiations. He failed. This article, written shortly before the meeting, gave the reasons why the meeting was bound to fail. Once hailed as the 'crown jewel' of globalization, the WTO has seen its power and legitimacy greatly reduced in recent years.[7]

Like the good count of Transylvania, the World Trade Organization's Doha Round of negotiations has died more than once. It first collapsed during the WTO ministerial meeting held in Cancún in September 2003. After apparently coming back from the dead, many observers thought it passed away a second time during the so-called Group of Four meeting in Potsdam in June 2007 – only to come back yet again from the dead. Now the question is whether the unraveling of the most recent 'mini-ministerial' gathering in Geneva was the silver stake that pierced the trade round's heart, rendering Doha dead forever.

post.com/wp-dyn/content/article/2006/04/23/AR2006042301016.html.

7. Originally published in *Foreign Policy in Focus*, August 5, 2008, www.fpif.org/articles/the_dracula_round.

Stampeded into the WTO

When the Uruguay Round that established the World Trade Organization was negotiated from 1986 to 1994, developing countries were largely bystanders. Governments that had been members of the General Agreement on Tariffs and Trade (GATT) were dragooned into its successor organization by the threat that if they did not come in on the ground floor, they would be subjected to a painful accession process should they decide to join it later. In the meantime, they were told, they would, like North Korea, become isolated from global trade. Preferring the devil they knew to the devil they didn't, most GATT members signed a document that subordinated all dimensions of a nation's economic life to the goal of expanding international trade.

Most had not had the time to really absorb the fine print of the 500-plus pages, something that was evident in Indonesia's case. When the Indonesian government declared in 1997 that it would build up its car industry by applying the so-called 'local content' policy, which mandated the sourcing of a growing portion of a car's parts to local industries, the United States, the European Union, and Japan – the big car corporations' home countries – informed it that this would violate the Trade-Related Investment Measures agreement (TRIMs) of the Uruguay Round and that they would haul Indonesia to a WTO dispute-settlement court. Smaller countries than Indonesia, with minuscule trade bureaucracies, were even more disadvantaged.

From Seattle to Doha

In any event, by November 1999, when the WTO's third ministerial meeting took place in Seattle, developing countries had come to a collective realization that they had bargained away significant space for development in signing on to the Uruguay Round and thus were in no mood to agree to launching another round to liberalize global trade, as the big trading powers demanded. At the same time, farmers, environmentalists, workers, anti-HIV/AIDS activists, and other global civil society movements were up in arms against the doctrine of 'trade über Alles' – as Ralph Nader described it – that was enshrined in the WTO. It was this synergy between the massive protests in the streets and the rebellion of developing countries at the Seattle Convention Center that resulted in the spectacular collapse of the so-called Seattle Round before it could even launch.

But the EU and United States were undeterred. The Fourth Ministerial Meeting in Doha, Qatar, in November 2001 saw developing countries subjected to tremendous pressure to agree to the launching of a new round in order to 'save' the global economy following the September 11 events. But there was more than moral pressure in the name of the anti-terrorist struggle involved. As Aileen Kwa and Fatoumata Jawara documented in their now classic book *Behind the Scenes at the WTO*, not-too subtle threats of retaliation for recalcitrance were combined with offers of massive aid packages.[8] Most countries were excluded from decision-making, which was effectively confined to a select group of about thirty to thirty-five governments handpicked by the EU and United States. The result was the 'Doha Development Round,' which had little to do with development and everything to do with expanding developed-country access to developing country markets.

The bitter experience of being subjected to divide-and-conquer tactics in Doha proved to be a turning point for developing-country politics in the WTO. Alliances were formed – among them, the Group of 20 led by Brazil, India, South Africa, and China – to demand cuts in developed-country agricultural subsidies and greater access to developed country markets, and the Group of 33 led by Indonesia and the Philippines to push for the creation of 'special products' that would be exempted from tariff reductions and

---

8. *Behind the Scenes at the WTO* (London: Zed Books, 2004).

for 'special safeguard mechanisms' like protective tariffs against surges of highly subsidized agricultural imports from the developed countries.

Collapse in Cancún

The lead-up to the 2003 Cancún Ministerial also featured debates among social movements engaged in the WTO process. Even after Seattle, there were still some non-governmental organizations that entertained the idea that the WTO could serve as a mechanism to bring about development. They believed that the designation 'Doha Development Round' provided an opening. Greater market access to developed-country markets for developing-country products could be achieved if the WTO free-trade agenda in agriculture was supported, some development organizations contended. Others argued that, on the contrary, Doha had shown that development was far down the list of concerns of the big trading powers and that the central task was to derail the WTO negotiations or to 'get the WTO out of agriculture,' as the international peasant organization Via Campesina puts it.

The NGO reformers' case wasn't helped by the United States and the EU, which became even more inflexible when it came to cutting their massive agricultural subsidies. The EU was also impatient to begin substantive WTO discussions on the creation of disciplines on the so-called 'New Issues' of investment, government procurement, competition policy, and trade facilitation. This effort to bring into the WTO ambit what many regarded as non-trade-related issues sparked the creation of the Group of 90 that opposed inclusion of these items in the WTO agenda. It was the walkout by some members of this grouping when some developed countries insisted on discussing the 'New Issues' that led to the collapse of the Cancún Ministerial on September 14, 2003, though the ground had been tilled by the stalemate in agriculture.

If lack of organization led to their being outmaneuvered in Doha, effective coalition-building enabled the developing countries to outmaneuver the developed countries in Cancún, with technical support from NGOs and moral support from social movements seeking to shut down the meeting in a protest atmosphere much like Seattle's.

Realizing that the WTO was no longer a playground the United States could control along with the EU, then-US trade representative Robert Zoellick described the debacle in Cancún as one where 'the rhetoric of the "won't do" overwhelmed the concerted efforts of the "can do." "Won't do" led to impasse.'[9] A few days later, he warned, 'As the WTO members ponder the future, the US will not wait: we will move towards free trade with can-do countries.'[10] That was taken to mean that the United States would now concentrate its efforts on obtaining bilateral free-trade agreements. These words also marked the beginning of a US assault on the G20, which succeeded in driving Colombia, Peru, El Salvador, Guatemala, and Costa Rica out of the formation a month after the Cancún collapse. The G20, however, held.

From Cancún to Potsdam

Cancún may have taken the wind out of Doha's sails, but over 2004 and 2005 negotiations revived, with both the United States and the EU trying a new tack. The two had brought in Brazil and India, the leaders of the G20, into a formation called FIPS or Five Interested Parties (the United States, the EU, and Australia, along with Brazil and India), which for a time managed to contain the opposition. Though the EU and the United States had their differences, especially on the question of agricultural subsidies, they

---

9. Press briefing, September 14, 2003.
10. Robert Zoellick, 'America Will Not Wait for the Won't-Do Countries,' *Financial Times*, September 21, 2003.

nevertheless agreed on an approach whose contours were etched out in the so-called July 2004 Framework that the EU and the United States forced through, with the acquiescence of G20 leaders Brazil and India, at a surprise General Council meeting in the dead of summer in Geneva: minor concessions on agricultural subsidies in return for big concessions from the developing countries in opening up their industrial sectors (or 'non-agricultural market access') and services.

The Declaration of the Hong Kong Ministerial in December 2005 was based on this inequitable approach, but the developed countries played the old divide-and-rule game by giving different sweeteners to different parties. They promised the G90 that it would get the 'Round for Free' and 'Aid for Trade.' The Round for Free referred to the promise that the G90 countries would have duty-free, quota-free market access to developed countries. Upon closer inspection of the agreement, however, it was revealed that the United States, in fact, maintained tariffs on those products that were of greatest interest to the G90 countries. The G20, on the other hand, received a 'pledge' from the EU that it would end agricultural subsidies by 2013. But in the area of non-agricultural market access, the harsh 'Swiss formula' was in place, which was a tariff reduction formula that would drastically bring down developing countries' industrial tariffs.

The Hong Kong Ministerial ended with a deal in place but with massive dissatisfaction among developing-country delegates, with some raising objections that the format of the final plenary made it difficult for opposition to be heard. There were also massive protests in the streets, which were only broken up by the police making more than 900 arrests. Still, the Hong Kong Ministerial could have ended up like Cancún had the Venezuelan government not reneged on its promise to NGOs that it would vote against the declaration, which would have rendered it null and void owing to the WTO's consensus rule.

The Hong Kong Declaration, however, masked continuing, indeed widening, divisions that were very difficult to bridge. In fact, in July 2006, a few months after the deal in Hong Kong, talks broke off in Geneva and were suspended for the rest of the year. In an effort to break the deadlock, the United States and the EU tried to work out a deal with Brazil and India, the acknowledged leaders of the Group of 20, in talks at Potsdam in June 2007. The US position was, however, a non-starter: not only did it not want to make substantive cuts in its domestic subsidies but it sought to discredit the agreement on the designation of Special Products and the implementation of a Special Safeguard Mechanism forged in Hong Kong. Also, neither the United States nor the EU was willing to depart from their position that the industrializing countries of the South had to make proportionally greater cuts in their industrial tariffs than the industrialized countries in return for US and EU 'concessions' in agricultural subsidies.

Geneva: the final, final collapse?

The collapse of the so-called 'G4' talks in Potsdam placed the Doha Round on life support. Faced with the prospect that any further postponement of a conclusion to the Round would make the organization he headed irrelevant, director general Pascal Lamy took a gamble and roused the fatally weakened organization to another late summer tryst in Geneva, this time to a 'mini-ministerial,' despite the fact that little had happened in the interim to bring the positions of the developed and developing countries any closer.

Indeed, President Nicolas Sarkozy of France and other EU leaders told EU trade commissioner Peter Mandelson to stop talking about further bringing down the EU's substantial subsidies. As the talks got under way, US trade representative Susan Schwab also made it clear that the United States wouldn't agree to reduce subsidies below $15 billion. More decisive in determining the outcome was

Washington's opposition to a very reasonable G33 formula tabled by India for imposing protective tariffs against agricultural import surges under the Special Safeguard Mechanism agreed to at the 2005 Hong Kong Ministerial.

Completely underestimating developing-country concerns that food imports had undermined food self-sufficiency at a time of rising food prices owing to global food shortages, the United States brought on another WTO disaster with its single-minded focus on dumping its subsidized agricultural surpluses on foreign agricultural markets.

Not helpful in bringing about a deal was Lamy's maneuver of limiting the decision-making to seven countries, which drew sharp criticism from many among the already circumscribed number of thirty-five countries that had been invited to the mini-ministerial, including from host country Switzerland. If ever there was a global meeting that was dead on arrival, this was it.

Lamy gambled and lost. The WTO is now in a worse position than before, with the prospect that it will evolve like the old League of Nations in the 1930s: present but powerless. That is, it is dead to all intents and purposes. The great need now is to supplant this anachronistic body with new institutional arrangements for global trade that promote equity and development along with sustainability.

In retrospect, the United States and the EU, used to getting their own way in global trade negotiations, went a bridge too far in the Doha talks. Instead of being open to real compromise, their intransigence and drive to expand their control of global markets brought about the organizing for self-defense of the developing countries at the WTO. Greed backfired, instigating instead a change in the equation of global economic power.

Nevertheless, just as Dracula could get resurrected in a B-movie sequel, there is no 100 percent guarantee that the WTO's Doha Round won't rise again.

U20: will the global economy resurface?

The following essay was written shortly before the G20 assembled in London in April 2009 to address the growing global financial crisis. Likening the global economy to a depth-charged submarine, it posed the question of whether the crew of leaders and managers of global capitalism had what it took to resurface the economy. It said that lacking the legitimacy of the original Bretton Woods multilateral system, the G20's prospects for stabilizing the global economic system and saving globalization were dim. Later developments proved it to be accurate.[11]

The Group of 20 (G20) is making a big show of getting together to come to grips with the global economic crisis. But here's the problem with the upcoming summit in London on April 2: it's all show. What the show masks is a very deep worry and fear among the global elite that it really doesn't know the direction in which the world economy is heading and the measures needed to stabilize it.

The latest statistics are exceeding even the gloomiest projections made earlier. Establishment analysts are beginning to mention the dreaded 'D' word and there is a spreading sense that a tidal wave just now gathering momentum will simply overwhelm the trillions of dollars allocated for stimulus spending. In this environment, the G20 conveys the impression that they're more commanded by than in command of developments. (In addition to the seven wealthy industrial nations that belong to the G7, the G20 includes China, India, Indonesia, Mexico, Brazil, Argentina, Russia, Saudi Arabia, Australia, South Korea, Turkey, Italy, and South Africa.).

Indeed, perhaps no image is more evocative of the current state of the global economy than that of a World War II German U-Boat depth-charged in the North Atlantic by British destroyers. It's

---

11. Originally published in *Foreign Policy in Focus*, March 30, 2009, www.fpif.org/articles/u-20_will_the_global_economy_resurface.

going down fast, and the crew doesn't know when it will hit rock bottom. And when it does hit the ocean floor, the big question is: will the crew be able to make the submarine rise again by pumping compressed air into the severely damaged ballast tanks, like the sailors in Wolfgang Petersen's classic film *Das Boot*? Or will the U-Boat simply stay at the bottom, its crew doomed to contemplate a fate worse than sudden death?

The current capitalist crew manning the global economy doesn't know whether Keynesian methods can re-inflate the global economy. Meanwhile, an increasing number of people are asking whether using a clutch of social-democratic-like reforms is enough to repair the global economy, or whether the crisis will lead to a new international economic order.

A New Bretton Woods?

The G20 meeting has been trumpeted as a new 'Bretton Woods.' In July 1944, in Bretton Woods, New Hampshire, representatives of the state-managed capitalist economies designed the postwar multilateral order with themselves at the center.

In fact, the two meetings couldn't be further apart. The London meeting will last one day; the Bretton Woods conference was a tough 21-day working session.

The London meeting is exclusive, with 20 governments arrogating to themselves the power to decide for 172 other countries. The Bretton Woods meeting tried hard to be inclusive to avoid precisely the illegitimacy that dogs the G20's London tryst. Even in the midst of global war, it brought together forty-four countries, including the still-dependent Commonwealth of the Philippines and the tiny, now-vanished Siberian state of Tannu Tuva.

The Bretton Woods Conference created new multilateral institutions and rules to manage the postwar world. The G20 is recycling failed institutions: the G20 itself, the Financial Stability Forum

(FSF), the Bank of International Settlements and 'Basel II,' and the now 65-year-old International Monetary Fund (IMF). Some of these institutions were established by the elite Group of 7 after the 1997 Asian financial crisis to come up with a new financial architecture that would prevent a repetition of the debacle brought about by IMF policies of capital account liberalization. But instead of coming up with safeguards, all these institutions bought the global financial elite's strategy of 'self-regulation.'

Among the mantras they thus legitimized were that capital controls were bad for developing economies; short-selling, or speculating on the movement of borrowed stocks, was a legitimate market operation; and derivatives, or securities that allow betting on the movements of an underlying asset, 'perfected' the market. The implicit recommendation of their inaction was that the best way to regulate the market was to leave it to market players, who had developed sophisticated but allegedly reliable models of 'risk assessment.'

In short, institutions that were part of the problem are now being asked to become the central part of the solution. Unwittingly, the G20 are following Marx's maxim that history first repeats itself as tragedy, then as farce.

Resurrecting the Fund

The most problematic component of the G20 solution is its proposals for the International Monetary Fund (IMF). The United States and the European Union are seeking an increase in the capital of the IMF from $250 billion to $500 billion. The plan is for the IMF to lend these funds to developing countries to use to stimulate their economies, with US treasury secretary Tim Geithner proposing that the Fund supervise this global exercise. If ever there was a non-starter, this is it.

First of all, the representation question continues to exercise much of the global South. So far, only marginal changes have been made in the allocation of voting rights at the IMF. Despite the clamor for greater voting power for members from the global South, the rich countries are still overrepresented on the Fund's decision-making executive board, and developing countries, especially those in Asia and Africa, are vastly underrepresented. Europe holds a third of the chairs in the executive board and claims the feudal right to have a European always occupy the role of managing director. The United States, for its part, has nearly 17 percent of voting power, giving it veto power.

Second, the IMF's performance during the Asian financial crisis of 1997, more than anything, torpedoed its credibility. The IMF helped bring about the crisis by pushing the Asian countries to eliminate capital controls and liberalize their financial sectors, promoting both the massive entry of speculative capital and its destabilizing exit at the slightest sign of crisis. The Fund then pushed governments to cut expenditures, on the theory that inflation was the problem, when it should have been pushing for greater government spending to counteract the collapse of the private sector. This pro-cyclical measure ended up accelerating the regional collapse into recession. Finally, the billions of dollars of IMF rescue funds went not to rescuing the collapsing economies but to compensate foreign financial institutions for their losses, a development that has become a textbook example of 'moral hazard' or the encouragement of irresponsible lending behavior.

Thailand paid off the IMF in 2003 and declared its 'financial independence.' Brazil, Venezuela, and Argentina followed suit, and Indonesia also declared its intention to repay its debts as quickly as possible. Other countries likewise decided to stay away, preferring to build up their foreign exchange reserves to defend themselves against external developments rather than contract new IMF loans.

This led to the IMF's budget crisis, for most of its income was from debt payments made by the bigger developing countries.

Partisans of the Fund say that the IMF now sees the merit of massive deficit spending and that, like Richard Nixon, it can say 'we are all Keynesians now.' Many critics do not agree. Eurodad, a non-governmental organization that monitors IMF loans, says that the Fund still attaches onerous conditions to loans to developing countries. Very recent IMF loans also still encourage financial and banking liberalization. And despite the current focus on fiscal stimulus, with some countries, like the United States, pushing for governments to raise their stimulus spending to at least 2 percent of GDP, the IMF still requires low income borrowers to keep their deficit spending to no more than 1 percent of GDP.

Finally, there is the question of whether or not the Fund knows what it's doing. One of the key factors discrediting the IMF has been its almost total inability to anticipate the brewing financial crisis. In concluding the 2007 Article IV consultation with the United States, the IMF board stated that '[t]he financial system has shown impressive resilience, including to recent difficulties in the subprime mortgage market.'[12] In short, the Fund hasn't only failed miserably in its policy prescriptions, but, despite its supposedly top-flight stable of economists, has drastically fallen short in its surveillance responsibilities.

However large the resources the G20 provide the IMF, there will be little international buy-in to a global stimulus program managed by the Fund.

The way forward

The North's response to the current crisis, which is to revive fossilized institutions, is reminiscent of Keynes's famous saying: 'The

---

12. www.imf.org/external/np/sec/pn/2007/pn0792.htm.

difficulty lies not so much in developing new ideas as in escaping from old ones.' So, in Keynes's spirit, let's try to identify ways of abandoning old ways of thinking.

First of all, since legitimacy is a very scarce commodity at this point, the UN secretary general and the UN General Assembly, rather than the G20, should convoke a special session to design the new global multilateral order. A Commission of Experts on Reforms to the International Monetary and Financial System,[13] set up by the president of the General Assembly and headed by Nobel Prize laureate Joseph Stiglitz, has already done the preparatory policy work for such a meeting. The meeting would be an inclusive process like the Bretton Woods Conference, and, like Bretton Woods, should be a working session lasting several weeks. One of the key outcomes might be the setting up of a representative forum, such as the 'Global Coordination Council' suggested by the Stiglitz Commission, which would broadly coordinate global economic and financial reform.

Second, to immediately assist countries to deal with the crisis, the debts of developing countries to Northern institutions should be cancelled. Most of these debts, as the Jubilee movement reminds us, were contracted under onerous conditions and have already been paid many times over. Debt cancellation or a debt moratorium will allow developing countries access to greater resources and will have a greater stimulus effect than money channeled through the IMF.

Third, regional structures to deal with financial issues, including development finance, should be the centerpiece of the new architecture of global governance, not another financial system where the countries of the North dominate centralized institutions like the IMF and monopolize resources and power. In East Asia, the 'ASEAN Plus Three' Grouping, or 'Chiang Mai Initiative,' is a

---

13. www.un.org/apps/news/story.asp?NewsID=28958&Cr=financial&Cr1=crisis.

promising development that needs to be expanded, although it also needs to be made more accountable to the peoples of the region. In Latin America, several promising regional initiatives are already in progress, like the Bolivarian Alternative for the Americas and the Bank of the South. Any new global order must have socially accountable regional institutions as its pillars.

These are, of course, immediate steps to be made in the context of a longer-term, more fundamental and strategic reconfiguration of a global capitalist system now on the verge of collapsing. The current crisis is a grand opportunity to craft a new system that ends not just the failed system of neoliberal global governance but the Euro-American domination of the capitalist global economy, and put in its place a more decentralized, deglobalized, democratic post-capitalist order. Unless this more fundamental restructuring takes place, the global economy might not be worth bringing back to the surface.

PART III

COMPETING ALTERNATIVES

CHAPTER 8

KEYNESIANISM IN THE BREACH

Keynes: a man for this season?

In 2009, John Maynard Keynes appeared to be making a comeback, given the collapse of neoliberal economics. Every economist is 'a Keynesian in a foxhole,' said the neoliberal University of Chicago economist Robert Lucas. This essay reviews the pros and cons of Keynesian economics as a solution to the global economic crisis. Among other things, it raises the question of whether Keynesianism merely postpones rather than offers a solution to the crisis of capitalism in the era of globalization.[1]

One of the most significant consequences of the collapse of neo-liberal economics, with its worship of the 'self-regulating market,' has been the revival of the great English economist John Maynard Keynes.

Not only do Keynes's writings make him very contemporary. There is also the mood that permeates them, which evokes the loss of faith in the old and the yearning for something that is yet to be born. Aside from their prescience, his reflections on the condition of Europe after World War I resonate with our current mix of disillusion and hope:

---

1. Originally published in *Foreign Policy in Focus*, July 8, 2009, www.fpif.org/ articles/keynes_a_man_for_this_season.

In our present confusion of aims, is there enough clear-sighted public spirit left to preserve the balanced and complicated organization by which we live? Communism is discredited by events; socialism, in its old-fashioned interpretation, no longer interests the world; capitalism has lost its self confidence. Unless men and women are united by a common aim or moved by objective principles, each one's hand will be against the rest and the unregulated pursuit of individual advantage may soon destroy the whole.[2]

Governing the market

Government must step in to remedy the failure of the market. This is, of course, the great lesson that Keynes imparted, one derived from his wrestling with the problem of how to bring the world out of the Great Depression of the 1930s. Keynes argued that the market, left to itself, would achieve equilibrium between supply and demand far below full employment and could stay there indefinitely. To kick-start the economy into a dynamic process that would move it toward full employment, the government had to serve as a *deus ex machina* by spending massively to create the 'effective demand' that would restart and sustain the engine of capital accumulation.

As preemptive measures to stave off a depression, President Barack Obama's $787 billion stimulus package, like those of Europe and China, is classically Keynesian. The measure of Keynes's triumph after nearly thirty years in the wilderness is the marginal impact that Republicans, Russ Limbaugh, the Cato Institute and other species of neoliberal dinosaurs have made on the public discourse with their talk of 'passing on a huge debt to coming generations.'

The revival of Keynes is not, however, simply a policy matter. Two ideas have displaced the theoretical assumption of the individual rationally maximizing his or her interest from the center of economic analysis. One of these ideas driving current thinking

2. *The Collected Writings of John Maynard Keynes*, Volume XVII: *Activities 1920–1922: Treaty Revision and Reconstruction*, ed. Elizabeth Johnson (Basingstoke: Palgrave Macmillan for the Royal Economic Society, 1977), p. 450.

is the pervasiveness of uncertainty in the making of decisions, which investors try to deal with by assuming (improbably) that the future will be like the present, and by coming up with techniques to predict and manage the future based on these assumptions. The related Keynesian notion is that the economy is driven not by rational calculus but by 'animal spirits' on the part of economic actors – that is, by their 'spontaneous urge to action.'[3]

Key among these animal spirits is confidence, the presence or absence of which is at the center of the collective action that drives economic expansions and contractions. Not rational calculation but behavioral or psychological factors predominate. From this standpoint, the economy is like a manic depressive driven by chemical imbalances from one pole to the other, with government intervention and regulation playing a role akin to that of chemical mood-stabilizers. Investment isn't a matter of rational calculus but a manic process that Keynes described as 'a game of Snap, of Old Maid, of Musical Chairs, whose object is to pass on the Old Maid – the toxic debt – to one's neighbour before the music stops.' Here, notes Keynes's biographer Robert Skidelsky, 'is the recognisable anatomy of the "irrational exuberance," followed by blind panic, which has dominated the present crisis.'[4]

Unbridled investors and submissive regulators are not the only protagonists in the recent tragedy. The hubris of neoliberal economists also played a part, and here Keynes had some very relevant insights for our times. He saw economics as 'one of these pretty, polite techniques which tries to deal with the present by abstracting from the fact that we know very little about the future.' Indeed, he was, as Skidelsky notes, 'famously skeptical about econometrics,' with numbers for him being 'simply clues, triggers for the imagination,'[5]

3. See George A. Akerlof and Robert J. Shiller, *Animal Spirits: How Human Psychology Drives the Economy, and Why It Matters for Global Capitalism* (New Haven: Princeton University Press, 2009).

4. Robert Skidelsky, 'Keynes is Back,' *Prospect*, November 23, 2008.

5. Robert Skidelsky, *John Maynard Keynes: The Economist as Savior, 1920–1937* (London:

rather than the expressions of certainties or probabilities of past and future events.

With their model of rational *Homo economicus* in tatters and econometrics in disrepute, contemporary economists would do well to pay heed to Keynes's advice that if only 'economists could manage to get themselves thought of as humble, competent people on a level with dentists, that would be splendid!'[6] Yet, even as many welcome the resurrection of Keynes, others have doubts about his relevance to the current period. And these doubters are not limited to neoliberal diehards.

Limitations of Keynesianism

For one thing, Keynesianism is mainly a tool for reviving national economies, and globalization has severely complicated this problem. In the 1930s and 1940s, reviving industrial capacity in relatively integrated capitalist economies revolved around the domestic market. Nowadays, with so many industries and services transferred or outsourced to low-wage areas, the effects of Keynesian-type stimulus programs that put money into the hand of consumers to spend on goods has much less impact as a mechanism of sustained recovery. Transnational corporations and TNC-host China may reap profits, but the 'multiplier effect' in deindustrialized economies like the United States and Britain might be very limited.

Second, the biggest drag on the world economy is the massive gulf – in terms of income distribution, the pervasiveness of poverty, and the level of economic development – between the North and the South. A 'globalized' Keynesian program of stimulus spending, funded by aid and loans from the North, is a very limited response to this problem. Keynesian spending may prevent economic collapse and even spur some growth. But sustained growth demands radical

Allen Lane/Penguin, 1995), p. xix.
   6. *The Collected Writings of John Maynard Keynes*, Volume IX: *Essays in Persuasion*, Basingstoke: Palgrave Macmillan for the Royal Economic Society, 1972, p. 332.

structural reform – the kind that involves a fundamental recasting of economic relations between the central capitalist economies and the global periphery. Indeed, the fate of the periphery – the 'colonies' in Keynes's day – didn't elicit much concern in his thinking.

Third, Keynes's model of managed capitalism merely postpones rather than provides a solution to one of capitalism's central contradictions. The underlying cause of the current economic crisis is overproduction, in which productive capacity outpaces the growth of effective demand and drives down profits. The Keynesian-inspired activist capitalist state that emerged in the post-World War II period seemed, for a time, to surmount the crisis of overproduction with its regime of relatively high wages and technocratic management of capital–labor relations. However, with the addition of massive new capacity from Japan, Germany, and the newly industrializing countries in the 1960s and 1970s, its ability to do this began to falter. The resulting stagflation – the coincidence of stagnation and inflation – swept throughout the industrialized world in the late 1970s.

The Keynesian consensus collapsed, as capitalism sought to revive its profitability and overcome the crisis of overaccumulation by tearing up the capital–labor compromise, liberalization, deregulation, globalization, and financialization. In this sense, these neoliberal policies constituted an escape route from the conundrum of overproduction on which the Keynesian welfare state had foundered. As we now know, they failed to bring back a return to the 'golden years' of postwar capitalism, leading instead to today's economic collapse. It is not, however, likely that a return to pre-1980s' Keynesianism is the solution to capitalism's persistent crisis of overproduction.

The great lacuna

Perhaps the greatest obstacle to a revived Keynesianism is its key prescription for revitalizing capitalism in the context of the climate crisis, namely the revving up of global consumption and demand. While the early Keynes had a Malthusian side, his later work hardly addressed what has now become the problematic relationship between capitalism and the environment. The challenge to economics at this point is raising the consumption levels of the global poor with minimal disruption of the environment, while radically cutting back on environmentally damaging consumption or overconsumption in the North. All the talk of replacing the bankrupt American consumer with a Chinese peasant engaged in American-style consumption as the engine of global demand is both foolish and irresponsible.

Given the primordial drive of the profit motive to transform living nature into dead commodities, capitalism is unlikely to reconcile ecology and economy – even under the state-managed technocratic capitalism promoted by Keynes.

'We are all Keynesians again'?

In other words, Keynesianism provides some answers to the current situation, but it does not provide the key to surmounting it. Global capitalism has been laid low by its inherent contradictions, but a second bout of Keynesianism is not what it needs. The deepening international crisis calls for severe checks on capital's freedom to move, tight regulation of financial as well as commodity markets, and massive government spending. However, the needs of the times go beyond these Keynesian measures to encompass massive income distribution, a sustained attack on poverty, a radical transformation of class relations, deglobalization, and perhaps the transcendence of capitalism itself under the threat of environmental cataclysm.

'We are all Keynesians again' – to borrow but slightly modify Richard Nixon's much-quoted phrase – is the theme that unites Barack Obama, Paul Krugman, Joseph Stiglitz, George Soros, Gordon Brown, and Nicolas Sarkozy, though in the implementation of the master's prescriptions they may have differences. But an uncritical revival of Keynes might simply end up with another confirmation of Marx's dictum that history first occurs as tragedy, then repeats itself as farce. To solve our problems, we don't just need Keynes. We need our own Keynes.

The coming capitalist consensus

Along with a revival of Keynesianism was expected a reinvigoration of social democracy as an ideological and strategic response to the crisis. Though this did not materialize in the short term, and conservative parties came to power or retained it in Spain, Britain, and Germany, and Republicans gained control of the US House of Representatives in the United States in 2010, by early 2012 a social-democratic resurgence seemed be on the way with the victory of François Hollande of the Socialist Party in the presidental elections in France. This essay suggested that global social democracy underpinned by Keynesianism shares neoliberalism's bias for globalization, differentiating itself mainly by promising to promote globalization better than the neoliberals.[7]

Not surprisingly, the swift unraveling of the global economy combined with the ascent to the US presidency of an African-American liberal has left millions anticipating that the world is on the threshold of a new era. Some of president-elect Barack Obama's new appointees – in particular ex-treasury secretary Larry Summers to lead the National Economic Council, New York Federal Reserve Board chief Tim Geithner to head the Treasury, and former Dallas mayor Ron Kirk to serve as trade representative – have certainly elicited some skepticism. But the sense that the old neoliberal formulas are thoroughly discredited have convinced many that the new Democratic leadership in the world's biggest economy will

---

7. Originally published in *Foreign Policy in Focus*, December 24, 2008, www.fpif. org/articles/the_coming_capitalist_consensus.

break with the market fundamentalist policies that have reigned since the early 1980s.

One important question, of course, is how decisive and definitive the break with neoliberalism will be. Other questions, however, go to the heart of capitalism itself. Will government ownership, intervention, and control be exercised simply to stabilize capitalism, after which control will be given back to the corporate elites? Are we going to see a second round of Keynesian capitalism, where the state and corporate elites along with labor work out a partnership based on industrial policy, growth, and high wages – though with a green dimension this time around? Or will we witness the beginnings of fundamental shifts in the ownership and control of the economy in a more popular direction? There are limits to reform in the system of global capitalism, but at no other time in the last half-century have those limits seemed more fluid.

President Nicolas Sarkozy of France has already staked out one position. Declaring that 'laissez-faire capitalism is dead,' he has created a strategic investment fund of €20 billion to promote technological innovation, keep advanced industries in French hands, and save jobs. 'The day we don't build trains, airplanes, automobiles, and ships, what will be left of the French economy?' he recently asked rhetorically. 'Memories. I will not make France a simple tourist reserve.'[8] This kind of aggressive industrial policy aimed partly at winning over the country's traditional white working-class can go hand in hand with the exclusionary anti-immigrant policies with which the French president has been associated.

Global Social Democracy

A new national Keynesianism along Sarkozyan lines, however, is not the only alternative available to global elites. Given the need for global legitimacy to promote their interests in a world where

8. http://euobserver.com/economic/27157.

the balance of power is shifting towards the South, Western elites might find more attractive an offshoot of European social democracy and New Deal liberalism that one might call 'Global Social Democracy' or GSD.

Even before the full unfolding of the financial crisis, partisans of GSD had already been positioning it as alternative to neoliberal globalization in response to the stresses and strains being provoked by the latter. One personality associated with it is British prime minister Gordon Brown, who led the European response to the financial meltdown via the partial nationalization of the banks. Widely regarded as the godfather of the 'Make Poverty History' campaign in the United Kingdom, Brown, while he was still the British chancellor, proposed what he called an 'alliance capitalism' between market and state institutions that would reproduce at the global stage what he said Franklin Roosevelt did for the national economy: 'securing the benefits of the market while taming its excesses.' This must be a system, continued Brown, that 'captures the full benefits of global markets and capital flows, minimizes the risk of disruption, maximizes opportunity for all, and lifts up the most vulnerable – in short, the restoration in the international economy of public purpose and high ideals.'[9]

Joining Brown in articulating the global social-democratic discourse has been a diverse group consisting of, among others, the economist Jeffrey Sachs, George Soros, former UN secretary general Kofi Annan, the sociologist David Held, Nobel laureate Joseph Stiglitz, and even Bill Gates. There are, of course, differences of nuance in the positions of these people, but the thrust of their perspectives is the same: to bring about a reformed social order and a reinvigorated ideological consensus for global capitalism.

Among the key propositions advanced by partisans of GSD are the following:

---

9. http://webarchive.nationalarchives.gov.uk/+/http://www.hm-treasury.gov.uk/2633.htm.

- Globalization is essentially beneficial for the world; the neo-liberals have simply botched the job of managing it and selling it to the public.
- It is urgent to save globalization from the neoliberals because it is reversible and may, in fact, already be in the process of being reversed.
- Growth and equity may come into conflict, in which case one must prioritize equity.
- Free trade may not, in fact, be beneficial in the long run and may leave the majority poor, so it is important for trade arrangements to be subject to social and environmental conditions.
- Unilateralism must be avoided while fundamental reform of the multilateral institutions and agreements must be undertaken – a process that might involve dumping or neutralizing some of them, like the WTO's Trade-Related Aspects of Intellectual Property Rights agreement (TRIPs).
- Global social integration, or reducing inequalities both within and across countries, must accompany global market integration.
- The global debt of developing countries must be cancelled or radically reduced, so the resulting savings can be used to stimulate the local economy, thus contributing to global reflation.
- Poverty and environmental degradation are so severe that a massive aid program or 'Marshall Plan' from the North to the South must be mounted within the framework of the 'Millennium Development Goals.'
- A 'Second Green Revolution' must be put into motion, especially in Africa, through the widespread adoption of genetically engineered seeds.
- Huge investments must be devoted to push the global economy along more environmentally sustainable paths, with government taking a leading role ('Green Keynesianism' or 'Green Capitalism').

- Military action to solve problems must be de-emphasized in favor of diplomacy and 'soft power,' although humanitarian military intervention in situations involving genocide must be undertaken.

The limits of Global Social Democracy

Global Social Democracy has not received much critical attention, perhaps because many progressives are still fighting the last war – that is, against neoliberalism. A critique is urgent, and not only because GSD is neoliberalism's most likely successor. More important, although GSD has some positive elements, it has, like the old social-democratic Keynesian paradigm, a number of problematic features.

A critique might begin by highlighting problems with four central elements in the GSD perspective.

First, GSD shares neoliberalism's bias for globalization, differentiating itself mainly by promising to promote globalization better than the neoliberals. This amounts to saying, however, that simply by adding the dimension of 'global social integration,' an inherently socially and ecologically destructive and disruptive process can be made palatable and acceptable. GSD assumes that people really want to be part of a functionally integrated global economy where the barriers between the national and the international have disappeared. But would they not in fact prefer to be part of economies that are subject to local control and are buffered from the vagaries of the international economy? Indeed, today's swift downward trajectory of interconnected economies underscores the validity of one of the anti-globalization movement's key criticisms of the globalization process.

Second, GSD shares neoliberalism's preference for the market as the principal mechanism for production, distribution, and consumption, differentiating itself mainly by advocating state action to address market failures. The kind of globalization the world needs, according to Jeffrey Sachs in *The End of Poverty*, would entail 'harnessing ... the remarkable power of trade and investment while acknowledging and addressing limitations through compensatory collective action.'[10] This is very different from saying that the citizenry and civil society must make the key economic decisions and the market, like the state bureaucracy, is only one mechanism of implementation of democratic decision-making.

Third, GSD is a technocratic project, with experts hatching and pushing reforms on society from above, instead of being a participatory project where initiatives percolate from the ground up.

Fourth, GSD, while critical of neoliberalism, accepts the framework of monopoly capitalism, which rests fundamentally on deriving profit from the exploitative extraction of surplus value from labor, is driven from crisis to crisis by inherent tendencies toward overproduction, and tends to push the environment to its limits in its search for profitability. Like traditional Keynesianism in the national arena, GSD seeks in the global arena a new class compromise that is accompanied by new methods to contain or minimize capitalism's tendency toward crisis. Just as the old social democracy and the New Deal stabilized national capitalism, the historical function of Global Social Democracy is to iron out the contradictions of contemporary global capitalism and to relegitimize it after the crisis and chaos left by neoliberalism. GSD is, at root, about social management.

Obama has a talent for rhetorically bridging different political discourses. He is also a 'blank slate' when it comes to economics. Like FDR, he is not bound to the formulas of the *ancien régime*. He is a pragmatist whose key criterion is success at social management. As such, he is uniquely positioned to lead this ambitious reformist enterprise.

---

10. *The End of Poverty: How We Can Make it Happen in Our Lifetime* (Harmondsworth: Penguin, 2005), p. 357.

Reveille for progressives

While progressives were engaged in full-scale war against neoliberalism, reformist thinking was percolating in critical establishment circles. This thinking is now about to become policy, and progressives must work double time to engage it. It is not just a matter of moving from criticism to prescription. The challenge is to overcome the limits to the progressive political imagination imposed by the aggressiveness of the neoliberal challenge in the 1980s combined with the collapse of the bureaucratic socialist regimes in the early 1990s. Progressives should boldly aspire once again to paradigms of social organization that unabashedly aim for equality and participatory democratic control of both the national economy and the global economy as prerequisites for collective and individual liberation.

Like the old postwar Keynesian regime, Global Social Democracy is about social management. In contrast, the progressive perspective is about social liberation.

CHAPTER 9

RESISTANCE
AND TRANSFORMATION

Elites vs greens in the global South

Written shortly after the United Nations-sponsored international conference on climate change in Bali in December 2007, this essay counters the image common in the North that people in the South are sold on having rapid growth at all costs. Instead, it portrays a Southern terrain marked by strong environmental movements that have challenged Southern elites' efforts to promote globalization and reproduce the Nothern growth model in their societies.[1]

Last month's conference on climate change in Bali, Indonesia, brought the North–South fault line in climate politics into sharp relief. While US intransigence on the question of mandatory cuts in greenhouse gas emissions took center stage, not far behind was the issue of what commitments fast-growing developing countries like China and India should make in a new, post-Kyoto climate change regime.

The developing world's stance toward the question of the environment has often been equated with the pugnacious stance of former Malaysian prime minister Mahathir bin Mohamad, who

---

1. Originally published in *Foreign Policy in Focus*, January 17, 2008, www.fpif.org/articles/elites_vs_greens_in_the_global_south.

famously said at the Rio Conference on the Environment and Development in June 1992,

> When the rich chopped down their own forests, built their poison-belching factories and scoured the world for cheap resources, the poor said nothing. Indeed they paid for the development of the rich. Now the rich claim a right to regulate the development of the poor countries... As colonies we were exploited. Now as independent nations we are to be equally exploited.[2]

The North has interpreted Mahathir as speaking for a South that doesn't have much of an environmental movement and that seeks to catch up whatever the cost. Today, China has emerged as the prime exemplar of this Mahathirian obsession with rapid industrialization that has minimal regard for the environment.

In fact, the environmental costs of rapid industrialization are of major concern to significant sectors of the population of developing countries. The environmental movement, moreover, has been a significant actor in the debates in which many countries are exploring alternatives to the destabilizing high-growth model. While the focus of this piece is Asia, many of the same trends can be observed in Latin America, Africa, and other parts of the global South.

The environmental movement in the NICs

Among the most advanced environmental movements are those in South Korea and Taiwan, which were once known as 'newly industrializing countries' (NICs) or 'newly industrializing economies.' This should not be surprising since the process of rapid industrialization in these two societies from 1965 to 1990 took place with few environmental controls, if any. In Korea, the Han River that flows through Seoul and the Nakdong River flowing through Pusan were so polluted by unchecked dumping of industrial waste that they were close to being classified as biologically dead. Toxic

---

2. *Asean Bulletin* 9, 1992, pp. 107–8.

waste dumping reached critical proportions. Seoul achieved the distinction in 1978 of being the city with the highest content of sulphur dioxide in the air, with high levels being registered as well in Inchon, Pusan, Ulsan, Masan, Anyang, and Changweon.

In Taiwan, high-speed industrialization had its own particular hellish contours. Taiwan's formula for balanced growth was to prevent industrial concentration and encourage manufacturers to set up shop in the countryside. The result was a substantial number of the island's factories locating on rice fields, along waterways, and beside residences. With three factories per square mile, Taiwan's rate of industrial density was seventy-five times that of the United States. One result was that 20 percent of farm land was polluted by industrial waste water and 30 percent of rice grown on the island was contaminated with heavy metals, including mercury, arsenic, and cadmium.

In both societies, farmers, workers, and the environment bore the costs of high-speed industrialization. Both societies saw the emergence of an environmental movement that was spontaneous, quite militant, drew participants from different classes, and linked environmental demands with issues of employment, occupational health, and agricultural crisis. Direct action became a weapon of choice. 'People have learned that protesting can bring results; most of the actions for which we could find out the results had achieved their objectives,' sociologist Michael Hsiao points out.

> The polluting factories were either forced to make immediate im-
> provement of the conditions or pay compensation to the victims.
> Some factories were even forced to shut down or move to another
> location. A few preventive actions have even succeeded in forcing
> prospective plants to withdraw from their planned construction.[3]

The environmental movements in both societies were able to force government to come out with restrictive new rules on toxics,

---

3. Walden Bello and Stephanie Rosenfeld, *Dragons in Distress: Asia's Miracle Economies* •
in Crisis (San Francisco: Food First, 1990), p. 213.

industrial waste, and air pollution. Ironically, however, these successful cases of citizen action created a new problem, which was
the migration of polluting industries from Taiwan and Korea to
China and Southeast Asia. Along with Japanese firms, Korean and
Taiwanese enterprises went to Southeast Asia and China mainly for
two reasons: cheap labor and lax environmental laws.

Environmental struggles in Southeast Asia

Unlike in Korea and Taiwan, environmental movements already
existed in a number of the Southeast Asian countries before the
period of rapid industrialization, which in their case occurred in
the mid-1980s to the mid-1990s. These movements had emerged
in the previous decade in struggles against nuclear power, as in
the Philippines; against big hydroelectric dams, as in Thailand,
Indonesia, and the Philippines; and against deforestation and
marine pollution, as in Thailand, Malaysia, and the Philippines.
These were epic battles, like the struggle against the Chico River
Dam in the northern Philippines and the fight against the Pak Mun
Dam in the northeast of Thailand, which forced the World Bank to
withdraw its planned support for giant hydroelectric projects – an
outcome that, as we shall see later on, also occurred in struggle
against the Narmada Dam in India. The fight against industrial
development associated partly with foreign firms seeking to escape
strict environmental regulations at home opened up a new front in
an ongoing struggle to save the environment.

Perhaps even more than in Northeast Asia, the environmental
question in Southeast Asia went beyond being a middle-class issue.
In the Chico struggle, the opposition were indigenous people,
while in the fight against the Pak Mun Dam it was small farmers and fisherfolk. The environmental issue was also more coher-
ently integrated into an overarching critique. Movements in the
Philippines, for instance, viewed deforestation as an inevitable

consequence of a strategy of export-oriented growth imposed by World Bank–International Monetary Fund structural adjustment programs that sought to pay off the country's massive foreign debt with the dollars gained from exporting the country's timber and other natural resources and manufactures produced by cheap labor. The middle class, workers, the urban poor, and environmentalists were thrust into a natural alliance. Meanwhile, transnational capital, local monopoly capital, and the central government created an anti-environmental axis.

The environmental movements in Southeast Asia played a vital role not only in scuttling projects like the Bataan nuclear plant but in ousting the dictatorships that reigned there in the 1970s and 1980s. Indeed, because authoritarian regimes did not perceive the environment as 'political,' organizing around environmental and public health issues was not initially proscribed. Thus, environmental struggles became an issue around which the anti-dictatorship movement could organize and reach new people. Environmental destruction became one more graphic example of a regime's irresponsibility. In Indonesia, for example, the environmental organization WALHI went so far as to file a lawsuit for pollution and environmental destruction against six government bodies, including the Ministry of the Environment and Population. By the time the dictatorships wised up to what was happening, it was often too late: environmentalism and anti-fascism fed on one another.

The environmental movement is at an ebb throughout the region today, but consciousness about threats to the environment and public health is widespread and can be translated into a new round of activism if the right circumstances come together.

Environmental protests in China

The environmental movement in China exhibits many of the same dynamics observed in the NICs and Southeast Asia. The environmental crisis in China is very serious. For example, the ground water table of the North China plain is dropping by 1.5 meters (5 feet) per year. This region produces 40 percent of China's grain. As environmentalist Dale Wen remarks, 'One cannot help wonder about how China will be fed once the ground aquifer is depleted.'[4]

Water pollution and water scarcity; soil pollution, soil degradation and desertification; global warming and the coming energy crisis – these are all by-products of China's high-speed industrialization and massively expanded consumption.

Most of the environmental destabilization in China is produced by local enterprises and massive state projects such as the Three Gorges Dams, but the contribution of foreign investors is not insignificant. Taking advantage of very lax implementation of environmental laws in China, many Western corporations have relocated their most polluting factories into the country and have exacerbated or even created many environmental problems. Wen notes that the Pearl River Delta and Yangtze River Delta, the two Special Economic Zones where most transnational subsidiaries are located, are the most seriously affected by heavy metal and POPs (persistent organic pollutants) pollution.

Global warming is not a distant threat. The periodical *Frontline* reports that the first comprehensive study of the impact of the sea level rise of global warming – by Gordon McGranahan, Deborah Balk, and Bridget Anderson – puts China as the country in Asia most threatened if the sea level rises up to 10 meters over the next century.[5]

Some 10 percent of China's population, or 144 million people, live in low-elevation coastal zones, and this figure is likely to increase as a result of the export-oriented industrialization strategies

4. Walden Bello interview with Dale Wen, *Focus on the Global South*, www.focusweb. org/interview-with-dale-wen.

5. R. Ramachandran, 'Coming Storms,' *Frontline* 24(7), 2007, www.frontlineonnet. com/fl2407/stories/20070420016090000.htm.

pursued by the government, which have involved the creation of numerous Special Economic Zones.

'From an environmental perspective,' the study warns,

> there is a double disadvantage to excessive (and potentially rapid) coastal development. First, uncontrolled coastal development is likely to damage sensitive and important ecosystems and other resources. Second, coastal settlement, particularly in the low-lands, is likely to expose residents to seaward hazards such as sea level rise and tropical storms, both of which are likely to become more serious with climate change.[6]

The recent spate of super-typhoons descending on the Asian mainland from the Western Pacific underlines the gravity of this observation.

As in Taiwan and Korea fifteen years earlier, unrestrained export-oriented industrialization in China has brought together low-wage migrant labor, farming communities whose lands are being grabbed or ruined environmentally, environmentalists, and the proponents of a major change in political economy called the 'New Left.' Environment-related riots, protests, and disputes in China increased by 30 percent in 2005 to more than 50,000, as pollution-related unrest has become 'a contagious source of instability in the country,' as one report put it.

Indeed, a great many of the recorded protests fused environmental, land-loss, income, and political issues. According to the Ministry of Public Security, 'mass group incidents' have grown from 8,700 in 1995 to 87,000 in 2005, most of them in the countryside.[7] Moreover, the incidents are growing in average size from ten or fewer persons in the mid-1990s to fifty-two people per incident in 2004. Notable were the April 2005 riots in Huashui, where an estimated 10,000 police officers clashed with desperate villagers,

---

6. Ibid.
7. Fred Bergsten et al., *China: What the World Needs to Know now about the Emerging Superpower* (Washington: Center for Strategic and International Studies and Institute for International Economics, 2006), pp. 40-41.

who succeeded in repelling strong vested interests polluting their lands. As in Taiwan, people have discovered the effectiveness of direct action in rural China. 'Without the riot, nothing would have changed,' said Wang Xiaofang, a 43-year-old farmer. 'People here finally reached their breaking point.'

As in Southeast Asia, struggles around the environment and public health may be leading to a more comprehensive political consciousness.

The strength of China's environmental movement must not be exaggerated. Indeed, its failures often outnumber its successes. Alliances are often spontaneous and do not go beyond the local level. What Dale Wen calls a national 'red–green' coalition for change remains a potential force, one that is waiting to be constructed.[8] Nevertheless, the environmental movement is no longer a marginal actor and it is definitely something that the state and big capital have to deal with. Indeed, the ferment in the countryside is a key factor in making the current Chinese leadership more open to suggestions from the so-called 'New Left' for a change of course in economic policy from rapid export-oriented growth to a more sustainable and slower domestic-demand led growth.

The environmental movement in India

As in China, the environment and public health have been sites of struggle in India. Over the last twenty-five years, the movement for the environment and public health has exploded in that country, contributing to a deepening of Indian democracy. Also, many of the leaders of environmental struggles in India have also become key figures in the international movements for the environment.

Although environmental and public health struggles go way back, perhaps the single biggest event that propelled the movement

---

8. Interview with Dale Wen.

to becoming a critical mass was the Bhopal gas leak on December 3, 1984. This tragedy released 40 tons of methyl isocynate, killed 3,000 people outright, and ultimately caused between 15,000 and 20,000 deaths. The struggle for just compensation for the Bhopal victims continues to this day.

Today struggles proliferate in this vast country. There is the national campaign against Coca-Cola and Pepsi-Cola plants for drawing ground water and contaminating fields with sludge. There are local struggles against intensive aquaculture farms in Tamil Nadu, Orissa, and other coastal states. There is a non-violent but determined campaign by farmers against GMOs, which has involved the uprooting and burning of fields planted to genetically engineered rice.

The most influential element of India's mass-based environmental movement has been the anti-dam movement. Dams have often represented the modernist vision that guided many Third World governments in their struggle to catch up with the West. The technological blueprint for power development for the post-World War II period was that of creating a limited number of power generators – giant dams, coal or oil-powered plants, or nuclear plants – at strategic points to generate electricity that could be distributed to every nook and cranny of the country. Traditional or local sources of power that allowed some degree of self-sufficiency were unfashionable. If you were not hooked up to a central grid, you were backward.

Centralized electrification with its big dams, big coal-fired plants, and nuclear plants became the rage. Indeed, there was an almost religious fervor about this vision among leaders and technocrats, who defined their life's work as 'missionary electrification' or the connection of the most distant village to the central grid. Jawaharlal Nehru, the dominant figure in postwar India, called dams the 'temples of modern India,' a statement that, as Indian author Arundhati Roy points out, made its way into primary school textbooks in every Indian language. Big dams have become such an article of faith that 'to question their utility amounts almost to sedition,' Roy writes in her brilliant essay *The Cost of Living*.[9]

In the name of missionary electrification, India's technocrats, Roy observes, not only built 'new dams and irrigation schemes ... [but also] took control of small, traditional water-harvesting systems that had been managed for thousands of years and allowed them to atrophy.'[10] Here Roy expresses an essential truth: that centralized electrification preempted the development of alternative power-systems that could have been more decentralized, more people-oriented, more environmentally benign, and less capital-intensive.

The key forces behind central electrification were powerful local coalitions of power technocrats, big business, and urban-industrial elites. Despite the rhetoric about 'rural electrification,' centralized electrification was essentially biased toward the city and industry. Especially in the case of dams, it involved expending the natural capital of the countryside and the forests to subsidize the growth of urban-based industry. Industry was the future. Industry was what really added value. Industry was synonymous with national power. Agriculture was the past.

While these interests benefited, others paid the costs. Specifically, the rural areas and the environment absorbed the costs of centralized electrification. Tremendous crimes have been committed in the name of power generation and irrigation, says Roy, but these were hidden because governments never recorded these costs. Roy calculates that in India large dams have displaced some 33 million people in the last fifty years, 60 percent of whom were either untouchables or indigenous peoples.

Things changed when the government announced its plans to dam the mighty Narmada River in the late 1970s. Instead of quietly

---

9. Arundhati Roy, *The Cost of Living* (London: Flamingo, 1999).
10. Ibid.

accepting the World Bank-backed enterprise, the affected people mounted a resistance that continues to this day. The Narmada Bachao Andolan movement, led by Medha Patkar, at the Sardar Sarovar Dam, and Alok Aggarwal and Silvi at the Maheshwar Dam drew support from all over India and internationally. The resistance of the people, most of them Adivasis or indigenous people, succeeded in forcing the World Bank to stop funding the project. Saddled with delays, the dam's completion has become uncertain. The Supreme Court, for instance, ordered rehabilitation for all those affected by the Sardar Sarovar Dam's construction, and in March 2005 ruled to halt construction on the dam until this had happened. Construction of the dam has now been halted at 110.6 meters, a figure that is much higher than the 88 metres proposed by the activists, and lower than the 130 meters that the dam is eventually supposed to reach. It is unclear at this point what the final outcome of the project will be or when it will be completed, though the entire project is meant to be finished by 2025. The fate of the Maheshwar Dam is similarly unclear.

Equally important was the broader political impact of the Narmada struggle. It proved to be the cutting edge of the social movements that have deepened India's democracy and transformed the political scene. The state bureaucracy must now listen to these movements or risk opposition. The political parties must heed their messages or risk being thrown out of power. Social movements in the rural areas played a key role in stirring up the mass consciousness that led to the defeat in 2004 of the neoliberal coalition led by the Hindu chauvinist BJP (Bharatiya Janata Party) that had campaigned on the pro-globalization slogan 'India Shining.' Its successor, the Congress Party-led coalition, has turned its back on the rural protest that led to its election. Following the same anti-agriculture and pro-globalization policies of the BJP, the coalition risks provoking an even greater backlash in the near future.

The environmental movement faces its biggest challenge today: global warming. As in China, the threat is not distant either in space or in time. The Mumbai deluge of 2005 came at a year of excessive rainfall that would normally occur once in a hundred years. The Himalayan glaciers have been retreating, with one of the largest of them, Gangotri, receding at what *Frontline* described as 'an alarming rate, influencing the stream run-off of Himalayan rivers.'[11]

Some 6 percent, or 63.2 million, of India's population live in low elevation coastal zones that are vulnerable to sea-level rise.

As in China, the challenge in India lies in building up a mass movement that might be unpopular not only with the elite but also with sections of the urban-based middle-class sectors. The middle class, after all, was the main beneficiary of the high-growth economic strategy that has been pursued since the early 1990s.

National elites and Third Worldism

The reason for tracing the evolution of a mass-based environmental movement in East Asia and India is to counter the image that the Asian masses are inert elements that uncritically accept the environmentally damaging high-growth export-oriented models promoted by their governing elites. As the geographer Jared Diamond notes in his influential book *Collapse*, people in the Third World

> know very well how they are being harmed by population growth, deforestation, overfishing, and other problems. They know it because they immediately pay the penalty, in forms such as loss of free timber for their houses, massive soil erosion, and ... their inability to afford clothes, books, and school fees for their children.[12]

It is the national elites that spout the ultra-Third Worldist line that the South has yet to fulfill its quota of polluting the world while

---

11. R. Ramachandran, 'Himalayan Concerns,' *Frontline* 24(4), 2007, www.flonnet.com/fl2404/stories/20070309006201000.htm.

12. *Collapse: How Societies Choose to Fail or Succeed* (New York: Viking, 2005).

the North has exceeded its quota. They insist on an exemption for the big rapidly industrializing countries from mandatory limits on the emission of greenhouse gases under a new Kyoto Protocol. When the Bush administration refuses to ratify the Kyoto Protocol because it does not bind China and India, and the Chinese and Indian governments say they will not tolerate curbs on their greenhouse gas emissions because the United States has not ratified Kyoto, they are in fact playing out an unholy alliance to allow their economic elites to continue to evade their environmental responsibilities and free-ride on the rest of the world.

This alliance has now become formalized in the so-called 'Asia Pacific Partnership' created last year by China, India, Japan, Korea, and the United States as a rival to the UN-negotiated Kyoto Protocol. Having recently recruited Canada, which is now led by Bush clone Stephen Harper, this grouping seeks voluntary, as opposed to mandatory, curbs on greenhouse gas emissions. This dangerous band of renegade states simply wants to spew carbon as they damn well please, which is what voluntary targets are all about. They are the core of the Major Economies Meeting slated later this month in Honolulu that many fear is designed to derail the recently agreed 'Bali Roadmap.'

The need for global adjustment

There is no doubt that the burden of adjustment to global warming will fall on the North. This adjustment will have to be made in the next ten to fifteen years, and it might need to be much greater than the 50 percent reduction from the 1990s' level by 2050 promoted by the G8 for the developed countries. Some experts predict that necessary reductions will be closer to a 100–150 percent reduction from 1990 levels. However, the South will also have to adjust, proportionately less than the North but also rather stringently. Bringing in China, now the second biggest emitter of greenhouse gases, into a regime of mandatory reductions would be a first step in this process.

The South's adjustment will not take place without the North taking the lead. But it will also not take place unless its leaders junk the export-oriented, high-growth paradigm promoted by the World Bank and most economists.

People in the South are open to an alternative to a model of growth that has failed both the environment and society. For instance, in Thailand, a country devastated by the Asian financial crisis and wracked by environmental problems, globalization and export-oriented growth are now bad words. To the consternation of the pro-market *Economist*, Thais are more and more receptive to the idea of a 'sufficiency economy' promoted by King Bhumibol, which is an inward-looking strategy that stresses self-reliance at the grassroots and the creation of stronger ties among domestic economic networks, along with 'moderately working with nature.'

Thailand may be an exception in terms of the leadership role for a more sustainable path played by an elite, and even there the commitment of that elite to an alternative path is tentative. Clearly, one cannot depend on the elites and some sections of the urban middle class to decisively change course. At best, they will procrastinate. The fight against global warming will need to be propelled mainly by an alliance between progressive civil society in the North and mass-based citizens' movements in the South.

As in the North, the environmental movements in the South have seen their ebbs and flows. As with all social movements, it takes a particular conjunction of circumstances to bring an environmental movement to life after being quiescent for some time or to transform diverse local struggles into one nationwide movement. The challenge facing activists in the global North and the global South is to bring about those circumstances that will trigger the formation of a global mass movement that will decisively confront the most crucial challenge of our times.

Defy the creditors and get away with it

This essay was written shortly after the unexpected passing of former Argentine president Nestor Kirchner in late October 2010 to remind the world of his exemplary leadership in the fight against finance capital.[13]

The unexpected death a few days ago of Nestor Kirchner not only deprived Argentina of a remarkable, albeit controversial leader. It also took away an exemplary figure in the global South when it came to dealing with international financial institutions.

Kirchner defied the creditors. More importantly, he got away with it.

The collapse

The full significance of Kirchner's moves must be seen in the context of the economy he inherited on his election as Argentine president in 2003. The country was bankrupt, having defaulted on $100 billion of its debt. The economy was in a depression, its gross domestic product having declined by over 16 percent that year. Unemployment stood at 21.5 percent of the workforce, and 53 percent of Argentines had been pushed below the poverty line. What was once the richest country in Latin America in terms of per capita income plunged below Peru and parts of Central America.[14]

Argentina's crisis stemmed from its faithful adherence to the neoliberal model. The financial liberalization that served as the proximate cause of the collapse was part and parcel of a broader program of radical economic restructuring. Argentina had been the poster child of globalization, Latin-style. It brought down its trade barriers faster than most other countries in Latin America and liberalized its capital account more radically. It followed a

13. Originally published in *Foreign Policy in Focus*, November 3, 2010, www.fpif.org/articles/defy_the_creditors_and_get_away_with_it.

14. Michael Cohen, 'A Season of Hope in Argentina,' *Challenge* 46(5), 2003, pp. 37-58.

comprehensive privatization program involving the sale of 400 state enterprises – including airlines, oil companies, steel, insurance companies, telecommunications, postal services, and petrochemicals – a complex responsible for about 7 percent of the nation's annual domestic product.

In the most touching gesture of neoliberal faith, Buenos Aires adopted a currency board and thereby voluntarily gave up any meaningful control over the domestic impact of a volatile global economy. This system tied the quantity of pesos in circulation to the quantity of incoming dollars. This policy, as the *Washington Post* writer Paul Blustein observed, handed over control of Argentina's monetary policy to Alan Greenspan, the US Federal Reserve chief, who was on top of the world's supply of dollars.[15] This was, effectively, the dollarization of the country's currency.

The US Treasury Department and its surrogate, the International Monetary Fund (IMF), either urged or approved of all of these measures. In fact, even with financial liberalization called into question in the wake of the Asian financial crisis of 1997–98, then-secretary of the treasury Larry Summers extolled Argentina's selling off of its banking sector as a model for the developing world: 'Today, fully 50 percent of the banking sector, 70 percent of private banks, in Argentina are foreign-controlled, up from 30 percent in 1994. The result is a deeper, more efficient market, and external investors with a greater stake in staying put.'[16]

As the dollar rose in value, so did the peso, making Argentine goods non-competitive both globally and locally. Raising tariff barriers against imports was not an option owing to the technocrats' commitment to the neoliberal tenet of free trade. Instead, borrowing heavily to fund the dangerously widening trade gap, Argentina spiraled into debt. The more it borrowed, the higher the interest

---

15. 'What Befell Argentina,' *Washington Post*, August 8, 2003.
16. 'What the New U.S. Treasury Chief Has in Store for Asia,' *Business World*, July 26, 1999.

rates rose as international creditors grew increasingly alarmed. Money began leaving the country. Foreign control of the banking system facilitated the outflow of much-needed capital by banks that became increasingly reluctant to lend, both to the government and to local businesses.

Backed by the IMF, the neoliberal government nevertheless continued to keep the country in the straitjacket that the peso–dollar currency board arrangement had become. As George Soros observed, Argentina 'sacrificed practically everything on the altar of maintaining the currency board and meeting international obligations.'[17]

The crisis unfolded with frightening speed in late 2001, forcing Argentina to go to the IMF for money to service its mounting debt. After earlier providing loans, the IMF refused its pupil this time, leading to the government's $100 billion debt default. Businesses collapsed, people lost jobs, capital left the country, and riots and other forms of citizen unrest toppled one government after another.

Kirchner's gamble

When Kirchner won the elections for the presidency in 2003, he inherited a devastated country. He saw the choice as debt or resurrection, putting the interests of the creditors first or prioritizing economic recovery. Kirchner offered to settle Argentina's debts but at a steep discount. He would write off 70–75 percent, repaying only 25–30 cents to the dollar. The bondholders screamed and demanded that the IMF discipline Kirchner. Kirchner repeated his offer and warned the bondholders that this was a one-time offer that they had to accept or lose the rights to any repayment. He told the creditors that he would not tax poverty-ridden Argentines to pay off the debt and invited them to visit his country's slums to

---

17. *George Soros on Globalization* (New York: Public Affairs, 2005), p. 143.

'experience poverty first hand.' Faced with his determination, the IMF stood by helplessly and a majority of the bondholders angrily accepted his terms.

Indeed, Kirchner played hardball not only with the creditors but with the IMF. He told the Fund in early 2004 that Argentina would not repay a $3.3 billion installment due to the IMF unless it approved a similar amount of lending to Buenos Aires. The IMF blinked and came up with the money. In December 2005, Kirchner paid off the country's debt to the IMF in full and booted the Fund out of Argentina.

For over two decades, since the Third World debt crisis in the early 1980s, developing-country governments had considered defying the creditors. There had been a few quiet defaults on payments, but Kirchner was the first to publicly threaten the lenders with a unilateral haircut and make good on that promise. Stratfor, the political risk analysis firm, pointed out the implications of his high-wire act:

> If Argentina walks away from its private and multilateral debts successfully – meaning it doesn't collapse economically when it is shut out of international markets after repudiating its debt–then other countries might soon take the same path. This could finish what little institutional and geopolitical relevance the IMF has left.[18]

And, indeed, Kirchner's act contributed to the erosion of the credibility and power of the Fund in the middle of this decade.

Recovery

Argentina did not collapse. Instead, it grew by a remarkable 10 percent per year over the next four years. This was no mystery. A central cause of the high rate of growth was the financial resources

---

18. Stratfor, 'Global Briefing Kit,' February 4, 2004.

that the government reinvested in the economy instead of sending outside as debt service. Kirchner's historic debt initiative was accompanied by other moves to throw off the shackles of neoliberalism: the adoption of a managed float for the Argentine peso, domestic price controls, export taxes, sharply increased public spending, and caps on utility rates.

Kirchner did not confine his reforms to the domestic sphere. He undertook high-profile initiatives with other progressive leaders in Latin America, such as the sinking of the Washington-sponsored Free Trade of the Americas and efforts to bring about greater economic and political cooperation. Emblematic of this alliance was Venezuela's $2.4 billion purchase of Argentine bonds, which enabled Argentina to pay off all of the country's debt to the IMF.

Along with Hugo Chávez of Venezuela, Lula of Brazil, Evo Morales of Bolivia, and Rafael Correa of Ecuador, Kirchner was one of several remarkable leaders that the crisis of neoliberalism produced in Latin America. Mark Weisbrot, who captured his continental significance, writes that Kirchner's moves 'have not generally won him much favor in Washington and in international business circles, but history will record him not only as a great president but also as an independence hero of Latin America.'[19]

---

19. Mark Weisbrot, 'Kirchner Rescued Argentina's Economy, Helped Unite South America,' *MRzine*, http://mrzine.monthlyreview.org/2010/weisbrot271010.html.

The Arab revolutions and the
democratic imagination

Written shortly after the ouster of the dictator Hosni Mubarak in Egypt in early 2011, this essay is an attempt to place the Arab Spring in the recent history of movements for democracy and to draw out the positive and negative lessons that the pro-democracy forces in the Middle East can learn from previous efforts at democratic transformation in a world dominated by global elites promoting failed models of representative democracy and disastrous neoliberal economic policies promoting globalization.[20]

The Arab democratic uprisings have brought a rush of nostalgia to many people who staged their own democratic revolutions years earlier. As they watched events unfold in Cairo's Tahrir Square on Al Jazeera and CNN, that feeling of 'all that is solid melting into thin air,' as Marx would have put it, returned to many of those who went to the barricades during the original People Power Revolution in the Philippines in 1986.

People who threw personal security to the winds and rushed to face down Ferdinand Marcos's armored personnel carriers in February 1986 could also relate to what the Egyptian Internet activist Wael Ghonim said about the key psychological moment in an uprising: 'We knew we would win when people began to break through the psychological barrier, when they decided that it was better to die for a cause than to live without dignity... We're stronger than those [Mubarak's] guys because they fear for their lives while we're ready to give ours.'

Breaching the psychological barrier of fear was coupled with another feeling that ran through the crowds in both Tahrir Square and Manila: the sense that people were truly determining their destiny, that they were taking matters into their own hands. This was the

20. Originally published in *Foreign Policy in Focus*, March 16, 2011, www.fpif.org/articles/the_arab_revolutions_and_the_democratic_imagination.

primordial democratic moment, the pristine moment of self-rule that is so inadequately conveyed by theoretical treatises on democracy.

Along with nostalgia, however, came a keen sense of missed opportunities. To many who participated in the popular democratic revolts that swept the Philippines and Latin America in the 1980s and Eastern Europe in 1989, the euphoria of people power was short-lived, giving way, as events unfolded, to concern, disappointment, then cynicism. The critical juncture occurred when the managers of the political transition transformed the raw power of direct democracy that overthrew dictatorships into representative electoral democracy to simplify the mechanics of democratic governance.

The conundrum of representative democracy

Some of the classical theorists of democracy were troubled by this transition. Rousseau distrusted representative democracy because he sensed it would replace the 'General Interest' or 'General Will' of the people with what he called the 'Corporate Will' of their elected representatives. Marx and Engels were famously contemptuous of representative democracy because, in their view, it simply concealed the ruling economic interests of the bourgeoisie behind the fig leaf of parliamentary politics. Perhaps most critical was the political sociologist Robert Michels, who saw elections evolve from being a method by which the people replaced their leaders to a mechanism through which leaders manipulated people to acquire permanent power. Michels went on to assert that representative democracies could not escape the 'iron law of oligarchy.'[21]

The fears of these classical theorists of political science became realities in the post-uprising systems of governance that emerged in the 1980s and 1990s. For the expectant citizens of the new

21. In Robert Michels, *Political Parties: A Sociological Study of the Oligarchical Tendencies of Modern Democracy* (1911) (New York: Collier Books, 1962).

democracies in the Philippines and Latin America, people power euphoria gave way to Western-influenced parliamentary electoral regimes, in which traditional economic elites promptly came to hold sway. Competitive politics flourished, but with factions of the elite competing among themselves for the right to reign. Progressive politics was marginalized within systems dominated by conservative or centrist elite agendas. Corruption greased the wheels of the system.

Structural adjustment via democracy

Even as traditional elites hijacked the resurgent parliamentary systems, the United States and the multilateral agencies subverted them to push through austerity programs that the authoritarian regimes they previously supported had no longer been able to impose on recalcitrant citizenries. It soon became clear that Washington and the multilateral agencies wanted the new democratic regimes to use their legitimacy to impose repressive economic adjustment programs and debt management policies. In Argentina, for instance, the international financial institutions pressured the post-dictatorship government of Raul Alfonsin to abandon neo-Keynesian policies, implement tax reforms, liberalize trade, and privatize enterprises. When the government quailed, the World Bank suspended disbursements of a structural adjustment loan to bring it into line.

In Peru, the government of Alberto Fujimori was elected on a populist anti-International Monetary Fund (IMF) platform. But on assuming office, it proceeded to impose a neoliberal program that included steep increases in the rates charged by state enterprises as well as radical trade liberalization. These measures provoked a deep recession, leading to popular discontent that in turn provided an excuse for Fujimori to suspend the constitution and reinstitute strongman rule.

In the Philippines, one of the key reasons Washington abandoned Ferdinand Marcos was its realization that the dictatorship's lack of legitimacy made it an ineffective instrument for repaying the country's $26 billion foreign debt and for implementing the IMF–World Bank structural adjustment program. Not even the economic crisis accompanying the end of the regime stopped the Bank and the Fund from demanding that the fledgling government of President Corazon Aquino make debt repayment its top economic priority. The government submitted, issuing a law that affirmed the 'automatic appropriation' of the full amount needed to service the foreign debt yearly from the national budget. With some 30 to 40 percent of the budget going to debt servicing, the government was deprived of vital investment capital, throttling economic growth and leaving the country floundering as its neighbors sprinted ahead during the years of the so-called Southeast Asian Miracle.

In Eastern Europe and the old Soviet Union, the euphoria of 1989 gave way in the 1990s to hard times, as the IMF took advantage of the transition from communism to impose 'shock therapy,' or the rapid and comprehensive imposition of market processes. The process led to a tripling of the number of people living in poverty to 100 million. Although in Eastern Europe most liberal democratic regimes were able to survive the association with radical adjustment, in Russia and its former dependencies in Central Asia the mafia capitalism that shock therapy spawned led people to tolerate if not support the return or persistence of authoritarian regimes, such as that of Vladimir Putin in Russia. By 2010, according to one analysis, some 80 percent of the residents of the former Soviet Union were still living or were back under authoritarian regimes.

Reviving the democratic imagination

The political imagination narrowed, with democracy emptied of its direct, unmediated character, dominated by competing elites, and unable to shake off its association with radical, poverty-creating market reform.

The first significant challenge to the ossification of the democratic impulse took place in Latin America, where in the first decade of the new century the disenchantment with neoliberalism, the emergence of innovative populist political parties and movements, and the mobilization of civil society all combined to open up new avenues for popular intervention in the political process in Venezuela, Ecuador, and Bolivia.

The Arab Revolution extends this challenge to the democratic imagination to create institutions that will promote greater direct intervention by citizens, sustain popular participation in decision-making, block the subversion of the electoral process by elite interests and money politics, and re-establish the primordial link between liberty, fraternity, and equality that has animated all great democratic upheavals since the French Revolution.

The Arab Revolution has two things going for it in meeting this challenge of liberating the democratic imagination. First, the youth who spearheaded it are less bound to respect the prescriptions of traditional representative democracy and likely to be more innovative in entertaining the possibilities offered by information technology in elaborating new, more direct forms of representation, much like they used information technology to subvert the traditional mechanisms of repression and mobilize the crowds that overthrew the repressive dictatorships.

Second, neoliberal pro-market reforms are in severe disrepute, which was not the case in the 1980s and 1990s. The liberalization of capital flows has provoked several crises, including the current global downturn, while trade liberalization has resulted in the displacement of local agricultural producers and local manufacturers by foreign imports. More than at any other time since the Reagan-Thatcher neoliberal revolution in the 1980s, radical free-market solutions lack credibility. Owing to the lack of alternative frameworks, however, neoliberal policies remain the default mode among economists and technocrats.

The revolutionary democrats of the Arab world have an opportunity to bring about the next stage in the global democratic revolution. Will they accept the challenge, or will they withdraw back to private life, as some have indicated, leaving older generations of politicians to come to center-stage with their tired, archaic Western models of representative democracy?

The World Social Forum at the crossroads

The World Social Forum, founded in 2001, was, in many ways, the most significant institution produced by the anti-globalization movement. This essay seeks to analyze its significance, its contributions, and its limitations as a movement for social transformation. Strategies for alternative development, such as deglobalization, were among those that were debated and refined at the annual WSF global assembly and in regional meetings.[22]

A new stage in the evolution of the global justice movement was reached with the inauguration of the World Social Forum (WSF) in Pôrto Alegre, Brazil, in January 2001. The WSF was the brainchild of social movements loosely associated with the Workers' Party (PT) in Brazil. Strong support for the idea was given at an early stage by the ATTAC movement in France, key figures of which were connected with the newspaper *Le Monde diplomatique*. In Asia, the Brazilian proposal, floated in June 2000, received the early enthusiastic endorsement of, among others, the research and advocacy institute Focus on the Global South, based in Bangkok.

---

22. Originally published in *Focus on the Global South*, www.focusweb.org/node/1327.

Pôrto Alegre was meant to be a counterpoint to 'Davos,' the annual event in a resort town in the Swiss Alps where the world's most powerful business and political figures congregate annually to spot and assess the latest trends in global affairs. Indeed, the highlight of the first WSF was a televised transcontinental debate between George Soros and other figures in Davos with representatives of social movements gathered in Pôrto Alegre.

The world of Davos was contrasted to the world of Pôrto Alegre, the world of the global rich with the world of the rest of humanity. It was this contrast that gave rise to the very resonant theme 'Another world is possible.'

There was another important symbolic dimension: while Seattle was the site of the first major victory of the transnational anti-corporate globalization movement – the collapse amidst massive street protests of the third ministerial meeting of the World Trade Organization – Pôrto Alegre represented the transfer to the South of the center of gravity of that movement. Proclaimed as an 'open space,' the WSF became a magnet for global networks focused on different issues, from war to globalization to communalism to racism to gender oppression to alternatives. Regional versions of the WSF were spun off, the most important being the European Social Forum and the African Social Forum; and in scores of cities throughout the world, local social forums were held and institutionalized.

The functions of the WSF

Since its establishment, the WSF has performed three critical functions for global civil society.

First, it represents a space – both physical and temporal – for this diverse movement to meet, to network, and, quite simply, to feel and affirm itself.

Second, it is a retreat during which the movement gathers its energies and charts the directions of its continuing drive to confront and roll back the processes, institutions, and structures of global capitalism. Naomi Klein, author of *No Logo*, underlined this function when she told a Pôrto Alegre audience in 2002 that the need of the moment was 'less civil society and more civil disobedience.'[23]

Third, the WSF provides a site and space for the movement to elaborate, discuss, and debate the vision, values, and institutions of an alternative world order built on a real community of interests. The WSF is, indeed, a macrocosm of so many smaller but equally significant enterprises carried out throughout the world by millions who have told the reformists, the cynics, and the 'realists' to move aside because, indeed, another world is possible ... and necessary.

Direct democracy in action

The WSF and its many offspring are significant not only as sites of affirmation and debate but also as direct democracy in action. Agendas and meetings are planned with meticulous attention to democratic process. Through a combination of periodic face-to-face meetings and intense email and Internet contact in between, the WSF network was able to pull off events and arrive at consensus decisions. At times, this could be very time-consuming and also frustrating, and when you were part of an organizing effort involving hundreds of organizations, as we at Focus on the Global South were during the organizing of the 2004 WSF in Mumbai, it could be very frustrating indeed.

But this was direct democracy, and direct democracy was at its best at the WSF. One might say, parenthetically, that the direct democratic experiences of Seattle, Prague, Genoa, and the other big mobilizations of the decade were institutionalized in the WSF or Pôrto Alegre process.

---

23. Speech at World Social Forum, Pôrto Alegre, February 1, 2002.

The central principle of the organizing approach of the new movement is that getting to the desired objective is not worth it if the methods violate democratic process, if democratic goals are reached via authoritarian means. Perhaps Subcomandante Marcos of the Zapatistas best expressed the organizing bias of the new movements:

> The movement has no future if its future is military. If the EZLN [Zapatistas] perpetuates itself as an armed military structure, it is headed for failure. Failure as an alternative set of ideas, an alternative attitude to the world. The worst that could happen to it apart from that would be for it to come to power and install itself there as a revolutionary army.[24]

The WSF shares this perspective.

What is interesting is that there has hardly been an attempt by any group or network to 'take over' the WSF process. Quite a number of 'old movement' groups participate in the WSF, including old-line 'democratic centralist' parties as well as traditional social democratic parties affiliated with the Socialist International. Yet none of these has put much effort into steering the WSF towards more centralized or hierarchical modes of organizing. At the same time, despite their suspicion of political parties, the 'new movements' never sought to exclude the parties and their affiliates from playing a significant role in the Forum. Indeed, the 2004 WSF in Mumbai was organized jointly by an unlikely coalition of social movements and Marxist–Leninist parties, a set of actors that are not known for harmonious relations on the domestic front.

Perhaps a compelling reason for the modus vivendi of the old and new movements was the realization that they needed one another in the struggle against global capitalism and that the strength of the fledgling global movement lay in a strategy of decentralized

---

24. 'The Punch Card and the Hourglass,' *New Left Review* 9 (May–June 2001).

networking that rested not on the doctrinal belief that one class was destined to lead the struggle but on the reality of the common marginalization of practically all subordinate classes, strata, and groups under the reign of global capital.

What constitutes 'open space'

The WSF has, however, not been exempt from criticism, even from its own ranks. One in particular appears to have merit. This is the charge that the WSF as an institution is unanchored in actual global political struggles, and this is turning it into an annual festival with limited social impact.

There is, in my view, a not insignificant truth to this. Many of the founders of the WSF have interpreted the 'open space' concept in a liberal fashion; that is, for the WSF not to explicitly endorse any political position or particular struggle, though its constituent groups are free to do so.

Others have disagreed, saying the idea of an 'open space' should be interpreted in a partisan fashion, as explicitly promoting some views over others and as openly taking sides in key global struggles. In this view, the WSF is under an illusion that it can stand above the fray, and this will lead to its becoming some sort of neutral forum, where discussion will increasingly be isolated from action. The energy of civil society networks derives from their being engaged in political struggles, say proponents of this perspective. The reason that the WSF was so exciting in its early years was because of its affective impact: it provided an opportunity to re-create and reaffirm solidarity against injustice, against war, and for a world that was not subjected to the rule of empire and capital. The WSF's not taking a stand on the Iraq War, on the Palestine issue, and on the WTO is said to be making it less relevant and less inspiring to many of the networks it had brought together.

Caracas versus Nairobi

This is why the Sixth WSF held in Caracas in January 2006 was so bracing and reinvigorating: it inserted some 50,000 delegates into the storm center of an ongoing struggle against empire, where they mingled with militant Venezuelans, mostly the poor, engaged in a process of social transformation, while observing other Venezuelans, mostly the elite and middle class, engaged in bitter opposition. Caracas was an exhilarating reality check.

This is also the reason why the Seventh WSF held in Nairobi was so disappointing, since its politics was so diluted and big business interests linked to the Kenyan ruling elite were so brazen in commercializing it. Even Petrobras, the Brazilian state corporation that is a leading exploiter of the natural resource wealth of Latin America, was busy trumpeting itself as a friend of the Forum. There was a strong sense of going backward rather than forward in Nairobi.

The WSF is at a crossroads. Hugo Chávez captured the essence of the conjuncture when he warned delegates in January 2006 about the danger of the WSF becoming simply a forum of ideas with no agenda for action. He told participants that they had no choice but to address the question of power: 'We must have a strategy of 'counter-power.'[25] We, the social movements and political movements, must be able to move into spaces of power at the local, national, and regional level.'

Developing a strategy of counter-power or counter-hegemony need not mean lapsing back into the old hierarchical and centralized modes of organizing characteristic of the old left. Such a strategy can, in fact, be best advanced through the multilevel and horizontal networking that the movements and organizations represented in the WSF have excelled in advancing in their particular struggles.

---

25. www.ipsterraviva.net/tv/wsf2005/viewstoryb968-2.html?idnews=170.

Articulating their struggles in action will mean forging a common strategy while drawing strength from and respecting diversity.

After the disappointment that was Nairobi, many long-standing participants in the Forum are asking themselves: is the WSF still the most appropriate vehicle for the new stage in the struggle of the global justice and peace movement? Or, having fulfilled its historic function of aggregating and linking the diverse counter-movements spawned by global capitalism, is it time for the WSF to fold up its tent and give way to new modes of global organization of resistance and transformation?

CONCLUSION

DEGLOBALIZATION: AN IDEA
WHOSE TIME HAS COME?

Except perhaps in the US and Britain, capitalism has elicited significant distrust among citizens in most societies. Perhaps most people's attitude towards it, especially after the collapse of the socialist alternative in the early 1990s, is akin to that of Winston Churchill's towards democracy: it's bad but all other systems are worse.

In the last fifteen years, however, the devastating consequences of neoliberalism have convinced more and more people that global capitalism cannot be reformed. Already, when the global powers were digging their heels in against real reforms at the World Trade Organization, the International Monetary Fund, and the World Bank in the early part of the last decade, skepticism about reform was widespread. With the onset of the global financial crisis, followed by the reversal of the faint efforts at Keynesian stabilization in 2009 and 2010, the search for alternatives to global capitalism has intensified. This section will survey some of the alternative micro- and macro-strategies, concluding with a discussion of the paradigm of deglobalization.

Micro-level alternatives

There is a rich history of efforts to create alternatives to the existing system. There have been attempts to present comprehensive macro-

alternatives, and we will focus on them later in this chapter. Our discussion will begin with initiatives at the micro- or local level, of which there have been many.

Participatory budgeting

Among the most famous of these micro-alternatives to conventional practice is participatory budgeting in the city of Pôrto Alegre and more than 140 cities and municipalities in Brazil. Participatory budgeting (PB) has been described as 'a means of overcoming the limits of representative democracy through mechanisms that increase civil society mobilization beyond corporatism and mere consultation.'[1] The impact in many places in Brazil where it has been tried has been an increase in popular empowerment and organizing, as well as improvements in public facilities and better conditions for the poor.[2] As one study notes, 'The main strength of the PB in Porto Alegre and Belo Horizonte seems to be the insertion of marginalized people and communities, albeit only a minority of them, into the political process for the first time. But allowing these citizens the right to decide (and not only to be heard) may well have a long-term impact on Brazil's unequal balance of power.'[3]

Since its beginnings in Pôrto Alegre, some 1,200 municipalities in Latin America, Asia, Africa, Europe, and North America have adopted participatory budgeting.[4]

When it comes to alternative ways of organizing the different dimensions of the economy, there is a wide range of family ventures, co-operatives, and small-scale enterprises that have emerged to propose alternative organizational arrangements in such areas as production, credit, transport, energy, and agriculture.

---

1. Celine Souza, 'Participatory Budgeting in Brazilian Cities: Limits and Possibilities in Building Democratic Institutions,' *Environment and Urbanization* 13(1), April 2001, p. 178.
2. Wikipedia, 'Participatory Budgeting,' http://en.wikipedia.org/wiki/Participatory_budgeting.
3. Souza, 'Participatory Budgeting in Brazilian Cities,' pp. 183-4.
4. Wikipedia, 'Participatory Budgeting.'

The Mondragon experiment

One of the most successful and famous enterprises is the Mondragon network of worker co-operatives in Spain. Mondragon, which features 85,000 worker-owners, is the world's biggest co-operative network, with some 256 co-operatives around the world, most of them in the Basque region in Northern Spain. It is associated with respected global brand commodities such as Orbea bikes, which won gold at the Beijing Olympics, Fagur fridges, Brandt ovens, Eroski shops, and the forthcoming electric City Car. One attractive feature of Mondragon is its egalitarian pay scales, with top management not allowed to earn more than six times the lowliest janitor, in comparison to the differentials in transnational corporations, which average 202 times. Mondragon mostly prohibits offshore manufacturing, pushing it, according to one manager, 'to keep climbing the technology ladder and improve core engineering here.'[5] Profits are 'largely reinvested or sunk into research centers, though a chunk is spent on social projects. Worker dividends are paid into retirement accounts. The whole system is run by an elected Congress, known as 'the supreme expression of sovereignty.'[6]

Community currency systems

There have been efforts to create community currency (CC) arrangements – that is, systems of exchange among members of a community or regions that rest on a commonly accepted measure of value among community members. While the aim of some systems is to lessen vulnerability to external forces that impact on communities via national and international currencies, the objective of others has been more ambitious, which is to encourage local production though local exchange. Ever since the establishment

---

5. 'Spain's Astonishing Coop Takes on the World,' *Telegraph*, February 16, 2011, www.telegraph.co.uk/finance/economics/8329355/Spains-astonishing-co-op-takes-on-the-world.html.

6. Ibid.

of the famous Local Currency Trading System (LETS) in Comox Valley, Vancouver, to counter the effects of massive unemployment owing to the closure of a local industry, other communities have experimented with local currencies. It is estimated that there are currently over 4,000 associations in forty countries, with almost 1 million members. However, as Jerome Blanc has observed, community currency systems

> as a rule ... concern less than one per cent of the population, though the figure rises to three per cent in some small countries such as New Zealand. In Argentina, CC systems involved over ten per cent of the population in 2002, following the spectacular collapse of the country's economy and prior to their own equally spectacular collapse...[7]

Community renewable energy ventures

Renewable energy and conservation systems are being promoted in many countries by communities and co-operatives. One of the most serious efforts is the so-called 'Transition Town' of Totnes, in Southwest England. It has put into effect a program called 'Transition Streets,' which is a detailed street-by-street approach to energy efficiency, community building, and domestic micro-energy generation. Managing the so-called energy transition is a Renewable Energy Society, which owns and profitably runs the renewable generating capacity of the region. Totnes now has a town-approved 'Energy Descent Action Plan,' which is a 'multi-staged plan for reducing dependence on fossil fuels in all significant areas...'[8] Trying to close the loop of an alternative system of living, Totnes now also has its own local currency and a food co-operative.

---

7. Jerome Blanc, 'Community and Complementary Currencies,' in Keith Hart, Jean-Louis Laville, and Antonio David Cattani, eds, *The Human Economy* (Cambridge: Polity Press, 2010), p. 305.
8. Richard Heinberg, *The End of Growth* (British Columbia: New Society Publishers, 2011), pp. 271-2.

Organic farming and fair trade networks

Organic farming has been one of the most successful alternative enterprises, and it was pioneered and pushed by small farmers who came into contact with their consumers in urban farmers' markets. Now urban agriculture, mainly carried out by families, promises to be a second stage of the organic farming 'revolution' that has been made possible by a combination of a desire for healthy living and anti-corporate consciousness expressed in a growing disdain for junk food. In fact the scale of urban agriculture – organic and non-organic, but mainly carried out by small producers – is now huge. As one report puts it,

> urban gardening and farming are experiencing a renaissance in North America. Significant amounts of food are cultivated by entrepreneurial producers, community gardeners, backyard gardeners, and even food banks, in vacant lots, parks, greenhouses, roof tops, balconies, window sills, ponds, rivers, and estuaries. The potential to expand urban production is enormous. One third of the 2 million farms in the United States are located within metropolitan areas, and produce 35 percent of U.S. vegetables, fruit, livestock, poultry, and fish.[9]

Associated with alternative food production has been the fair-trade movement, aimed at providing tropical commodities like coffee to people in the North while enabling participating farmers in the South to earn decent profits by eliminating most of the middlemen. Describing its aims, one analyst writes:

> Recognizing that cutting down physical distance within the food system is not always possible for some products that can only be grown in tropical climates, fair trade does explicitly aim to reduce mental distance in the system. It does this by cutting down the number of middle agents in the international exchange

---

9. Anne Bellows, Katherine Brown, and Jac Smit, 'Health Benefits or Urban Agriculture,' https://docs.google.com/viewer?a=v&q=cache:2E4rcEgkSPoJ:www.foodsecurity.org/UA-HealthFactsheet.pdf+benefits+of+urban+agriculture&hl.

of commodities, and through education of both consumers and producers about the alternative supply chain. It also raises the awareness on the part of farmers, by showing them precisely how their products are traded through the network with transparency regarding their level of compensation. Fair trade products, then, serve important functions beyond the commodity itself for both consumer and producer.[10]

It is estimated that in 2008 sales of fair-trade products totaled over $4.5 billion, and involved some 1.2 million farmers and farm workers, represented by 800 producer organizations that were linked in fair-trade networks in an estimated fifty-eight countries. Including families and dependents, the direct beneficiaries of free trade are said to number some 6 million people in developing countries.[11]

Microcredit

Microfinance or microcredit, which is associated with Bangladeshi activist Muhammad Yunus, is another widely acknowledged successful alternative, in this case to conventional banking. Through its dynamics of lending predicated on the collective responsibility for repayment of the loan by a group of women borrowers, microcredit is said to have enabled many poor women to become small entrepreneurs and to roll back pervasive poverty. For his achievements in this area, which was pioneered by the Grameen Bank, Yunus received the Nobel Peace Prize in 2008.

The vicissitudes of success

While boasting of successes – and these are not insignificant – many of these alternatives to corporate enterprises operating in a market system have faced great difficulties either in sustaining themselves or in living up to their original objectives.

---

10. Jennifer Clapp, *Food* (Cambridge: Polity Press, 2012), p. 170.
11. Ibid., p. 171.

The contradictions of Mondragon

In the case of Mondragon, for instance, the imperatives of globalized capitalist competition have created a paradox that might ultimately be unsustainable. With Mondragon's expansion, only some 40 percent of its current workforce are owner-members, the rest being ordinary employees. The vast majority of Mondragon's subsidiaries, including foreign subsidiaries, belong to the category of employees. As Erik Olin Wright notes,

> In effect, therefore, the owners-members of the cooperatives within MCC [Mondragon Cooperative Corporation] have become, collectively, capitalist employers of the workers within the subsidiary firms. This global configuration of economic and class relations within the conglomerate structure of the Mondragon cooperatives is in deep tension with its cooperativist principles.[12]

Microcredit and the perils of cooptation

After being hailed as a pioneering approach in the 1990s by progressive development practitioners, microlending has had a checkered history more recently. For one, research shows that it appears to be mainly the moderately poor rather than the very poor who benefit, and not very many can claim they have permanently left the instability of poverty. Likewise, not many would claim that the degree of self-sufficiency and the ability to send children to school afforded by microcredit are indicators of their graduating to middle-class prosperity. As economic journalist Gina Neff notes, 'after 8 years of borrowing, 55% of Grameen households still aren't able to meet their basic nutritional needs – so many women are using their loans to buy food rather than invest in business.'[13]

---

12. Erik Olin Wright, *Envisioning Real Utopias* (London: Verso, 2010), pp. 244-5.
13. Gina Neff, 'Microcredit, Macroresults,' *Left Business Observer*, www.leftbusinessobserver.com/Micro.html.

Indeed, one of those who have thoroughly studied the phenomenon, Thomas Dichter, says that the idea that microfinance allows its recipients to graduate from poverty to entrepreneurship is inflated. He sketches out the dynamics of microcredit:

> It emerges that the clients with the most experience got started using their own resources, and though they have not progressed very far – they cannot because the market is just too limited – they have enough turnover to keep buying and selling, and probably would have with or without the microcredit. For them the loans are often diverted to consumption since they can use the relatively large lump sum of the loan, a luxury they do not come by in their daily turnover.

He concludes: 'Definitely, microcredit has not done what the majority of microcredit enthusiasts claim it can do – function as capital aimed at increasing the returns to a business activity.'[14] And so the great microcredit paradox is that, as Dichter puts it, 'the poorest people can do little productive with the credit, and the ones who can do the most with it are those who don't really need microcredit, but larger amounts with different (often longer) credit terms.'[15]

Most studies appear to confirm that microcredit is a great tool as a survival strategy, but it is not the key to development, which involves not only massive capital-intensive, state-directed investments to build industries but also an assault on the structures of inequality such as concentrated land ownership that systematically deprive the poor of resources to escape poverty. Microcredit schemes end up coexisting with these entrenched structures, serving as a safety net for people excluded and marginalized by them, but not transforming them.

The conversion of microfinance into a silver bullet for development instead of simply being seen as a poverty containment strategy owes itself to the embrace of the establishment, especially the World

---

14. www.microfinancegateway.org/content/articles/detail/31743.
15. Ibid.

Bank. As Ananya Roy has pointed out, nowadays the 'agenda of microfinance is established and controlled in a monopolistic fashion by the World Bank and its network of experts.'[16] It has become, in her view, a key element in the Bank's 'neoliberal populism':

> Microfinance celebrates the people's economy but it also entails, to borrow a phrase from Marxist geographer David Harvey, an effort to 'bring all human action into the domain of the market ... to value market exchange as an ethic in and of itself.' By 'neo-liberal populism,' I thus mean the ways in which microfinance seeks to democratize capital and simultaneously convert the microcapital of the poor into new global financial flows.[17]

Perhaps one of the reasons there is such enthusiasm for micro-credit in establishment circles these days is that it is a market-based mechanism that has enjoyed some success where other market-based programs have crashed. Structural adjustment programs promoting trade liberalization, deregulation, and privatization have brought greater poverty and inequality to most parts of the developing world over the last quarter century, and have made economic stagnation a permanent condition. Many of the same institutions that pushed and are continuing to push these failed macro-programs (sometimes under new labels like 'Poverty Reduction Strategy Papers'), like the World Bank, are often the same institutions pushing microcredit programs. Viewed broadly, microcredit can be seen as the safety net for millions of people destabilized by the large-scale macro-failures engendered by structural adjustment.

Organic farming and the wolf

As in the case with microfinance, the perceived success of organic agriculture threatens to derail it in a corporate-driven global economy. Miguel Altieri warns that if organic farming were pushed

---

16. Ananya Roy, *Poverty Capital* (New York: Routledge, 2010), p. 32.
17. Ibid.

simply as an alternative technology that hopes to coexist with
corporate agriculture, it is setting itself up for a takeover:

> The acceptance of the present structure of agriculture as a given
> condition restricts the possibility of implementing alternatives
> that challenge such a structure. Thus, options for a diversified
> agriculture are inhibited by, among other factors, the present
> trends to farm size and mechanization. Implementation of such
> mixed agriculture would only be possible as part of a broader
> program that includes land reform and machinery designed
> for polycultures. Merely introducing alternative agricultural
> designs will do little to change the underlying forces that led to
> monoculture production, farm size expansion, and large-scale
> mechanization in the first place.[18]

Altieri's warning is not about a potential problem but an urgent
current threat, for corporate agriculture has increasingly 'gone
organic.' With organic agriculture now being a $40 billion market
in the United States, a number of supermarkets and corporations
have acquired organic brands and small firms, set up partnerships
with organic companies, or established their own organic lines.
These firms include some major multinationals, such as Cadbury,
Schweppes, Coca-Cola, Danone, Deal, Heinz, Kellogg, Kraft, and
Sara Lee. According to one report, these paragons of industrial agriculture 'increasingly dominate' the organic food sector.[19] Without
actively battling corporate agriculture and without ensuring the
social dimensions of alternative agriculture – small-scale production, family or communal ownership, community solidarity between
farmers and consumers, short distance from farm to table – and
focusing on technological issues alone, alternative agriculture is in
danger of ending up a mere arm of corporate industrial agriculture
to gain a 'niche market.'

---

18. Miguel Altieri, 'Ecological Impacts of Industrial Agriculture and the Possibilities for
Truly Sustainable Farming,' in Fred Magdoff, John Bellamy Foster, and Frederick Buttel,
eds, *Hungry for Profits* (New York: Monthly Review Press, 2000), p. 89.

19. 'The Battle for the Soul of the Organic Movement,' CNN, October 9, 2006, http://
edition.cnn.com/2006/WORLD/europe/10/10/tbr.organic.

Alternative systems

A broader, overarching system to support micro-efforts to move away from the hegemony of the corporate-driven market and towards more cooperative exchange mediated by the market is necessary. As Boris Kagarlitsky has noted,

> Cooperatives and municipal enterprises are creating the primary infrastructure for a new economic participation. But they cannot remain self-sufficient, in isolation from one another. Local control is ineffective if each 'site' operates separately from the others. A unifying network and democratic coordination are essential.[20]

There have been a number of proposals for systems operating on different principles that would not coexist with but rather would supplant the prevailing corporate-driven market system. With the collapse of the socialist system in the Eastern Europe and the former Soviet Union, however, prescribing comprehensive alternatives to capitalism has often met with skepticism, sometimes even from sympathetic quarters. 'Utopian' is the pejorative word that has often greeted these initiatives. The current global crisis, however, has weakened the once confident assertion of the establishment that 'There is no alternative' to global capitalism, or TINA. The new spirit of mental liberation from conservative 'realist' thinking is captured by the World Social Forum's slogan: 'Another World is Possible.'

In the next few pages, we will focus on two complementary comprehensive alternative paradigms with which the author has been intimately engaged: 'food sovereignty'[21] and 'deglobalization.'

---

20. Boris Kagarlitsky, *The Revolt of the Middle Class* (Moscow: Cultural Revolution, 2006), p. 297.
21. The following section is based on Chapter 7, pp. 135-44, of my *The Food Wars* (London: Verso, 2009).

Food sovereignty

The food sovereignty paradigm is associated with the global farmers' network Via Campesina and has the distinction of being elaborated mainly by farmer and peasant activists. As the name implies, the perspective is focused mainly on the agri-food system, though it would have profound implications for other sectors of the economy.

What are the elements of the food sovereignty paradigm? From the writings of Via Campesina, its leaders, organic intellectuals like Annette Desmarais, Via's allies, and the broader coalitions it participates in, a number of themes emerge.

First, the goal of agricultural policy should be food self-sufficiency, wherein the country's farmers produce most of the food consumed domestically – a condition not covered by the concept of 'food security,' which US corporate representatives have defined as the capacity of fill a country's food needs through either domestic production or imports. The radical implications of this premiss are noted by Jennifer Clapp:

> By removing farmers from the global trading system altogether, the food sovereignty movement focuses on local needs and local food markets, thus freeing smallholders from the unfair and unbalanced trade rules that are upheld by the WTO Agreement on Agriculture.[22]

Second, a people should have the right to determine their patterns of food production and consumption, taking into consideration 'rural and productive diversity,' and not allow these to be subordinated to unregulated international trade.[23]

---

22. Jennifer Clapp, *Food* (Cambridge: Polity Press, 2012), p. 175.
23. Via Campesina, 'Food Sovereignty and International Trade,' position paper approved at the Third International Conference of the Via Campesina, Bangalore, India, October 3–6; cited in Annette Desmarais, *La Via Campesina and the Power of Peasants* (London: Pluto Press, 2007), p. 34.

Third, production and consumption of food should be guided by the welfare of farmers and consumers, not the needs of profit of transnational agribusiness.

Fourth, national food systems must produce 'healthy, good quality and culturally appropriate food primarily for the domestic market,'[24] and avoid what Bové has called *malbouffe* or internationally standardized or 'junk food.'[25]

Fifth, a new balance must be achieved between agriculture and industry, the countryside and the city, to reverse the subordination of agriculture and the countryside to industry and urban elites, which has resulted in a blighted countryside and massive urban slums of rural refugees.

Sixth, the concentration of land by landlords and transnational firms must be reversed and equity in land distribution must be promoted through land reform, though access to land should be possible beyond individual ownership, allowing more communal and collective forms of ownership and production that promote a sense of ecological stewardship.

Seventh, agricultural production should be carried out mainly by small farmers or cooperative or state enterprises, and the distribution and consumption of food should be governed by fair pricing schemes that take into consideration the rights and welfare of both farmers and consumers. Among other things, this means an end to dumping by transnational firms of subsidized agricultural commodities, which has artificially brought down prices, resulting in the destruction of small farmers. It would also mean, according to activist scholar Peter Rosset, 'a return to protection of the national food production of nations ... rebuilding national grain reserves ... public sector budgets, floor prices, credit and other

---

24. Quoted in ibid.
25. José Bové, 'A Farmers' International?' *New Left Review* 12 (November–December 2001), www.newleftreview.org/A2358.

forms of support' that 'stimulate the recovery of [countries'] food production capacity.'[26]

Eighth, industrial agriculture based on genetic engineering and the original chemical-intensive Green Revolution should be discouraged because monopoly control over seeds advances the corporate agenda and because industrial agriculture is environmentally unsustainable.

Ninth, traditional peasant and indigenous agricultural technologies contain a great deal of wisdom and represent the evolution of a largely benign balance between the human community and the biosphere. Thus evolving agro-technology to meet social needs must have traditional practices as a starting point rather than considering them obsolete practices to be overthrown.

The food sovereignty perspective valorizes elements – peasant agriculture, small-scale production, the environment – that have been devalued by capitalism and simply considered as barriers to progressive modes of economic organization. The characteristics of peasant agriculture – the closeness to the land, the organic tie between family and farm, the focus on the local market, the labor-intensity of production, the sense of working with rather than dominating nature – are elements that have evolved to respond to the needs of ecological stability, community, and governance, and are not to be thrown away in the cavalier way that industrial capitalist agriculture has done.

This valorization is not a defensive mechanism, one meant to postpone the passing of a doomed mode of production, but looks to the future, as one of the elements of a larger process of transformation. As Philip McMichael puts it,

> food sovereignty in theory and practice represents a political, ecological, and cultural alternative to a 'high modernist' corporate agriculture premised on standardized inputs and outputs

---

26. Peter Rosset, quoted in Philip McMichael, 'Food Sovereignty in Movement: The Challenge to Neo-Liberal Globalization,' draft MS, Cornell University, 2008.

and serving a minority of the world's population... [T]he principle of food sovereignty embodies neither a return to traditional agriculture, nor a return to a bucolic peasant culture – rather, it is a thoroughly modern response to the current neoliberal conjuncture, which has no sustainable solutions to its thoroughly modern problems.[27]

Desmarais echoes the same theme of food sovereignty representing not a rejection of modernity but an espousal of an alternative modernity:

The peasant model advocated by the Via Campesina does not entail a rejection of modernity, or of technology and trade, accompanied by a romanticized return to an archaic past steeped in rustic traditions. Rather, the Via Campesina insists that an alternative model must be based on certain ethics and values in which culture and social justice count for something and concrete mechanisms are put in place to ensure a future without hunger. The Via Campesina's alternative model entails recapturing aspects of traditional, local, or farmers' knowledge, and combining that knowledge with new technology when and where it is appropriate to do so.[28]

She points out that

[b]y integrating careful borrowings with traditional practice, peasants and small-scale farmers everywhere are reaffirming the lessons from their histories and reshaping the rural landscape to benefit those who work the land as they collectively redefine what food is produced, how it is produced, and where and for whom.[29]

It is well and good to affirm the benign character of peasant agriculture, as Demarais does, but does it really respond to the great demands on agriculture in our time? Even scholars sympathetic to the plight of the peasantry or rural workers, such as Henry Bernstein, claim that advocacy of the peasant way 'largely

---

27. McMichael, 'Food Sovereignty in Movement.'
28. Desmarais, *La Via Campesina and the Power of Peasants*, p. 38.
29. Ibid., pp. 38-9.

ignores issues of feeding the world's population, which has grown so greatly almost everywhere in the modern epoch, in significant part because of the revolution in productivity achieved by the development of capitalism.'[30]

Advocates of the peasant way respond, first of all, that the superiority in terms of production of industrial capitalist agriculture is not sustained empirically. Miguel Altieri and Clara Nicholls, for instance, point out that, although conventional wisdom is that small farms are backward and unproductive, in fact

> research shows that small farms are much more productive than
> large farms if total output is considered rather than yield from
> a single crop. Small integrated farming systems that produce
> grains, fruits, vegetables, fodder, and animal products outproduce
> yield per unit of single crops such as corn (monocultures) on
> large-scale farms.[31]

Moreover, when one factors in the ecological destabilization that has accompanied the generalization of industrial agriculture, the balance of costs and benefits lurches sharply towards the negative. For instance, a recent study by Worldwatch Institute has found that in the United States food now travels between 1,500 and 2,500 miles from farm to table, as much as 25 percent farther than two decades ago.[32] The study found that Americans are

> spending far more energy to get food to the table than the energy
> we get from eating the food. A head of lettuce grown in the Salinas
> Valley of California and shipped nearly 3,000 miles to Washing-
> ton, DC, requires about 36 times as much fossil fuel energy in
> transport as it provides in food energy when it arrives.[33]

30. Henry Bernstein, 'Agrarian Questions from Transition to Globalization,' in A. Haroon Akram-Lodhi and Cristobal Kay, eds, *Peasants and Globalization* (New York: Routledge, 2009), p. 255.
31. Miguel Altieri and Clara Nicholls, 'Scaling up Agroecological Approaches for Food Sovereignty in Latin America,' *Development* 51(4) (December 2008), p. 474.
32. Worldwatch Institute, 'Globetrotting Food will Travel Farther Than Ever This Thanksgiving,' 2011, www.worldwatch.org/node/1749.
33. Ibid.

In contrast, a typical meal – some meat, grain, fruits, and veg-etables – using local ingredients entails four to seventeen times less petroleum consumption in transport than the same meal bought from the conventional food chain.[34]

Indeed, the ability of peasant or small-scale agriculture to combine productivity and ecological stability constitutes a key dimension of its superiority over industrial agriculture. A detailed but simple explanation as to why this is so is given by Tony Weis:

> Increased mechanization goes hand in hand with monocultures, which leave bare ground between planted rows. Conversely, small farms tend to make more intensive use of such space by cropping patterns that integrate complementary plant species ... as well as integrating small livestock populations and using ecologically benign animal draught. Denser multicropped patterns that are frequently rotated, occasionally fallowed and integrated with small livestock and draught animal populations foster decomposition-assisting soil micro-organisms, detritivores, and invertebrates, which enhance the biological regulation of soil fertility, pests, weeds, and disease cycles with fewer chemicals and fertilizers than monocultures. This ability to renew and even enhance soils over time is also a function of the radically different time scales of farm management: because small farms are often drawing on knowledge passed down through generations on the land, they tend to be organized with a much longer-term objective of equilibrium, in contrast with how industrial monocultures are governed by an annual balance sheet.[35]

Jan van der Ploeg notes that the logic of the peasant mode of pro-duction is different from capitalist logic, and that the technological challenge is to build on the elements of this model rather than supplant them with technology associated with capitalism. There is progress in peasant agriculture, but that lies in a process where the use of technology is selective and is not disruptive of the mode

---

34. Ibid.

35. Tony Weis, *The Global Food Economy: The Battle for the Future of Farming* (London: Zed Books, 2007), p. 167.

of production but is 'in synch' with it. Technological development in peasant agriculture is not about standardizing production but about building into the production process the capacity to deal with diversity. Technology is, in a very real sense, path-dependent: its development takes different paths in different production paradigms. As van der Ploeg notes, in peasant farming,

> Technology is not only about linking artifacts and governing material flows – it is as much about interlinking people in specific ways in order to obtain the right kind of conditions and flows. Thus, skill is all about being able to overview, observe, handle, adjust, and coordinate extended domains of the social and natural world. This is done by building upon the specificities of different elements of the social and natural world. It is probably in this latter aspect (building on encountered and/or created specificities) that the main difference between skill-oriented and mechanical technologies resides. Continuous adjustments are neither feasible nor desirable. If you produce coca cola, then only coca cola comes out of your plant. A better or worse coca cola is unthinkable and would be immediately perceived as a disaster. As objectified patterns of 'through flow,' mechanical technologies assume a standardized inflow, as much as they produce a standardized outflow. They cannot deal with specificity or variation. Specificity is a deviation, a threat and even, potentially, a destructive factor.[36]

Advanced science and peasant agriculture are not in contradiction. It is in the way one incorporates science into small-scale farming that the challenge lies. According to Weis, 'to significantly increase the scale of organic and near organic practices will require much more scientific research and training geared toward better understanding how agro-ecosystems operate and work and how key dynamics can be enhanced.'[37] As an example, research into the functional complementaries of various insects can improve

---

36. Jan Douwe van der Ploeg, *The New Peasantries: Struggles for Autonomy and Sustainability in an Era of* Globalization (London: Earthscan, 2008), p. 172.

37. Weis, *The Global Food Economy*, p. 170.

integrated pest management, while greater knowledge of soils and the dynamics of nutrient recycling can enlighten farmers on the best cropping patterns and rotations, nitrogen-fixing plants, and green manures to use to upgrade soil fertility.[38]

Other examples of how modern technologies can be blended with traditional patterns of agriculture are the recovery and transfer of the system of raised farming beds in shallow lakes and marshes perfected by the Aztecs from the Mexico City suburbs to the lowland tropics of the country; the restoration, building, and improvement of Indian terraces in the Peruvian Andes; and the discovery and rebuilding of a system of raised beds with canals that evolved on the high plains of the Andes. In all cases, the harvest on the reconstructed fields compared favorably with that from regular, chemically fertilized soils.[39]

With the unraveling of global finance and the consequent collapse of the integrated global economy that is the legacy of the neoliberal era, food sovereignty has become acutely relevant to a world disillusioned with neoliberalism and capitalism and desperately looking for alternatives.

Farmers and peasants have long fed their local and national communities. Capitalism, especially in its neoliberal form, worked to consign them to the dustbin of history, replaced by a capital-intensive monoculture geared mainly to a global supermarket of elite and middle-class consumers. In its goal of completely transforming the world's system of food production and distribution, one of the rationales advanced by industrial agriculture for the displacement of peasants and small farmers is that they do not have the capacity to feed the world. In fact, small farmers and peasants do not have ambitions to feed the world, their horizons being limited to providing food for their local and national communities. It is by

---

38. Ibid.
39. Altieri and Nichols, 'Scaling up Agroecological Approaches for Food Sovereignty in Latin America,' pp. 476-7.

providing sustenance as best they can to their communities that peasants and farmers everywhere can be said to feed the world. And, despite the claims of its representatives that corporate agriculture is best at feeding the world, the creation of global production chains and global supermarkets, driven by the search for monopoly profits, has been accompanied by greater hunger, worse food, and greater agriculture-related environmental destabilization all around than at any other time in history.

Peasants and small farmers, however, are resilient, and at this time of global crisis they present a vision of autonomy, diversity, and cooperation that may just be the key elements of a necessary social and economic reorganization. As environmental crises multiply, the social dysfunctions of urban industrial pile up, and globalization drags the world to a global depression, the 'peasant's path' has increasing relevance to broad numbers of people beyond the countryside. Indeed, one finds movements of 're-peasantization,' as entrepreneurial farmers abandon capitalist farming and increasing numbers of urbanites take up small-scale agriculture. One might even consider the possibility that, as van der Ploeg puts it, 'the emergence of urban agriculture in many parts of the world signals the emergence of new numbers of (part-time) peasants and a simultaneous spatial shift of the peasantry from the countryside toward the big metropolises of the world.'[40]

From globalization to deglobalization

Like food sovereignty, deglobalization is a paradigm that emerged in the struggle against corporate-driven globalization in the late 1990s and during the first decade of the twenty-first century. When the organization Focus on the Global South first articulated it publicly in 2000, deglobalization was widely perceived as unrealistic, even in civil society circles that saw globalization as irreversible

40. Van der Ploeg, *The New Peasantries*, p. 37.

and inevitable. By the end of the decade, however, as the global financial collapse radiated from New York to the rest of the world, *The Economist* asserted that deglobalization, a term it attributed to this author, might not be far-fetched after all. According to *The Economist*, the 'integration of the world economy is in retreat on almost every front.' Global supply chains, it said, 'like any chain ... are only as strong as their weakest link. A danger point will come if firms decide that this way of organizing production has had its day.'[41]

The economics of the supply chain was not the only problem. The vulnerability of the global supply chain to natural disasters, brought home by the 2011 earthquake in Japan and the massive flooding in Thailand that was most likely triggered by climate change. The twin disasters, in countries that hosted critical component suppliers for automobile and electronic TNCs, revealed the fragility of the decentralized, globalized lean supply chain that most TNCs had adopted from Toyota and perfected in the era of globalization.[42] The disasters caused massive disruption throughout the global supply chain, resulting in billions of dollars in losses. According to a supply chain expert, 'These recent "Black Swan" or unprecedented natural disaster events have obviously exposed vulnerabilities among indus- try supply chains... The question now is, has the quest for lowest-cost production and hyper-lean supply chains overridden and exposed vulnerability to significant business risk?'[43]

Similar concerns were raised, both by governments and by multilateral agencies, about the soundness of global food supply chains, given rising concerns about tainted inputs from China, climate-related disruptions, and possible terrorist disruptions. One report on Britain's food system, for instance, notes:

41. 'Turning their Backs on the World,' *The Economist*, February 19, 2009, www.economist. com/node/13145370?story_id=13145370.

42. Bill Powell, 'The Global Supply Chain: So Very Fragile,' *Fortune*, December 12, 2011, http://tech.fortune.cnn.com/2011/12/12/supply-chain-distasters-disruptions.

43. Ibid.

Commercial pressures also demand that the food-chain be as lean as possible, and consequently dependent upon every section functioning properly. Within that food chain, the UK has come to rely overwhelmingly on large supermarkets and their logistics networks. By its very nature, therefore, the British food-chain is vulnerable to shocks and disruptions, whether natural, accidental or malicious.[44]

The concerns about the vulnerabilities – economic, financial, and physical – of global supply chains have been accompanied by increasing concern among both political and economic elites that the process of transnationalizing ownership of firms to promote their global reach has gone too far. With the onset of the financial crisis, President Nicolas Sarkozy of France called in 2010 for an industrial policy to prevent the country's industries from being further eroded by the offshoring strategies of globalized man- agements.[45] By the beginning of 2012, with indefinite economic stagnation in both the US and Europe being a certainty, and with the so-call BRICS (Brazil, Russia, India, China, and South Africa) slowing down, the retreat from globalization had become more of a certainty in many quarters. As Nader Mousavizadeh and George Kell wrote in the *International Herald Tribune*, 'we are enter- ing a period of competitive sovereignty, replacing two decades of consensus around the universal benefits of globalization – however uneven and unequal its path.'[46]

Even more interesting was the fact that deglobalization as an eco- nomic strategy entered the mainstream of French politics during the campaign for the presidency in 2011-12. Crediting the author for the concept, Socialist Party candidate Arnaud Montebourg pushed for deglobalization as an alternative strategy for France, provoking

---

44. George Grant, *Shocks and Disruption: The Relationship between Food Security and National Security* (London: Henry Jackson Society, 2012), p. 29.

45. See 'Europe's Dark Secret,' *The Economist*, July 22, 2010, www.economist. com/node/16646168.

46. Nader Mousavizadeh and George Kell, 'Getting Down to Business in Rio,' *International Herald Tribune*, June 15, 2002, p. 8.

a spirited public debate about alternatives to globalization. Why did deglobalization resonate with the electorate? According to one account, this was because

> the country has lost millions of jobs to the emerging economies of eastern and central Europe and farther away to China and other low-wage economies with no social protections. And France has not developed alternative sources of jobs and wealth, finding itself, like many European economies, with a crisis of structural youth unemployment.[47]

Montebourg was later appointed minister for reindustrialization in the government of François Hollande, who succeeded Sarkozy as president in May 2010.

With deglobalization entering the mainstream, the danger is that the term might be hijacked to promote strategies that are different in intent from that which we are proposing. It is, therefore, imperative that we set forth clearly the concepts and values that inform the paradigm and the concrete measures it proposes.

According to the dominant neoliberal paradigm, the best way to organize the economy is to strive for constant large increases in the gross domestic product through efficient production. Efficient production is defined as turning out a product consumers demand at the least unit cost. And achieving such an outcome depends on a market-driven system that is not 'distorted' by artificial barriers like tariffs, investment rules like nationality requirements, and labor unions. The transnational corporation whose different subsidiaries or suppliers are distributed globally so as to benefit from labor cost, geographical, and other advantages that turn out a commodity at the lowest unit cost has become the paradigmatic organization of production in the age of globalization.

---

47. Pierre Haski, 'Is France on Course to Bid Adieu to Globalization?' Yale Global Online, July 21, 2011, http://yaleglobal.yale.edu/content/france-bid-adieu-globalization.

With this form of organization and the institutions facilitating it creating so much social and ecological dislocation, seen in, among other things, increasing inequalities within and among countries and in more and more ecological destabilization, different efforts are under way to formulate an alternative paradigm of economic organization. Yet alternatives are often judged, either explicitly or implicitly, by the criterion of whether they can perform better than or as well as corporate capital in terms of delivering the best product at the lowest unit cost.

Precisely because the pursuit of narrow efficiency has had de-stabilizing social and ecological by-products, the alternative must explicitly disavow it as a central principle in its approach to reorganizing economic life. This position finds support historically if we follow Karl Polanyi's thesis that the unregulated market emerged from a process of 'disembedding' the market from the broader social system, so market relations came to drive the whole system. In the wake of the Great Depression, which was one of the events that ended the first period of globalization that began around 1815, society began to reassert its supremacy over the market, a process that Polanyi called the second moment of the double movement, with the state becoming the prime agency of this process of 're-embedding' the market in broader social relations.[48]

Something fundamentally similar is necessary today, with the current crisis of neoliberalism. Unlike classical socialism, deglobalization does not call for the abolition of the market and its replacement by central planning. What it does call for is the 're-embedding' of market relations in society, meaning that social relations must reflect the subordination of market efficiency to the higher values of community, solidarity, and equality. The market's role in exchange and the allocation of resources is important, but this must be not only balanced but subordinated to the maintenance

---

48. Karl Polanyi, *The Great Transformation* (Boston MA: Beacon Press, 1957).

and enhancement of social solidarity. Acting to balance and guide the market must not only be the state but also civil society, and in place of the invisible hand as the agent of the common good must come the visible hand of democratic choice. In place of the economics of narrow efficiency, we propose what we might call 'effective economics.'

The deglobalization paradigm also asserts that a 'one size fits all' model like neoliberalism or centralized bureaucratic socialism is dysfunctional and destabilizing. Instead, diversity should be expected and encouraged, as it is in nature. Having said this, shared principles of alternative economics do exist, and they have already substantially emerged in the struggle against and critical reflection over the failure of both centralized socialism and capitalism and the enormous challenge posed by the environmental crisis. We make no claim for discovering these principles. They have emerged in a collective process marked by the participation of individuals, organizations, and communities that do not believe in intellectual property rights.

What one might call the fourteen key principles of the deglobalization perspective are the following:

1. Production for the domestic market rather than production for export markets must again become the center of gravity of the economy.
2. The principle of subsidiarity should be enshrined in economic life by encouraging production of goods at the level of the community and at the national level if this can be done at reasonable cost in order to preserve community.
3. Trade policy – that is, quotas and tariffs – should be used to protect the local economy from destruction by corporate-subsidized commodities with artificially low prices.
4. Industrial policy – including subsidies, tariffs, and trade – should be used to revitalize and strengthen the manufacturing sector.

5. Long-postponed measures of equitable income redistribution and land redistribution (including urban land reform) must be implemented to create a vibrant internal market to serve as the anchor of the economy and produce local financial resources for investment.

6. De-emphasizing growth, emphasizing the upgrading of the quality of life, and maximizing equity will reduce environmental disequilibrium.

7. The power and transportation systems must be transformed into decentralized systems based on renewable resources.

8. A healthy balance must be mainained between the country's carrying capacity and the size of its population.

9. Environmentally congenial technology must be developed and diffused in both agriculture and industry.

10. A gender lens must be applied in all areas of economic decision-making so as to ensure gender equity.

11. Strategic economic decisions must not be left to the market or to technocrats. Instead, the scope of democratic decision-making in the economy should be expanded so that all vital economic issues – such as which industries to develop or phase out, what proportion of the government budget to devote to agriculture, etc. – become subject to democratic discussion and choice. This will entail the demystification of economics and a return to its origins as political economy and moral economy.

12. Civil society must constantly monitor and supervise the private sector and the state, a process that should be institutionalized.

13. The property complex should be transformed into a 'mixed economy' that includes community co-operatives, private enterprises, and state enterprises, and excludes transnational corporations.

14. Centralized global institutions like the IMF and the World Bank should be replaced with regional institutions built not on free

trade and capital mobility but on principles of cooperation that, to use the words of Hugo Chávez in describing the Bolivarian Alternative for the Americas (ALBA), 'transcend the logic of capitalism.'

The foregoing must be seen as general principles. How they are concretely articulated will depend on the values, rhythms, and strategic choices of each society. Also, their coherence is not strictly economic in character. Indeed, their coherence is as much ethical in nature since the aim is to reconstruct the economy so as to better achieve greater community, equity, and justice.

Parts of the deglobalization paradigm aren't really new or radical. Its pedigree in the area of trade relations includes the writings of Keynes, who, at the height of the Great Depression, bluntly stated: 'We do not wish ... to be at the mercy of world forces working out, or trying to work out, some uniform equilibrium, according to the principles of *laissez faire* capitalism.' Indeed, he continued,

> [over] an increasingly wide range of industrial products, and perhaps agricultural products also, I become doubtful whether the economic cost of self-sufficiency is great enough to outweigh the other advantages of gradually bringing the producer and the consumer within the ambit of the same national, economic and financial organization. Experience accumulates to prove that most modern mass-production processes can be performed in most countries and climates with almost equal efficiency.

And, with words that have a contemporary ring, Keynes asserted:

> I sympathize ... with those who would minimize rather than with those who would maximize economic entanglement between nations. Ideas, knowledge, art, hospitality, travel – these are the things which should of their nature be international. But let goods be homespun whenever it is reasonably and conveniently possible; and, above all, let finance be primarily national.[49]

---

49. John Maynard Keynes, 'National Self-Sufficiency,' *Yale Review* 22(4) (June 1933), pp. 755-69.

Yet deglobalization is, taken as a whole, radical. It goes beyond Keynesianism, for its intent is not to stabilize corporate-driven capitalism by reforming it with technocratic management but to bring about an economy that runs on different principles, where cooperation rather than competition is the engine of the economy, and where the market, while continuing to serve as a medium of exchange and a mechanism for the allocation of resources, is guided and steered by values, the state, and civil society toward the social good.

We are not Keynesians, but we cannot resist concluding with a statement Keynes made in 1933, in the depths of the Great Depression, that captures, remarkably, our own situation today:

> The decadent international but individualistic capitalism, in the hands of which we found ourselves after the war, is not a success. It is not intelligent, it is not beautiful, it is not just, it is not virtuous. In short, we dislike it, and we are beginning to despise it. But when we wonder what to put in its place, we are extremely perplexed.[50]

Deglobalization and its related paradigm of food sovereignty seek to provide a path out of our current perplexity. Whether they succeed or not remains to be seen, but we are confident they point in the right direction.

---

50. Ibid.

INDEX